THE *Morality* OF *Laughter*

THE *Morality* OF
Laughter

F. H. BUCKLEY

THE UNIVERSITY OF MICHIGAN PRESS
Ann Arbor

Copyright © by the University of Michigan 2003
All rights reserved
Published in the United States of America by
The University of Michigan Press
Manufactured in the United States of America
⊗ Printed on acid-free paper

2006   2005   2004   2003   4   3

A CIP catalog record for this book is available from the British Library.

Library of Congress Cataloging-in-Publication Data

Buckley, F. H. (Francis H.), 1948–
        The morality of laughter / F.H. Buckley.
            p.   cm.
        Includes bibliographical references and index.
        ISBN 0-472-09818-7 (cloth : alk. paper)
            1. Laughter—Moral and ethical aspects.
        2. Comic, The—Moral and ethical aspects.   I. Title.

    BH301.C7 B83   2003
    179—dc21   2002015815

To Esther & Sarah

Contents

 Preface

All theories, dear friend, are grey
But green is the tree of life.
Goethe, *Faust*

This book had its origin in an elevator at the University of Chicago Law School, where I was a visiting fellow. On the elevator with me was Nobel laureate Ronald Coase, a founder of the law and economics movement associated with that school and with the law school where I now teach. The elevator stopped on the way down, and a U. of C. fundraiser stepped aboard with a donor in tow. "This is Ronald Coase," she enthused. "He invented the Coase theorem!" Smiles, and a shaking of hands all around. "This is Frank Buckley . . . ," she continued. And in the embarrassed silence which followed I resolved to have a theorem too.

But where to theorize? The areas in which I taught were already well-stocked with theories, so I had to move on. Yet wherever I turned in the useful sciences of law and economics, my side had already won. Over the last twenty-five years, economics has made a slow march through most of the social sciences, breaking through all redoubts and planting its banners atop every public policy bastion. Today, economics is what heraldry was to Sir Walter Scott. "Not know economics! Of whatever was your mother thinking!"

If economics has won the day in the social sciences, it has had little success in the humanities, and the border between the two is the front line of a cultural war. Disputes about culture are not a new phenomenon. In the nineteenth century the antagonists were Darwin's Bulldog, Thomas Huxley, and Matthew Arnold. Fifty years ago Lord Snow proclaimed the preeminence of the hard sciences, and for his show of sham culture was savaged by literary scholar F. R. Leavis. (Of Leavis's jeremiad, Roger Kimball wrote: "It's not just that no two stones of Snow's argument are left standing: each and every pebble is pulverized; the fields are salted; and the entire population is sold into slavery.")[1]

Some things are different today. The political positions were reversed in the past. Arnold and Leavis were cultural conservatives, while their scientific opponents attacked established religion (Huxley) or espoused marxisant politics (Snow). The differences have also become heightened of late. But in one respect the two groups are more alike today than formerly. The older school of humanists had a fairly clear vision about some of life's basic goods, particularly the value of high culture. Today, few scholars have much to say about life-style choices or culture. On the right, conservative economists are seldom willing to second-guess personal preferences that do not impose physical costs on third parties. On the left, academics in the humanities prescribe a thick set of rules about politics but are studiously neutral about how we should live. As a result, the civilizing mission of the university has largely been ignored by scholars right and left.

Clifford Geertz has asked for a "useful miracle" that would give academics a common language and bring peace to the culture wars.[2] None of us is a miracle worker, but a modest start might be made through humane studies that look to a common culture for instruction on how to live. The modern obsession with politics blinds us to the far more interesting question of what we should do with our lives. The politician cannot help us there, but the humanist can.

The humanist sees culture from the inside, not as an inert artifact but as a living code whose authority is felt within, not as a grey theory but as a green tree of life. One of the strongest cultural signals about how to live comes from laughter, whose sting we can never ignore. We can bear poverty, illness, even shame, but not ridicule, and the strategies we employ to immunize ourselves from it constitute a thick code of conduct that I call the morality of laughter. There are religious, legal, and moral codes that condemn the imposition of harm on others, but the morality of laughter is different for it teaches the individual how to extract joy from his own life. Friedrich Nietzsche recognized the difference and called the study of laughter the gay science.

I would write of laughter, then. But how could I do so when academic conventions (with an eye to self-preservation) frown on any attempt at humor? Yet if laughter is banned in the useful sciences, I might examine its utility in the gay sciences. I would read Swift, Pope, and *The Onion* (with its campaign for a "Leave Your Daughters at Work" day). And then—the icing on the cake—my theory of laughter would require me to mock people I dislike.

I argue that laughter announces and enforces a code of behavior through the jester's signal of superiority over a butt. There is no laughter without a butt, and no butt without a message about a risible inferiority. I label this the *Positive* superiority thesis, and discuss it in part I. The *Normative* superiority thesis, which I examine in part II, makes the stronger claim that our laughter communicates a true superiority and that the butt is truly an inferior person. While the two theses tend to run together, it is important to distinguish them, for the first is far more plausible than the second. Those who laugh are sometimes inferior brutes, and even evil ones as well, and in such cases we should disregard the message. Yet we should not be over-quick to dismiss the claim that laughter offers valuable lessons on how to live. We have every incentive to heed the comic muse—Thalia—and ordinarily have little choice in the matter. Laughter forces itself on us, and few emotions are stronger than the fear of being a butt. Lastly, part III examines the experience of laughter and asks why its message might mislead or be ignored.

I describe the Positive thesis in chapter 1 and examine objections to it in chapters 2 and 3. Superiority is a necessary but not a sufficient condition of laughter: we always signal superiority when we laugh, but may feel superior without laughing. Chapter 2 examines the other necessary elements of laughter: sociability, surprise, and playfulness. Chapter 3 considers the claim that we may laugh without superiority. Where is the superiority in wordplay or in the joke told on oneself? If valid, such objections would be fatal to the Positive thesis. I argue, however, that a signal of superiority may always be found in every honest laugh, or at least in one that proceeds from a mental stimulus and not a merely physical cause, such as tickling or inhaling nitrous oxide.

If the Positive thesis were rejected, we would have to abandon the Normative thesis as well. It would be difficult to see how laughter might be used to signal a true superiority unless the jester saw himself as superior. But one might accept the Positive and reject the Normative thesis. The wit might be a very inferior fellow. What he cannot do, however, is laugh if he thinks himself inferior.

Evil and vulgar people can and do laugh, as I note in chapter 4, and the Normative thesis cannot be accepted without reservation. The laughter of the gutter signals a false superiority. But this means only that we should be discriminating about laughter, as we are of every medium of information. It does not imply that we should disregard the signal of laughter, and in part II I defend a soft version of the Normative thesis, in which the general effect of laughter is benign. By highlighting comic vices, laughter teaches us a superior life-plan, of grace and suppleness, that is immune from ridicule.

Chapter 5 examines the admiration we naturally feel for the wit and the comic norms that we can elicit from his message. If the Normative thesis were false, even in the soft form that I defend, our instinctive respect for those who wear what Nietzsche called the rose-wreath crown of laughter would be puzzling.

In identifying a butt, laughter's message is both negative and positive. We are told what not to do if we wish to avoid becoming a butt, and also what to do if we wish to immunize ourselves against laughter. Laughter identifies comic virtues as well as comic vices. Chapter 6 examines the *social virtues* of integrity, moderation, fortitude, and temperance, and chapter 7 describes the *charismatic virtues* of grace, taste, and learning. For both sets of virtues, the prescribed behavior is a mean between contrasting extremes that constitute comic vices, one for an excess and the other for an insufficiency of the comic virtue.

Comic virtues teach us how to extract joy from life, and their message is necessarily complex. Rigid and narrow rules cannot possibly do justice to the endless variety of opportunities that life offers us for joy. Henri Bergson turned this into a law: mechanistic rules are ridiculous, and the more they treat people like machines the more they are risible. Chapters 8 to 10 apply this insight to machine law, machine scholarship, and machine art. Fashionable nonsense that would have been laughed out of court a generation ago now thrives in a jurisprudence that at times has lost all common sense. Machine theories that fail to recognize man's humanity flourish in the academy unless, as happens too seldom, they are punctured by ridicule. Modern art that denies the artistic impulse of a human creator, and modern buildings and cities that aspire to the condition of a machine, have conspired to produce an inhuman wasteland because we forgot to laugh at ugliness.

Chapter 11 examines why laughter norms might err. The impulse to laugh might arise through base motives, factual mistakes, or errors of judgment. In particular, comic norms are contested through a battle for the middle ground of comic virtue. If virtue is a mean, it is often unclear where the *juste milieu* might lie, and what constitutes excessive and inadequate virtue. Underclass laughter asserts that its butts are excessively virtuous, while haughty laughter derides inadequate virtue. From each extreme, the two groups trade off laughter in an effort to show that they have comic virtue on their side and that their opponents are ridiculous.

Chapter 12 describes five cases of resistance to laughter, beginning with the vain man who thinks too highly of himself to notice that he has become a butt. Next, the acedic or depressed man has lost interest in laughter's message. Third, the cynic assumes the thick-skinned pose of one who has risen above laughter. Fourth, those who seek power may also find that in doing so they have abandoned laughter. Power offers its own pleasures, but not the rapture of laughter, and might exclude laughter as a means of enforcing its will. Lastly, the modern puritan focuses exclusively upon politics and condemns laughter for distracting us from the serious pursuit of remedying injustice.

Chapter 13 describes laughter's secondary effect, which I call *sociability*. By creating communities with common butts, laughter serves as a bonding device between wits and listeners. The listener who laughs takes the wit's side against the butt, and cements a relationship of trust between himself and the wit. In most laughter, three persons may be found: wit, listener, butt. This is not an original idea—Freud had it first. What is original is my argument that objections to the superiority theory may err by focusing on the relationship between wit and listener, forgetting that both regard the butt as inferior. Such objections see laughter's sociability but miss the element of superiority.

I conclude by situating the morality of laughter in a broader philosophical context. In the revival of interest in the passions, attention has focused on *eudaimonia*-happiness, which Aristotle thought the highest good. The morality of happiness is suspicious of extreme pleasures; for a science of joy one must turn to the Judaic and Christian traditions, to aestheticism, or to the morality of laughter. Through laughter, we might seek an integration of religious, aesthetic, and moral dimensions, which since Kierkegaard have seemed fragmented.

My project is a *teleological* one, for it assumes that (1) man has a natural end (*telos* in Greek) in which he realizes his potential, and (2) laughter's message of superiority assists him in reaching this end. A teleological account of laughter is necessarily a superiority explanation, since nonsuperiority theories are agnostic about what constitutes a good life. This may explain why superiority theories are out of fashion today. In an age of relativism that asks us not to be judgmental, the idea that laughter signals inferiority will seem very old-fashioned. And so it is. The morality of laughter provides an answer to one of the oldest questions in philosophy: How ought I to live? The question is little posed today, but our laughter is wiser than we are and forces us to seek an answer to it.

The search for a single touchstone to explain an institution or emotion is also an old-fashioned project. Scholars nowadays are more likely to insist on the multidimensionality of everything. There are no single explanations; instead, things must be seen from countless, different perspectives. There is nothing we might call "the risible," and any attempt to arrive at a definition is simplistic and reductive. It is not too much to say that the superiority thesis

> may be seen under the aspect of Foucauldian strategic reversal—of the unholy trinity of Parmenidean/Platonic/Aristotelean provenance; of the Cartesian-Lockean-Humean-Kantian paradigm of foundationalisms (in practice, fideistic foundationalisms) and irrationalisms (in practice, capricious exercises of the will-to-power or some other ideologically and/or psycho-somatically buried source) new and old alike . . .

and so on for seventy-eight more words before one comes to a lonely period. All this is from Roy Bhaskar's *Plato etc,*[3] which won first prize in the on-line Bad Writing Contest. (The dust jacket describes the book as the author's "most accessible book to date.")

Still, I regret the passing of the older project, whose search for a single explanation avoided the modern fuzziness of a plethora of Foucauldian/Parmenidian/Platonic/Kantian theories. A formal search for a single theory demands the discipline that comes from defending a thesis and attacking rival theories, and such efforts are valuable whether or not they are ultimately successful. They are also more joyful than a scholarship that has lost its desire to make a point or articulate an intelligible position. More than anything, on the centenary of Bergson's attempt to define the risible in *Le rire,* I regret the dearth of interest in the content of laughter's message of the good life.

The last few decades have seen a welcome revival of scholarly interest in how we should live, led by philosophers Alasdair MacIntyre, Charles Taylor, and Julia Annas. The events of 9-11 will accelerate this trend. The war on terrorism is not about politics. It is about heroism and evil, about how we should and how we should not live.

The inward turn may also be observed in France, where recent writers such as Pascal Bruckner, André Comte-Sponville, and Pascal Quignard offer fascinating insights into *la vie ordinaire*. The difference is that Continental philosophers do not write with the emotional flatness that one finds in modern Anglo-American scholarship. Even in England, the ideal of emotional neutrality is largely a twentieth-century phenomenon. Locke deprecated an emotional style but still wrote with passion, as did John Stuart Mill. So too did cultural critics John Ruskin and Matthew Arnold. Clearly, the expression of emotion is not incompatible with real scholarship. In particular, there is no reason for an emotional lobotomy in a book about the emotions. So long as the author is not diverted from the heavy work of analysis, he may tell us more about tragedy when he communicates the pathos of life. Similarly, a book about laughter might be strengthened by wit, and a discussion of joy by joyousness. Explanations of the risible might indeed be evaluated on the simple basis of whether they amuse. If I defend the Positive thesis, part of the reason is that rival theories of laughter seem consistently unfunny.

Where I have referred to an individual this is a work of fiction, and any resemblance to a real person is quite coincidental.

A great many people helped in the preparation of this book. I gratefully acknowledge the generous support of the George Mason Law and Economics Center, which (like Stephen Leacock's McGill) gives the scholar the leisure to step from the classroom and *think,* or (what is better still) not to think at all. For their most helpful suggestions, I also thank Julia Annas, Bob Anthony, Hadley Arkes, David Bernstein, John Cleese, Esther and Ben Geva, Mark Grady, Florence King, Ejan Mackaay, Geoff Miller, Eric Posner, Norman Siebrasse, Martin Wooster, colleagues at GMUSL and Université Panthéon-Assas Paris II, subscribers to the econlaw listserv, and anonymous referees. My editor at the University of Michigan Press, Jeremy Shine, was a font of useful suggestions and encouragement, as were two anonymous referees and my copy editor, Janice Brill.

To assist my research, Deborah Keene, Rae Best, and the staff at the GMUSL library purchased absurdly useless and entertaining books for me and pillaged local libraries through interlibrary loans. My daughter dutifully read every single Dave Barry and *Dilbert* book. Finally, through her editorial suggestions, Esther Goldberg made a book out of a series of disconnected musings.

PART ONE

The Positive Thesis

1 Laughter as Superiority

How much lies in Laughter: the cipher-key,
wherewith we decipher the whole man!

Thomas Carlyle, *Sartor Resartus*

What is lighter and more frivolous than laughter? And yet the most serious thinkers have puzzled over what makes us laugh. From Plato to Kant, philosophers have sought to define the risible, and even made jokes to explain their theories. Henri Bergson had a genuine sense of humor, and Freud's jokes (often Jewish ones) were delightful.

> The shnorrer supplicates the Jewish philanthropic baron for money to take the 'cure' at Ostend, as the physician has ordered him to take sea-baths for his ailment. The baron remarks that Ostend is an especially expensive resort, and that a less fashionable place would do just as well. But the shnorrer rejects this out of hand. 'Herr Baron, nothing is too expensive for my health!'

Or, "This girl reminds me of Dreyfus. The army does not believe in her innocence."[1]

But that was then. Modern scholars lack Kant's light touch, and laughter no longer is a subject of philosophic enquiry. One searches, almost in vain, through the pages of scholarly journals for any sign of wit, for writers today have little time for pasquinade, lampoon or satire. In learned reviews ridicule is thought in poor taste, and the young academic soon learns that humor is a bad career move.

The loss of a sense of humor has impoverished academic discourse, where nonsensical theories that could not survive the test of ridicule are now taken seriously. Before adopting a fashionable idea, we ought first to enquire whether it twigs our sense of humor. Now, if laughter usefully identifies nonsense, it warrants serious (well, not wholly serious) study. What is it that sparks our laughter? What do Menippean and Augustan satire, vulgar guffaw and polished laughter, have in common? What purposes might laughter serve, and when might it mislead?

In this book I stretch a few simple ideas as far as I can, to see if they break. That is the way in which ideas are tested—even the skeptic will admit that this is a useful exercise. Too often, scholars aspire to the condition of a judge: guarded, balanced, and impartial. The result is like an editorial in a sensible liberal newspaper, exquisitely fair and utterly predictable. If short on novel analysis, modern scholarship is *safe,* for it takes no sides and offends no one. It splits every issue down the middle, offering a neat little slice for everyone. The wonderful thing about such scholarship is that one needn't actually *read* it. It suffices to glance at the footnotes, to make sure that all the proper authorities are cited and in the proper order.

I shall takes sides, then, and argue that a *superiority* thesis best explains when we laugh. Laughter signals our recognition of a comic vice in another person—the butt. We do not share in the vice, for we could not laugh if we did. Through laughter, the butt is made to feel inferior, and those who laugh reveal their sense of superiority over him.

Superiority theories provide only one of the many explanations that have been advanced to explain laughter. In addition, there are incongruity theories, relief theories, hybrid and other theories. J. Y. T. Greig listed eighty-eight theories of laughter and comedy.[2] However, I take the world to divide neatly between superiority and nonsuperiority theories, with only the former affirming that laughter always signals a sense of superiority.

Since they describe different aspects of laughter, nonsuperiority theories might overlap with each other and with superiority explanations of laughter. Superiority refers to status differences between jester and butt, incongruity to a mental puzzle, and relief to an emotional state; and there is no reason why we might not find all three elements in a single laugh. The butt's defect might seem incongruous, and in laughing we might feel a sense of relief that we are superior to a comic vice. So understood, nonsuperiority theories would not pose a challenge to the superiority account of laughter. For my purposes, therefore, a rival theory is one that denies laughter's need for a sense of superiority.

I distinguish between positive and normative theories of superiority. Part I defends a *Positive* thesis, which asserts that in laughing we signal a

4

personal sense of superiority over a butt. The *Normative* thesis, which I examine in part II, makes the further claim that laughter communicates a true superiority, and that the butt is indeed inferior. I do not say that laughter's message of superiority is infallible. That would obviously be too strong, since the inferior may laugh as well, and rival groups may trade off laughter against each other. Nevertheless, our laughter contains valuable information about how to live. While the comic muse might at times mislead, we should still attend to her message. She is light and playful, but when ignored takes a most effective revenge.

The Positive and Normative theses are intimately connected. Were the Positive thesis false, it would be difficult to argue that laughter signals valuable standards of conduct, as the Normative thesis asserts. If laughter signals a true superiority, it must be because (1) those who laugh think themselves superior, and (2) they are right to think so. How could we pretend that our laughter derides the butt unless we think him inferior? But even if some laughter did not signal superiority, the Positive thesis might still account for the rest, and such laughter might signal the true superiority of the Normative thesis.

Superiority theories are incomplete, for they do not account for the sociable side of laughter. If relations of dominance were all there was to it, then why are jokes so often associated with feelings of solidarity and community? The answer is that laughter means something very different for the listener who laughs along with the joke than it does for the butt. Like Janus, laughter has two faces: from one side it smiles amiably at a listener; from the other it smirks at a butt who is ridiculed. The wit proposes a joke to the listener, who may either accept it by laughing or reject it by silence. By laughing the listener accepts a tie of solidarity—a *lien de rire*—with the wit. In this way laughter's superiority may coexist with a sense of sociability. The sociability thesis explains the relationship between wit and listener (see chap. 13), while the superiority thesis explains the relationship between (on the one hand) wit and listener and (on the other) the butt.

To test these ideas, self-examination suffices. We need simply ask ourselves what we find risible. In place of the philosopher's thought-experiment, I substitute the joke-experiment. My method, like that of Matthew Arnold, is to give fresh and free play to our sense of humor, suspending heavy seriousness to look candidly at the lightness and nastiness of laughter.

I adopt an introspective perspective because I see the study of laughter as a branch of literature or philosophy, not neurology or medicine. I offer little by way of scientific evidence for the Positive thesis. There have been interesting electroencephalogical studies of laughter that employ PET scans and MRI technology, but they are beyond the scope of this book. Nor do I distinguish between humor and laughter, though I am mindful that others have done so. Such studies identify laughter with its accompanying physiological processes. What they do not do, however, is identify the risible. Indeed, they tell us nothing about the things at which we laugh. They do not even tell us what laughter is, for the personal experience of laughter is quite different from the physiological events that correlate with it. Suppose that our laughter were found to be correlated with a particular neural event X. It would still be perfectly meaningful to say that X occurred and to deny that anything funny happened.

The reader must also look elsewhere for a sociological examination of laughter, or for psychological tests of risibility. Empirical studies have their place, and do support the Positive thesis.[3] In evaluating laughter, however, we may always second-guess empirical studies. We might pay graduate students to listen to *Seinfeld* and observe them for smiles and guffaws—but what if they lack a sense of humor, and laugh? If we needed a second opinion, we would be like the wine snob in Mordecai Richler's *Joshua Then and Now*. One night Joshua breaks into the oenophile's house and carefully washes the label off every Chateau Lafite and Chateau Margaux. Then he places each bottle back where he found it and leaves. Later he meets the forlorn wine snob. "But what does it matter," Joshua says. "You can still tell the difference, can't you?"

Because laughter rests on a normative foundation that tells us how we ought to behave, my intuitive approach is something more than empirical psychology writ small. Empirical tests have no place in normative disciplines such as laughter and ethics, whose claims can neither be proven nor disproven. Though 90 percent of the subjects of a psychological study might laugh, I may still say, "That's not funny!"

Normative questions are not resolved by telephoning randomly selected people at dinnertime. The moralist does not rest his arguments on an appeal to popular sentiments. To say that a thing is wrong is very different from saying that a majority of people condemn it. Indeed, to say something is wrong is to mean that it is wrong whatever others might think about the matter. So too with aesthetics. We do not fault John Ruskin for failing to ask Venetian tourists what they thought of John

Bellini. To insist on polling data about beauty is to move the discussion from aesthetics to demographics. Polling data can tell us what people value, but not what is valuable; what is thought beautiful, but not what is beautiful; what people laugh at, but not what is risible.

It is a precondition to ethical and aesthetic discourse that universal standards of morality and beauty exist. Someone who says "That is immoral but that is simply how we feel about things over here" shows that he does not understand how moral discourse works. And what is true of ethics and art is true of humor as well. Like ethics, comedy is a normative discipline that enunciates standards of behavior. And like art, comedy is a branch of aesthetics. The difference, as Aristotle observed, is that art is the study of beauty and comedy of ugliness (*Poetics* 1449a).

Hobbes and Bergson

The Positive thesis has been advanced by a surprising number of philosophers who agreed about little else. In the *Philebus,* Plato argued that the pleasure derived from comedy was based on malice and our enjoyment of others' misfortune. Aristotle also proposed a superiority explanation, defining the risible as a mistake or deficiency.[4] So too, in Descartes's dualist account of the passions laughter is produced by either a bodily impulse or a mental process, but in either case reveals one's sense of superiority to a butt.[5]

Notwithstanding the forerunners, the superiority thesis is most closely identified with Descartes's contemporary, Thomas Hobbes. The Hobbesian theory of laughter was based on a highly reductionist account of human action. We are prompted to action by our appetite for pleasure and aversion to pain. Nothing else counts, and good and evil are merely the names we give to things that please or displease us. The ability to procure the good or avoid the bad is "power," and among the passions Hobbes accorded priority to the search for power. "So that in the first place, I put for a generall inclination of all mankind, a perpetuall and restlesse striving of Power after power, that ceaseth onely in death."[6]

For Hobbes, power was power over other people. "Power simply is no more, but the excess of the power of one above that of another."[7] Possessing power over others is glory, and the sudden realization of that power produces laughter. It is a "sudden glory," a cry of triumph that signals our discovery of superiority to a butt, "and is caused either by some sudden act of their own, that pleaseth them; or by the apprehension of some deformed thing in another, by comparison whereof they suddenly applaud themselves."[8]

The Hobbesian account of motivation is thin, as we value a good many things besides the desire for relative status—how we rank compared to others. However, status is obviously very important to us. We are concerned not only with absolute status—our wealth, intelligence, and so on—but also with how we compare with others. Our sense of contentment might even depend more on relative than absolute status. A man on the dole might live like a prince when compared with fifth-century nobles, but as his principal reference group is his contemporaries he may burn with resentment. Tertullian has left us with a striking vision of relative preferences. One of the particular joys of Heaven, it seems, will be the ability to peer down from on high and observe the sufferings of the sinners in Hell.[9]

Relative status is greatly affected by ridicule. Even those who deny that the wit signals his superiority will admit that the butt is made to feel inferior. Relative to the wit, the butt is degraded; relative to the butt, the wit moves up a notch. The butt knows this, of course, and that is why he resents the joke; and it is not a great stretch to assume that the wit sees it the same way, as the Positive thesis asserts. Speaking for butts everywhere, Hazlitt said that our humiliation is the wit's triumph.[10]

The leading modern statement of the superiority thesis is Henri Bergson's *Le rire*.[11] Bergson defined the risible as a rigidity (*raideur*) of body or character. For the anglophone, this might at first seem a quirky Gallic *hommage* to Jerry Lewis. By rigidity, however, Bergson meant something more than a physical clumsiness. Instead, rigidity served as a metaphor for a want of suppleness in any aspect of life.

Consider the simplest of butts, the man who clumsily slips on the ice. He falls because he sought to walk after his grip gave way. A more agile man might have kept his balance by standing still, but the butt lacks the alertness to change gears quickly. So down he goes, to our great amusement; and in him Bergson saw the very type and model of all our laughter. The butt who cannot navigate the obstacles erected by social customs is like the man who cannot navigate a patch of ice. Both are comically inadequate to the dexterity society requires of us. They are marionettes, whose actions are circumscribed and mechanical.

Like machines, their actions follow a determined program. They keep on walking when their feet have left the ice, and that is why we find them comic.

By following a single program, said Bergson, the comic butt is a machine man. Our actions are risible to the exact extent that they remind us of a mechanical thing, and the most amusing people are those whose actions are least human and most mechanical. They have betrayed their nature, and for their *gran rifiuto* merit our deepest scorn.

The machine man is inadequate to life's complexities. He trusts in his rules and ignores the more reliable guide of experience, like the man in Molière's *Critique de L'École des femmes* who likes the sauce but wants to check it against the cookbook recipe. He takes a single principle and absurdly extends it beyond its reasonable scope, where erudition turns into pedantry, polish into slickness, and solidity into dullness. He is the miser who takes frugality to the point of vice; the gourmand who becomes a glutton; the health Nazi. (In Germany, the Fascists goose-step, notes John O'Sullivan; in America they jog.)

The rigid butt might usefully be contrasted with the tragic hero. An Othello or a Macbeth is an integrated, whole person, for all his flaws; the machine man of comedy is defined solely by his vice. Euclio and Harpagon are one-dimensional, cardboard characters, whose only feature is their avarice. Aristotle noted the difference in his *Poetics:* comic characters were stereotypes, while tragedies were usually based on well-known and developed mythic figures. Bergson made the similar point that, unlike comedies, tragedies seldom bear the name of the vice portrayed. Molière's *The Miser* is a comedy about avarice, but *Othello* was not called "Jealousy." Calling a play by the name of a vice tells us that the principal character is not a whole person but only a caricature, and this invites our laughter.

Plays sometimes hover between comedy and tragedy until the protagonist acquires a complex character and the impulse to laugh is stifled. Until the end of act I, we do not know which *King Lear* will be. It becomes a tragedy only when the mad king acquires wisdom and moral grandeur through an ability to see a universal message in his fall. Before then, the play might have taken a different turn and been called "The Foolish Father." Similarly, Falstaff is too complicated a figure to be truly comic. "Thou compound of sense and vice," apostrophized Samuel Johnson, "of sense which may be admired but not esteemed, of vice which may be despised, but hardly detested."[12] Like Johnson, we have no choice but to love Falstaff, and his fall is tragic when he is killed off in *Henry V.*

The Normative Foundation

Le rire's theory of laughter is normative as well as positive. Bergson sought to explain why we laugh by identifying a feature common to all butts; but at the same time he argued that rigidity ought to be risible and that the butt deserved to be ridiculed. Our laughter teaches him valuable lessons about life. Positive and Normative theories often run together, and we shall return to Bergson's machine men in part II, where I will argue that the Positive thesis's signal of superiority is based on a set of comic norms—standards of behavior that direct the butt to mend his ways. Laughter always sanctions a butt's comic vice and reveals a correlative comic virtue that immunizes us from laughter. However, it is a farther step to assert that comic norms deserve to be followed. The difference between Positive and Normative theories is that the first identifies a set of comic norms and the second urges us to adopt them. Some superiority theorists, like Bergson, defended both theories. But the two kinds of theories are very different, for Hobbes subscribed to the Positive thesis but rejected the Normative one (see chap. 4).

Even on the Positive thesis, laughter assumes a normative order from which the butt has deviated. The thesis holds that laughter signals our derision at a defective act or life. Since this entails a comparison with a superior life, comic vices assume comic virtues, and he who laughs must in his own way be a moralist. Through their laughter, wit and listener reaffirm a shared vision about how life should be lived and proclaim that the butt is guilty of a comic vice.

Laughter's ability to correct our morals—*castigare ridendo mores*—has long been employed as a literary device by satirists. In the Preface to *Absalom and Achitophel,* Dryden announced: "The true end of Satyre is the amendment of Vices by correction. And he who writes Honestly, is no more an Enemy to the Offendour, than the Physician to the Patient, when he prescribes harsh remedies to an inveterate Disease." Later, in his *Original and Progress of Satire,* Dryden said, "The Poet is bound, and that *ex Officio,* to give his Reader some one precept of moral virtue; and to caution him against some one particular vice or folly." And delivering his own eulogy, Swift said: "Tis plain, his writings were design'd / To *please,* and to *reform* Mankind" (*Life and Character of Dr. Swift*). All of this is consistent with the superiority thesis, for there is no satire without a butt who is satirized, no butt without a signal of inferiority, and no signal of inferiority without a normative message. Take away the moral criticism, said Northrop Frye, and one is left with irony or fantasy, with Kafka but not satire.[13]

Like comedy, tragedy also assumes a shared normative vision; but unlike comedy it transcends normative categories. The comic butt receives his just deserts; the tragic hero's fall is quite unwarranted. Lear's flaw is an inability to distinguish sincere affection from strategic fawning, and his punishment vastly exceeds any sanction he might have deserved for a most human blindness. Antigone is entirely without a flaw: she disregards an unjust order to leave her brother unburied and fulfills her moral and religious duties. For this she is sentenced to die, and meets her end without false hopes.

The audience must share the playwright's moral vision, since the fall is not tragic if it is deserved. But tragedy requires something more than a shared moral code, since it seeks something more than justice. *Phèdre* is often acclaimed the greatest tragedy, and what makes it tragic is its Jansenism, its belief that salvation is more than a matter of justice, that God might deny his grace to "righteous sinners" (*justes pécheurs*) like Racine's Phèdre.

Racine had studied at the Jansenist school at Port-Royal des Champs, but broke with his teachers when he lived "in the world" and wrote for the stage. Now, with his greatest play, he would make amends. In the Preface to *Phèdre,* Racine wrote that the heroine's sin was "more a punishment of the gods than an exercise of her will,"[14] and added that the play might safely be read by those with the strictest moral views. Racine's friend, Boileau, brought a copy of the play to Antoine Arnauld, the spiritual leader of Port-Royal, who agreed to meet with Racine. The poet fell to his knees before the Great Arnauld, who knelt beside him, and the two embraced. In his will, the poet asked to be buried at Port-Royal des Champs, at the feet of his teacher.

There is no tragedy when a play addresses an injustice or a social problem, like the didactic plays of Henrik Ibsen or Clifford Odets. "More pliant divorce laws could not alter the fate of Agamemnon," notes George Steiner. "Social psychiatry is no answer to Oedipus."[15] Instead, tragedy requires an audience that knows that, even when every demand for justice is met, life will still break your heart. Like Aeneas, we mourn for what never can be changed: tears in the nature of things, hearts touched by human transience.*

Tragedy is more conservative than comedy. Unlike comedy, tragedy does not seek to change the world; instead it accepts the possibility that injustice may triumph and offers a religious or heroic perspective that ennobles suffering. When this faith is lost, we may speak with Steiner of *The Death of Tragedy*. But comedy—particularly satire—also requires a normative vision, and were this lost we might speak of the Death of Comedy. This was why Evelyn Waugh denied he wrote satire:

> Satire is a matter of period. It flourishes in a stable society and presupposes homogenous moral standards—the early Roman Empire and eighteenth-century Europe. It is aimed at inconstancy and hypocrisy. It exposes polite cruelty and folly by exaggerating them. It seeks to produce shame. All this has no place in the Century of the Common Man where vice no longer pays lip service to virtue.[16]

The modern academy is often agnostic about norms and skeptical about truth. It prizes an irony in which perspective is all, where events like 9–11 can be made to look good or bad simply by being redescribed. Modernism is also strongly egalitarian and hostile to signals of inferiority. In this environment laughter cannot flourish. Yet outside the academy laughter fares better, for we are never really without a normative order or risible butts. Waugh himself produced some of the most amusing and biting satires ever written, appealing to a timeless moral code.

Laughter as a Signal

All consciousness is consciousness of something, said Edmund Husserl. Similarly, all laughter is laughter about something. The physical action of laughing defines the risible by conveying information from the wit to the butt about the latter's comic defect.

Laughter assumes an informational asymmetry between wit and butt.

---

*"Lacrimae rerum et mentem mortalia tangunt." *Aeneid* I.452.

The butt is unaware of his comic vice, said Plato; and the ridiculous might be described as the opposite of the inscription at Delphi: Know not thyself (*Philebus* 48). After the more alert wit points out the defect the butt might correct it, but until then he is risible. In this sense, laughter performs what economists call a signaling function, communicating information from one party to another.

If risibility is a kind of ignorance, one of the best defenses against being laughed at is a sense of humor that tells us when we are ridiculous. The heightened facility for detecting cant, the concern for clarity, the horror of posturing and pomposity, the love of common sense, all proceed from a sense of the ridiculous and protect one against laughter.

While the butt must be unaware of his comic vice, wit and listener must be in the know. The listener who does not see the wit will not get the joke and produce an honest laugh. Nor could the wit tell a joke without meaning to do so. At Trafalgar, Nelson's dying words to his captain were "Kiss me, Hardy." As that was a little de trop for the naval hagiographer, however, the tradition arose that Nelson's last thoughts were on fate and not love, and that what he had said was "Kismet, Hardy." One thing is certain: He did not mean both; if he had he would have died with a pun on his lips. Absent the specific intent, he did not jest. Nor did George IV, who misunderstood a courtier and thought Queen Caroline was dead. Alas, it was only Napoleon.

> "It is my duty to inform Your Majesty that your greatest enemy is dead."
> "Is she, by God."[17]

The difference in knowledge distinguishes comedy from tragedy. The comic defect is visible to everyone save the butt, and is essentially an intellectual error. The butt has adopted a comic vice (such as avarice) in the mistaken belief that it will bring him happiness, and our laughter tells him to guess again. However, when the butt knows of his mistake and refuses to change he is no longer comic. When he destroys his life, knowing what he is doing but unable to help it, he becomes tragic. On the heath, all illusions lost, Lear has no lessons to learn and is the greatest figure in English tragedy; but in act I, when he foolishly gives away his kingdom because he believes his daughters will care for him, he is comic.

The comic defect must be correctable, since the signal would otherwise be pointless. We do not laugh when the blind or lame stumble, but only when laughter might make a difference. What Swift said of his satire is generally true of most laughter.

> His Satyr points at no Defect,
> But what all Mortals may correct; . . .
> He spar'd a Hump or crooked Nose,
> Whose Owners set not up for Beaux
> True genuine Dulness mov'd his Pity
> Unless it offer'd to be witty.
> *(Verses on the Death of Dr. Swift)*

There is a vulgar laughter that mocks the dwarf and cripple. But for most of us a natural defect awakens our sympathy, and only correctable comic vices provoke our laughter.

Our laughter always contains the hope of redemption. When the butt is wholly mechanical, when nothing human remains, laughter is out of place. In a recent contest that recalled the steel-driving machine vs. John Henry, the IBM Deep Blue computer defeated Gary Kasparov before an audience of chess aficionados. The match had a great deal of drama, but had Deep Blue made a bad move no one would have laughed. We do not laugh at machines. However sophisticated the circuitry, however agile the movements, they remain machines and beyond the scope of ridicule.

Laughter provides us with a thought-experiment, like John Searle's Chinese Room argument, in the debate on the artificial intelligence of computers.[18] Searle sought to show that, however sophisticated they might be, computers do not think. Even if they can translate Chinese, they do not *understand* Chinese. Suppose that John Searle (who does not speak Chinese) is locked in a room with boxes of Chinese characters (the data base) and a rule-book (the program) for matching Chinese questions with answers. Someone slips a question in Chinese under the door. Searle consults his rule-book, assembles the answer in Chinese characters, and slips it back under the door. The answers he provides are all sensible and correct, and Chinese speakers would assume that another Chinese speaker had provided them. Now compare this to a computer that performs the same translation function. If the computer understands Chinese, then Searle understands Chinese. But Searle does not understand Chinese; therefore neither does the computer.

If Searle is right, computers cannot think; to which I would add, Nor are they risible. If the translation program flubs a word we would not laugh. Thinking and risibility are both human attributes and limited to conscious beings. We cannot feel anything for nonconscious objects, since consciousness is what makes it possible for something to matter for us.[19] Our emotions are nothing if not efficient, for we cannot love or ridicule machines which our passion or laughter cannot change.

Before one can laugh, it seems, a sense of humor is needed. Should he lack this, can the *agelast*—the man who does not laugh—be blamed? If "ought implies can," we cannot blame those who lack the ability to correct their faults. But this is surely wrong. As Aristotle noted, being moral is not simply a matter of right action; it also involves having the right sentiments. We can and do blame those whose feelings are inadequate, who cannot feel friendship, love, patriotism, anger, or joy when these are called for. Few things repel us more than someone like Camus's Meursault, the antihero of *L'Etranger,* who is entirely incapable of sympathy for others. Imagine someone who is chastised for smiling at a funeral. "I'm terribly sorry," he explains, "but the fact is I don't *feel* anything." Far from excusing the apparently heartless behavior, the comment exacerbates it. We do blame people for bad feelings and for the absence of feelings. In part this is because we bear a responsibility for shaping our feelings. Rather than glower, the agelast should permit himself to relax and enjoy the lightness of laughter. Alternatively, we might blame people for their feelings, whether or not they can change them, because they are constitutive of their identities and moral personhood. We blame the sociopath for his lack of affect and the narcissist for his overweening love of praise. These are vices at the heart of his soul, and in such cases we cannot hate the sin without hating the sinner. So too, we curl our lips in distaste at those who seem unable to experience the joy of laughter.

In sum, laughter signals the wit's sense of superiority and is a most effective technique for correcting the butt's errors. In the next two chapters we examine objections to the superiority account of laughter.

2   The Elements of Laughter

J'ai dit souvent que tout le malheur des hommes
vient d'une seule chose, qui est de ne savoir pas
demeurer en repose dans une chambre.
Blaise Pascal, *Pensées*

Objections to the Positive thesis might take one of two forms. First, it might be argued that superiority is not enough, that something more is needed. This is obviously true, since disdain communicates superiority but excludes laughter. Second, superiority might be thought unnecessary, in the sense that we can laugh without signaling superiority. But while superiority is not a sufficient condition of laughter, it seems to me a necessary condition. We can feel superior without laughing but cannot laugh without signaling superiority. Here we examine what is needed for laughter, in addition to superiority, while chapter 3 argues that superiority is a necessary condition of laughter.

While superiority is always a feature of genuine laughter, there is no reason why we should expect to find it in feigned laughter. After all, I can pretend to laugh whenever I feel like it, while flying a kite or reading Kant. There is nothing of superiority here, or in the embarrassed and sympathetic laughter that seeks to cover up another's social gaffe. But since I seek only to explain genuine and pleasureful laughter, I need not trouble myself further with counterfeit laughter.

I also exclude what James Beattie called "animal laughter," the innocent laughter of infants and the adult's laughter from tickling.[1] In the adult laughter which interests me, an intellectual stimulus prompts a physical response. Nothing else is quite like this mix of mental and physical elements. Humor is the only activity where a complex intellectual stimulus produces a massive and sharp physiological reaction.[2] As a mental event, laughter is quite different from the merely physical laughter produced by tickling. Researchers report that we cannot be put into the mood to be tickled as we can for a joke. Minor comics can warm us up for the star comic, but we cannot be warmed up for laughter through tickling.[3] And as a physical event, laughter is very different from our reaction to other complex stimuli. We might respond to art emotionally, but not with the immediate physical reaction of laughter.

Laughter's sheer physicality, the sense that it is forced out of us without reflection, explains why it might seem innocent. When we hear an off-color joke we have no choice but to laugh. We might feel shame when someone afterward says "I don't think that's funny!" but by then it's too late. The only effective avoidance technique is to train oneself to lie in wait for an approach of humor, and to grit one's teeth during the joke. Short of that, the joke takes hold of us and we belong to it.

There are four necessary conditions for genuine, adult laughter. One of these, superiority, we have already seen. But superiority will not suffice without three other conditions. (2) Laughter must arise in a *social* context; (3) it must be occasioned by a *surprise;* and (4) it requires a lightness or *playfulness* of spirit.

The failure to observe the distinction between sufficient and necessary conditions has led to unfair attacks on the Positive thesis. Were Hobbes right, said Francis Hutcheson, we would laugh whenever we encountered an inferior. "It must be a very merry state in which a fine gentleman is, when well-dressed, in his coach, he passes our streets, where he will see many ragged beggars. . . . It is a great pity that we had not an infirmary . . . to retire to in cloudy weather, to get an afternoon of laughter."[4] But these are cases where one of the other necessary conditions of laughter—playfulness—is absent. They are not counterexamples when superiority is seen as a necessary and not a sufficient condition of laughter.

Sociability

Laughter may be seen as a social phenomenon in four different ways. First, only people laugh. Little Fido might wag his tail in joy, but does not smirk, chortle, or grin. Laughter is not always pleasant but it is distinctly human.[5]

Second, if man is the animal who laughs, noted Bergson, he is also the animal at whom one laughs.[6] We do not laugh at animals unless they remind us of humans. Think of a trip to a zoo, and ask where laughter is heard. Not at the hippopotamus or turtle cages, however ungainly those animals might seem. But how quickly the atmosphere changes as we approach the monkey cage. We smile before we reach it, as we do before we hear the first joke when a beloved comedian takes the stage. We laugh at the dog who slips on the ice, or the penguin who belly flops into the water, when they reminds us of human pratfalls. More than any of this, we laugh at a dog in church, since this mocks a sacred ceremony.

Third, laughter is social since there is a natural desire to share a joke with others.[7] Laughter is a conduit for transmitting information throughout society, spreading the message of superiority. In quattro-cento Italy, a clever epigram traveled up and down the peninsula, and made its author famous by the time it returned a month later.[8]

Laughter is what economists call a social or public good, since my pleasure from laughter does not detract from that of those who laugh along with me. Just the opposite, since a joke asks to be retold and the retelling increases the pleasure all around. The miracle of laughter, like that of the loaves and fishes, is that it increases as more partake.

Jean-Jacques Rousseau complained that the theater isolates people by taking them from each other's company. In fact, the theater unites us, for it brings us together to share an emotional experience in common. In particular, few pleasures are more communal than shared laughter at a comedy. When we read a clever play at home alone, we merely smile; but at the theater we laugh aloud. And as we do, we look about to see if other people are enjoying it as much as we are. If they are, our pleasure is magnified. A morbid play, such as *A Long Day's Journey into Night,* can turn into a comedy when a few members of the audience begin to snicker at the family from Hell.

> That was the winter of senior year. Then in the spring something hap-
> pened to me. Yes, I remember. I fell in love with James Tyrone and was
> so happy for a time.

The miserly father who sends his consumptive child to die in a cheap hospital, the alcoholic son, the drug-addicted mother. How did we ever miss the joke?

Superiority theories explain why laughter needs sociability. The instinct to share the joke widens the audience, like the strengthening of a radio transmission, so that more people receive the message about how to live. In addition, the signal would not serve a purpose if directed at an animal that could not profit from it, and superiority theories therefore explain why animals are not risible unless they remind us of correctable human faults. Other explanations of laughter, which ignore its function of signaling information to the butt, cannot account for the need for sociability.

Finally, there is a fourth way in which laughter is social, which we examine in chapter 13. Laughter creates a bond between wits and listeners who share a joke, and enables them to forge bonds of trust. The heightened trust permits them to exploit opportunities of joint gain that otherwise would be lost.

In some jokes, however, the wit laughs at the listener, and the element of sociability seems absent. In shaggy-dog stories, the punch line is withdrawn and the joke is on the listener. Plato concludes *The Symposium* with the very first shaggy-dog story that brings a fascinating discussion between Socrates and Aristophanes to an abrupt end. Gentle reader, would you wish to know the relation between comedy and tragedy?

> Only Agathon, Aristophanes, and Socrates were still awake, drinking out of a large cup which they were passing around from left to right. Socrates was talking to them. Aristodemus couldn't remember exactly what they were saying—he'd missed the first part of their discussion, and he was half asleep anyway—but the main point was that Socrates was trying to prove that authors should be able to write both comedy and tragedy. He was about to clinch his argument, though to tell the truth, sleepy as they were, they were hardly able to follow his reasoning. In fact, Aristophanes fell asleep in the middle of the discussion, and very soon thereafter, as day was breaking, Agathon also drifted off. (*Symposium* 223b)

Something similar happens in Gogol's *The Inspector-General.* The leading citizens of an obscure country town are thrown into a panic when they learn (through a nosy postmaster) that a government inspector from St. Petersburg will visit them. But who is the inspector? Why, it must be Hlestakov, a sponger visiting their town. He orders everything on account, and doesn't pay his bills, so who else can he be? He is fawned on by everyone till he leaves town, leaving behind him a revealing letter that the postmaster obligingly reads aloud. The mistake comes out, to the shame of all, particularly the self-important chief of police, who imagines how Hlestakov will mock him. "He'll spread the story all over the earth! And I'll not only be a laughing-stock but some quill-driver, some paper-spoiler, will be found to put me in a comedy!" And then, as we laugh at him, the police chief turns on us in the audience. "What are you laughing at? You are laughing at yourselves!" he yells. "Damn you!" As stupid and venal as the characters in the play are, Gogol tells us that we are no better than they. A chilling moment, when the actor laughs at the playwright, who laughs at the audience!

Jokes such as these conflate the roles of listener and butt. Since there is a butt, they are not inconsistent with superiority explanations of laughter. But when the listener is the butt the element of sociability seems absent. Yet even in the most offensive of plays a sympathetic listener may be found, one who laughs along with the gibes because he does not see himself as the target. There is always an in-crowd that mocks the suburbanites back at the multiplex. "The barbs are aimed at them, not at us!" The more shocking the play, the more thrilling for the sophisticates.

Those with a degree of self-awareness might afterward wonder whether plays that pander to self-love are entirely healthy or risible. Yeats attended the tumultuous first night of Alfred Jarry's *Ubu Roi,* an adolescent revenge fantasy that even today has the power to shock. "Merdre," the play began—*shite*—and the audience exploded, split down the middle between with-it progressives and outraged conservatives. Fifteen minutes later, when the house had quieted down, Ubu began once more. "Shite," he said again, and the demonstrations started a second time. The pandemonium continued throughout, with Yeats always taking Jarry's side. But alone in his room afterward, remorse set in. After Mallarmé, Verlaine, Gustave Moreau, and his own verse, after every novel kind of modernism, Yeats wondered, what would come next? "After us the Savage God."[9]

Surprise

The successful comic must surprise us with his wit. Or, if that is too strong, his jokes cannot be expected and routine. A stale joke is not a joke. Surprise—the sudden turnabout—is why Pope's abrupt descent to whimsy in *The Rape of the Lock* amuses:

Here Thou, great Anna! whom three Realms obey
Dost sometimes Counsel take—and sometimes Tea.

Few things annoy more than the person who thinks himself amusing but who fails to surprise. We feel cheated, and our sense of the comic is blunted. The compulsive punster, the bore with his well-worn stock of anecdotes, the self-conscious stylist who speaks in dialect or in Johnsonian polysyllables, all reveal a spirit too easily satisfied with self. Our groans usefully teach them to remain silent.

The need for surprise explains why comics need a sense of timing, where they gauge the pause before a punch line. Blurted out, the joke falls flat; but a Jack Benny could prolong the gag and keep his audience in suspense. He first held back, drawing the audience to him in nervous expectation, and finally punctured the balloon at the moment of greatest tension. A great comic essayist—a Mark Steyn or Michael Kelly—also has a sense of timing. Through sarcasm and irony, he announces that something wicked will come this way, and the reader hugs himself in delight as he waits for the dénouement. As they say, it's all in the timing.

There is a kind of anticipatory laughter, where we laugh before we are surprised. Robertson Davies described a reading by Stephen Leacock, in which the audience laughed throughout, after jokes, during them, and before they were told.[10] We can be put in the mood for laughter. Otherwise, why would minor comics be hired to warm up the audience? Put in the right mood, waiting for the joke, we laugh more heartily.

When we anticipate laughter we feel something like the sensation of fear and exhilaration we experience as we queue up before the roller coaster. We see ourselves gripping the rail, white-knuckled, and sense a portion of the terror of the ride itself. Similarly, we queue up at the comedy club in a jovial mood, waiting to be amused, and already chuckling inside. Yet our laughter still requires surprise. We wait to be surprised, and not to be bored. Which is to say that we can anticipate a surprise and the emotions it will awaken in us, and still be surprised when it occurs.

The requirement of surprise is consistent with the Positive thesis, which does not assert that superiority alone can raise a laugh. However, two rival theories of laughter, which would dispense with the need for superiority, focus on the need for surprise. The first of these describes the risible as a response to an *incongruity:* We are led to anticipate one thing and are surprised by something quite unexpected. The second theory sees laughter as a response to the *relief* one feels when surprise dissipates without harm. I describe the two rival theories here, then ask whether incongruity or relief might raise a laugh in the absence of superiority (chap. 3).

The need for surprise underlies incongruity explanations of laughter. We live in an orderly world and expect things to line up according to established patterns. When they don't we might find the incongruity amusing. But while this might raise a laugh, incongruity is neither a sufficient nor a necessary condition for laughter, as we shall see in this and the next chapter.

Incongruity explanations were first advanced by James Beattie,[11] but are most closely associated with Kant, who defined laughter as "an affection arising from a strained expectation being suddenly reduced to nothing."[12] Not surprisingly, Kantian jokes cannot be described as sidesplitting.

> A rich relative wishes to arrange for an imposing funeral. He laments that he must fail: "the more money I give the mourners to look sad, the more pleased they look."

Kant's comment: "When we hear this story we laugh loud." Ho, Ho, Ho!

Incongruity is indeed a feature of many jokes and witticisms. For example, a paradox appears self-contradictory, but on closer inspection is found to contain a truth that reconciles the conflict, and this might be amusing. Oscar Wilde's confession that "I can resist everything except temptation" meant that he could resist gross but not beguiling sins. Similarly, the *credo quia impossibilia* (I believe because it is impossible) of Tertullian and St. Augustine puzzles at first glance, since impossible things defy belief. But the deeper point is that impossible things (like miracles) must be accepted on faith alone, if accepted at all.

In its internal structures, philosophical analysis may build on an incongruity or paradox, and thus might resemble joke-telling. The Cretan paradox ("All Cretans are liars," said Epimenides the Cretan) is amusing the first time it is heard. Later on, one recognizes that it is a serious philosophical puzzle for which philosophers have struggled to provide an answer. S. J. Perelman showed how the Cretan paradox might be employed in a joke when he observed:

> The botanical garden boasts many varieties of cactus not found anywhere, not even in the botanical garden.

Similarly, the reductio ad absurdum, where proposition *x* is proven by showing the impossibility of not-*x,* resembles a joke that we follow down its path, only to see that something very different was meant.

Mathematical puzzles have a similar internal structure. Because of this, John Paulos suggests that one might speak of "mathematical jokes" and as an example offers a story from Gauss's primary school days. To quiet the students, the teacher asked Gauss's class to find the sum of the first 100 integers, only to find that Gauss came up with the correct answer almost immediately: 5,050. Gauss had recognized that the first 100 numbers formed 50 pairs of numbers that each summed to 101 (1 and 100, 2 and 99, . . . , 50 and 51). From that, it was a simple matter to multiply 101 by 50! A delightful story, to be sure. But not a funny one. When students compete to prove who is the best mathematician, the evidence of superiority from winning might raise a triumphant laugh. But take away the competition with its element of superiority, and the mathematical joke is not funny. Cleverness and ingenuity may be captivating, but more than this is needed. We do not laugh when we finish the Sunday crossword puzzle, alone in a room, or when we beat our computer at chess. Were incongruity all it took, comedy clubs would close: their patrons would all be reading game theory.

The need for surprise also underlies the second rival theory, which identifies laughter with a sense of relief. Freud thought relief a crucial element in laughter, which arises, he said, "when the sum of psychic energy, formerly used for the occupation of certain psychic channels, has become unutilizable so that it can experience free discharge."[13] In simpler terms, a joke transforms a serious conflict into a trivial one and thereby releases emotional tension. This is particularly the case with jokes that express hostility to a butt, since these permit us to overcome our inhibitions. We should like to vent our hostility but are blocked by social norms or our superego. And then we find a way to evade these barriers by triumphing over our antagonist through a joke.

In fact, laughter is often accompanied by a feeling of relief. This is most obviously the case in Freudian laughter that triumphs over repressive norms. But even in other kinds of laughter there is usually a sense that we have dodged a bullet.

For most of us, the first experience of conscious laughter comes when we observe a pratfall. The child's first reaction is fear: "This walking business is trickier than I thought." When he is more adept at getting about he can afford to laugh at the clumsy butt. However, the laughter is mixed with a frisson of "There but for the grace of God . . ." That is why the spastic humor of Jerry Lewis so appeals to children. As they have only recently learned to navigate their way, they feel a deeper relief when the butt takes a tumble. For adults, there is ordinarily little relief or laughter at childlike antics. We are too superior to Jerry Lewis to laugh at him. If, however, the adult's clumsy act is followed by successive, unsuccessful attempts to extricate oneself, each plausible in itself, building on each other until a minor faux pas has been turned into a total catastrophe, one has the comedy of Mr. Bean.

Were the butt wholly inferior we would fail to see ourselves in him, and his fall would fail to amuse. We are insulated from laughter when we do not believe that the butt's misadventures could ever happen to us. But how different it is when we secretly fear that we share the comic vice. We are drawn into the comedy and wait in growing fear that we will be unmasked ourselves. Our laughter is loudest when the comic disaster is magnified and prolonged, to the point where it becomes excruciating. Will we be brought on stage, our fly open, our shirttail out? And then the tension is broken, like a thunderclap, when the butt stands exposed and we are safely hidden in the dark of the theater.

Burke defined the sublime as the strong passion we experience when presented with a tragic event: we empathize with the hero and then feel a shiver of relief when we realize that we have escaped his fall. From the sublime to the ridiculous is only one step, for our laughter signals a similar relief which is not unlike the catharsis of tragedy.

In the *Poetics,* Aristotle described *katharsis* as the emotional release experienced by spectators at a tragic play. Tragedy arouses strong emotions of sympathy and purges them through pity and fear. Comedy may also arouse a deep emotional response, as we squirm at the butt's predicament.[14] However, the comedic catharsis is very different from the purgation of tragedy. In tragedy, we sympathize with the hero and participate in his fall. We take his side against the gods and men who oppose him. But in comedy the release comes at the moment of laughter when our sympathy suddenly shifts from the butt to the jester: we recognize the butt as alien and identify with those who mock him.

We cannot shift our sympathy from the butt when we identify too closely with him. Our laughter requires a detachment or emotional distance from the butt. This is why thinking of a person as a thing—a marionette, a machine, a clown—facilitates laughter. We do not laugh at things, but laugh more easily at men who resemble things since our natural sympathy for them is weakened. We can prick them, and they do not bleed.

Playfulness

Laughter's surprise and relief are enhanced by its playfulness. The surprise of a quick-witted sally signals that we have moved from the dull and commonplace to a realm of higher drama. This is a source of tension, since we are not sure at first how things will turn out. But when the punch line comes we see that the wit does not threaten us, and our laughter is mingled with a sense of relief. We are now in the realm of play-activity and illusion (from *in lusio* or "in a game"). We have turned from the serious to the ludicrous (from *ludus* or "game"). We act out a drama, but with the knowledge that it is all in fun. The stage is set by Alfred Jarry in *Ubu Roi:* "The place is Poland, that is, nowhere."

Max Eastman described the sense of entering into a different mental state through laughter by suggesting that we laugh when we are "in fun."[15] Even Kant recognized the play-element in laughter.[16] We suspend belief that things matter, and enter into a theatrical world. In a comedy, the audience relaxes, forgets its work, and awaits the entertainment.

Comedy is naturally diverting, and we have an instinctive taste for diversion. All human misery, thought Pascal, comes from the inability to be happy alone in a room without diversions. This is why we cherish the inoffensive (and sometimes the offensive) eccentric. His peculiarities might be risible, but still they entertain; and when the entertainment is intentional we sense that we have stumbled onto a delightful play. The master-artist, who can play the role to the hilt with wit and verve, a Wilde or a Waugh, may be a national treasure. What is special about him is his sense of the theater: his foibles are not faults, but only a role he assumes to amuse us. People who see ordinary events *sub specie theatri* have a suppleness and cleverness that duller souls lack, and remind us that, of all things, the ability to find joy in life is our chief earthly good.

From seriousness, we flee naturally to play, to a self-arighting and self-delighting world that leaves mundane concerns behind. We permit ourselves to believe in things that are not, and to enter into a realm of magic that dispenses with inconvenient facts and uncomfortable constraints. We shuck off the weights of our moral and social fetters and ascend to a world that is kingly and divine. In play, said theologian Hugo Rahner, man reaches out for "that superlative ease, in which even the body, freed from its earthly burden, moves to the effortless measures of a heavenly dance."[17] Our sense of play in this world offers us a glimpse of joy in the next.

Play-activities bring us a respite from the serious business of life and give us a breathing space from earnest moralizing. As in Charles Lamb's day, we are bound up in "the exclusive and all-devouring drama of common life, where the moral point is everything," and naturally seek refuge in artificial comedies. Where the stage turns serious, "we must live our toilsome lives twice over, as it was the mournful privilege of Ulysses to descend twice into the shades."[18]

Our search for diversion may lead us to play-activities in unsuspected areas. In *Homo Ludens,* Johan Huizinga argued that all human culture had its origin in play. We naturally take sides, like children at a ballpark, for the fun of the game. We divide into parties, cliques, cabals, not to exploit some factional advantage, but simply for the drama of the contest, like the gamesmen of Stephen Potter.

One such game is that of wit and laughter. In *Les jeux et les hommes,* Roger Caillois divided games into four categories. We might play at *agon* (contest) games such as football and chess, in which sides are chosen and the parties actively compete to win; at *alea* (risk) games of chance such as roulette, in which there are winners and losers but no contest; at mimicry games such as cops and robbers, in which the parties take on roles; and at *ilinx* (dizziness) games such as skiing, in which players seek to induce a sense of vertigo or "voluptuous panic" in themselves. These rubrics, said Caillois, might overlap in a particular game. The game of life, of career and marriage, is as much *alea* and chance as it is *agon* and active competition. Had Caillois examined laughter, he would have noted that it combines all four elements. It is a contest in which wits strive for the wreath of Dionysus; a game of chance in which a lucky hit can topple a butt; a game of mimicry in which a clever wit has a stagelike presence; and a supremely intoxicating pleasure that we pursue for its vertiginous thrills.

While playfulness is distinct from laughter's superiority and sociability, the three requirements are nonetheless related. Because laughter is playful there is an instinctive desire to share in it, and this strengthens the bonds of solidarity between teller and listener, as the sociability thesis maintains. And since the incentive to share the message of laughter is strengthened, the signal of superiority is spread more quickly throughout a community.

Because of our love of play, satire is most amusing when it mocks high seriousness. This is why Oscar Wilde thought one needed a heart of stone not to laugh at the death of Little Nell. It is also why, after reading Wordsworth's treacly *Lucy Gray,* we instinctively reach for Byron's cynical *Don Juan.*

> I say, the future is a serious matter—
> And so—for God's sake—hock and soda-water!

The border between sympathy and laughter is an area of heightened tension, where conflicting impulses pull hard in opposite directions. We feel a special gratitude to dark comedy, which excuses indifference to pathos and pulls us into the camp of laughter. Life is serious enough, it tells us, enjoy yourselves. Man does not live by bread alone, said Lionel Trilling; he also needs strawberry jam.[19]

The playfulness of laughter explains a hidden link between tragedy and comedy. The same event might be both tragic and comic, if viewed first with empathy and then as a theatrical spectacle. Imagine yourself at a lecture, where the speaker is a stammerer. He bravely carries on, but seems always on the verge of a breakdown. We listen in growing horror for his collapse, but are secretly titillated by the performance. We cannot decide whether we are watching a tragedy or a comedy, whether we should sympathize or laugh.

In a working-class section of Montreal there is a *Palais des nains,* now closed, where formerly a visitor might have paid to see a house of dwarfs and their tiny furniture. Did the visitor laugh, once inside? No doubt he expected to, but I rather suspect that his laughter was stilled when he saw the dwarfs sipping tea and reading *Montréal-Matin,* just as the visitor did *chez lui.* Surely he would have felt some sympathy for the dwarfs. But is that why he paid to get in?

Laughter is inappropriate where play is inappropriate—in court, during mass, at funerals. Yet the desire for play makes laughter especially delicious during solemn occasions. The jest told from the bench or during a sermon is often greeted with far more laughter than its wit deserves. This is especially true of funerals, since the desire to affirm life's joy through play is strongest in the face of death. The funeral mass is anything but depressing: the ceremony is diverting, and the mourners are cheered. The service affirms life, not death. At dinner afterward, when a large family has gathered and relatives meet for the first time in years, the simplest anecdotes are greeted with gales of laughter. The sadness comes afterward, when the ceremony is over and the relatives have left, and we lack the strength to believe *non omnis moriar.*

The One Necessary Thing

Chi vuol esser lieto, sia,
Di doman, non c'é certezza.
Lorenzo di Medici, *Trionfo di Bacco*

Superiority is not a sufficient condition for laughter, as we saw in chapter 2. For example, we might fail to laugh at someone in pain because the element of playfulness is missing. But I do think that superiority is a necessary condition. When I examine the different things that provoke our laughter, superiority seems a key that unlocks every door.

I must therefore address five possible counterexamples, where we laugh but the element of superiority might not seem readily apparent. These are incongruities and wordplay, relief and exuberant laughter, innocent laughter, the absurd, and the joke told on oneself (self-deprecatory laughter).

Incongruity and Wordplay

In chapter 2 we noted Kant's explanation of the risible: we laugh whenever two incongruous ideas are juxtaposed. We would have to reject the Positive thesis if a mere incongruity, without a signal about relative status, could raise a laugh. But while incongruities are sometimes risible, not every contradiction will serve. Kant himself acknowledged that incongruities in nature are not amusing. Snowfall in July is incongruous, but not risible. Indeed, why should an incongruity make us *laugh*? One might puzzle over an oddly paired set of experiences, but puzzlement is not comic, even when it leads to a Kantian incongruity. The only kind of incongruity that is risible is one that expresses a sense of superiority.

If we laughed whenever our senses were surprised, we would giggle at musical "jokes," the bane of the music appreciation class, where different effects are incongruously linked. Haydn's *Surprise Symphony* is an example: a sleepy melody is followed by a thundering punctuation, like the sudden blossoming of azaleas that lie dormant the rest of the year. Incongruity yes, but laughter no, neither for the music nor the azaleas— at most a musicologist's wintry grin. Before music may amuse, something more than incongruity is needed. For example, an imbroglio conveys the idea of utter confusion by giving singers parts that sound harmonic but are in different rhythms and meters. What is amusing is not the incongruity but the apparent confusion of the singers. Similarly, a musical parody might be amusing, but only because a composer is mocked. Recall Erno von Dóhnanyi's parody (in *Variations for Piano and Orchestra*) of Richard Strauss. Thundering crescendos, a climax, a pause. And then the piano softly enters—playing "Baa, Baa, Black Sheep." Or think of Peter Schickele's spoofs as P. D. Q. Bach (a hitherto undiscovered work reveals the influence of Western swing on Baroque music in the *Gunfight at the O.K. Chorale*).

As these examples show, incongruity is risible only when it identifies a butt's inferiority. By itself, incongruity adds nothing, except the element of surprise that we identified as a necessary condition of laughter (chap. 2). Nor does the incongruity theory account for the other elements of laughter, notably sociability, as the superiority theory does. Kant does not explain why the incongruity is always about people—only the superiority thesis does that. Similarly, only the superiority thesis can explain the instinct to retell the joke.

One might seek to rescue the incongruity theory by broadening it to encompass the superiority theory. This was what Beattie did, in labeling all excessive behavior as incongruous.[1] However, every comic vice represents a deviation from a golden mean, and all laughter asserts a superiority over excessive behavior (see chap. 5). Beattie's move was simply to redefine incongruity as superiority.

Nevertheless, the incongruity thesis might at first glance seem better able to account for the play on words. There is a clear incongruity, but the element of superiority seems veiled. Instead, there is the delight that comes from recognizing that, like paradox, wordplay operates at more than one level.

Wordplay comes in many varieties, beginning with the simple pun, where the same sound has more than one meaning and where the sentence in which it appears means more than one thing. The simplest example involves the homonym (or polyseme), where a word has the same sound and spelling as another but a different meaning. Pascal's "Le coeur a des raisons que la raison ne connaît point" (The heart has its reasons that reason does not know) employs words with the same derivation but with different meanings to make a profound point about the limits of rationality. The homonym might also employ two words, written and pronounced the same way, but with different meanings and derivations. Walking down a street in London's East End, Sydney Smith heard two women railing at each other from windows on opposite sides of the street. "They will never agree," he said, "for they argue from different premises." Alternatively, the pun might employ a homophone—a word that has the same sound as another, but a different spelling and meaning. A famous example is Donne's play on his name in *A Hymne to God the Father*. "When thou hast done, thou hast not done, / For I have more." So too, Sir Charles Napier is said to have employed an elegant homophone to announce that (exceeding his authority) he had captured the Indian province of Sind: *peccavi* (I have sinned).

The paragram is a wordplay that works by an alteration of letters: "Absinthe makes the tart grow fonder," observed Ernest Dowson. Paragrams will be familiar to listeners of the BBC's *My Word* program, where the guests are asked to explain the derivation of a common saying and do so through a humorous story that finishes with a paragram. When done intentionally, this may be very clever indeed; when unintentional, it is a spoonerism. Dr. Spooner is said to have transposed "the queer old dean" for "the dear old queen," and to have sent down a student with "Sir, you have tasted two worms; you have hissed all my mystery lectures and you have been caught fighting a liar in the quad; you will leave Oxford on the next town drain."[2]

There are a wide variety of lesser wordplays, such as palindromes, oxymorons, and rebuses. Palindromes read the same right to left as left to right. Famous examples are the introduction in the Garden of Eden ("Madam, I'm Adam") and Napoleon's lament ("Able was I ere I saw Elba"). The oxymoron is a species of paradox where apparently contradictory words are placed together for ironic effect. When the term has passed into general usage—"guest host," "idiot savant," and "jumbo shrimp"—it is no longer amusing. But it is arresting where it captures an idea that cannot easily be otherwise expressed, such as the special charm of the *jolie laide*. The rebus is a sentence in which one word is represented by a picture. In a child's picture-book this is not amusing, but consider the memento an anonymous sculptor left of Louvois, the Invalides' finicky architect: a wolf peering down from on high. *Louvois = loup voit* (the wolf sees).

In an acyrologia, a mistake wholly changes the meaning of what was intended: one dog brags to another in a Gary Larson *Far Side* cartoon "I'm going to get tutored!" When unintentional, this is a malapropism, from Mrs. Malaprop's (Sheridan's *The Rivals*) disastrous attempts to appear learned ("Few gentlemen, nowadays, know how to value the ineffectual qualities in a woman!"). Even the lowly alliteration may amuse, particularly when it mocks itself. In *A Funny Thing Happened to Me on the Way to the Forum,* Pseudolus is amazed to learn that General Miles Gloriosis has violated Thrace three times. "He raped Thrace thrice?" Finally, there is the mock pedantry that ridicules long-ago Latin classes. In *Big Julie,* the Wayne and Shuster parody of *Julius Caesar,* Mafia kingpin Big Julie walks into a bar.

> BRUTUS: What are you having, Big Julie?
> BIG JULIE: I'll have a martinus.
> BRUTUS: You mean a martini.
> BIG JULIE: If I want two, I'll ask for two.

Does wordplay support the incongruity explanation of laughter and cast doubt on the Positive thesis? I think not, for three reasons. First, wordplay and incongruities are not particularly amusing in themselves, and ordinarily more clever than comic. Often they fail to reach even that level. In the *Dictionnaire philosophique,* Voltaire called puns the worst example of false wit. Similarly, in his *Preface to Shakespeare,* Johnson lamented Shakespeare's weakness for them. "A quibble [i.e., a pun] . . . is the golden apple for which he will always . . . stoop from his elevation."[3]

Second, where the pun is amusing, it is apt to contain a hidden message of superiority. For example, Voltaire said of J.-B. Rousseau's ode "To Posterity" that it would not reach its destination. Think also of the riposte to Sir Edward Coke (pronounced "Cook"), when he asked his nobly born wife why she swelled so soon after their marriage. "Madam, I perceive thou hast a bun in thy oven," said the dour lawyer. "Yes," said she, "or else why would I have married a cook?"[4]

Third, the diversion of wordplay results from a competition in which the winner demonstrates his superior wit. The lowly pun may thus have a malicious tinge when produced spontaneously in conversation, since it moves the conversation to a more exacting plane. The wit might respond with a sally; a slower mind with a smile; and the dullard with nothing at all, since he will not have caught the pun.

The conversational pun is like a classical allusion or epigram. An educated listener will recognize that a game of learning has begun and that something is expected of him: the author's name or, better still, a continuation of the verse. The somewhat less educated listener will squirm, particularly if he has intellectual pretensions. The uneducated or humorless listener will simply take the epigram to be a piece of pedantry that interferes with what he thought to be the subject of the conversation.

We enter into wordplay as we enter into a playground, with a feeling of tension and uncertainty. We put our abilities and character to the test, stripped for the race and striving for the wreath of laughter. Because punning is competitive, the contest is conducted in deadpan fashion. Should we smile as we deliver up our bon mot, we give the game away. Better to slip it in without signaling what we are about, for the further triumph when the pun is missed. All deadpan humor signals the wit's superiority over those who fail to get it.

Much of our conversation is a game, with the laurel going to the quick-witted. As of right, they assume the power to dictate the subject of conversation, to proclaim standards, to squelch intruders and mock the dullard. The modest and deferential soul who fails to recognize the competition simply does not know what his colleagues say of him behind his back. Amongst the sharpest minds, moreover, the competition is fiercest. Surrounded by Burke, Goldsmith, and Sheridan, Dr. Johnson dominated conversation by his learning, clarity, and wit. One day a new visitor, scarce able to stop the flow of words, stamped his feet to make his point. "Why do you stamp, Sir?" Johnson asked. "Sir," the stranger responded, "because you stamped; and I was resolved not to give you the advantage of a stamp in the argument."

In sum, incongruity is neither a sufficient nor a necessary condition for laughter. It is not sufficient because it fails to amuse unless an element of superiority is present. And it is not necessary either. The comic vices of pedantry, clumsiness, and cowardice represent a risible inferiority, but not an incongruity.

Relief and Exuberant Laughter

Is there a sense of superiority in simple, exuberant laughter? This is not good-natured, innocent laughter; instead it is raucous and life-affirming. It is a vital laughter that triumphs over adversity and affirms the pure sense of life. It arises naturally in festivals, triumphs, and weddings, and is always heartier than intelligent and polished laughter.

Exuberant laughter comes in two forms: *triumphant laughter*, where we exult in our success against an adversary, and *carnival laughter*, where we mock constraining social norms and authorities. Both kinds of laughter express our relief at surmounting an obstacle. In triumphant laughter we dodge another's bullet; in carnival laughter we surmount oppressive rules.

Triumphant laughter is unsociable, and does not ask to be retold. Indeed, it is often more than a little annoying, particularly to one's friends. It is not playful, and might represent the joy of victory over an opponent, like the laughter (*s'chok*) the Psalmist describes.

When the Lord restored the fortunes of Zion, we were like those who dream,
Then our mouth was filled with laughter, and our tongue with shouts of joy. (Psalm 126:1–2)

All triumphant laughter requires an element of superiority over competitors. The laughter of the soldier who conquers his enemies or the student who wins a prize is an *io paian*, an immediate and unreflective cry of triumph that assumes a relationship of superiority even if it at first seems self-referential. The soldier is engaged in the most deadly of competitions and knows that his survival is linked to the defeat of his foe; nor would the student laugh if everyone in the class had received the same grade as he. Were superiority irrelevant, those who triumph against nature might laugh in the same way. However, Robinson Crusoe did not laugh.

While triumphant laughter is consistent with the superiority explanation of laughter, the second kind of exuberant laughter poses a more serious challenge. This is the exhilarating *fou-rire* that flouts restrictive norms or mocks authorities. One example is the obscene joke, where our laughter overcomes societal norms of sexual repression as well as private inhibitions. Freud thought that obscene jokes might express a seduction technique, but they are better seen as a thumbing of one's nose at social conventions. The same is true of most ethnic jokes where we do not have strong feelings about the butt's inferiority and where the joy comes from defying a norm of political correctness. The secret pleasure comes from breaking a taboo, not from expressing an opinion about blondes, Newfies, or Irishmen.

The Russian critic Mikhail Bakhtin called the hilarity of transgressing social norms *carnival laughter*. The carnival celebrates revival and renewal, like a jubilee, where past fetters are broken and fresh starts made. Hierarchical relationships are relaxed: the lord pays homage to the servant, the fool reigns. Serious matters are suspended, things do not count, absolution is offered ex ante, and we enter into a world of play and joy. This is the laughter of the charivari, Mardi Gras, and the streaker. Like obscene laughter, it works as a safety valve. When narrow churchmen sought to suppress the medieval Feast of Fools, with its Lord of Misrule, the theological faculty of the Sorbonne successfully defended the carnival. "We do this . . . in order that folly, which is second nature to man and seems to be inborn, may at least once a year have free outlet. Wine casks would burst if we failed sometimes to remove the bung and let in air."[5]

The symbol of *carnivale* is the mask, which gives material expression to the desire for liberation from repressive codes. In their *carnivale*, the Venetians went about incognito in their *bauti*, composed of a voluminous cloak (*tabarro*), a black silk hood (*zendale*), a white mask (*volto*), and a tricorn hat. They wore it for assignations, conspiracies, and the most ceremonial occasions. They wore it for everyday trips to the market, since an adventure might lie down any innocent-looking canal or campo.

Stern moral codes and the carnival exist in symbiosis, each feeding on the other. Without the dispensation of carnival, strict rules would seem oppressive, and without strict rules the thrill of carnival would be lost. Carnival (literally, "farewell to flesh") was the feast of Mardi Gras (Fat Tuesday), and celebrated before the austerities of Ash Wednesday and Lent. Take away the sacred feast and the secular one would seem pointless.

As polar opposites, carnival and Sabbath have more in common than the workdays they displace. Whether sacred or secular, the feast reminds us that there is more to life than the grim satisfaction of a job well done, and that we have a Heavenly home far removed from mundane concerns. When his flock has forgotten this, the priest must feel a closer affinity to the jester than to the businessman. At the heart of Christianity is the sinner, said Charles Péguy, but the jester is closer still. No one is as competent as the jester in Christian affairs. No one, except the saint.

Bakhtin saw carnival laughter as egalitarian, in contrast to the satire of the superiority thesis. Scratching out a literary career in Stalinist Russia, Bakhtin could not have been expected to praise conservative satiric laughter; but carnival laughter is the people's laughter, he said, and expresses a pure equality from which no one is excluded.[6] So viewed, carnival laughter lacks a butt and is inconsistent with superiority explanations.

Nevertheless, carnival laughter is anything but innocent. It is lawless and violent. It celebrates the grotesque and degrades the human. It delights in abuses, curses, and billingsgate. It seeks to degrade those in authority, covering them with excrement, whipping them, and exposing their failings. It may even rejoice in cruelty. "Without cruelty there is no festival," said Nietzsche.[7] Carnival laughter is the laughter of peasants with pitchforks.

While reveling in the primacy of sensual pleasure and bodily functions, carnival laughter is also fascinated with death. Spirits ride, ghosts moan, and we dance with death, as we do in the Menippean comedies of Rabelais and Bergerac.[8] The name is taken from Menippus the Cynic, whose descent into the underworld was humorously described by Lucian. Diogenes dies first, and from the underworld calls on Menippus to commit suicide, so he can see how the big shots are cut down to size in Hades. And so Menippus kills himself. He arrives in Hades, where he tricks Charon out of his fare, mocks the dead heroes, and banters with Socrates. The same fascination with death can be seen throughout Rabelais, from the moment of Pantagruel's birth, when his mother dies and his father does not know whether to laugh or cry.

The great Menippean satire on death is Edgar Allan Poe's *Cask of Amontillado*, set in a carnival, which describes the macabre retribution a butt takes on a satirist, the ironically named Fortunato. The butt had been mocked by the satirist, but now in the carnival the wheel will turn. The butt slyly brings Fortunato home to visit his wine cellar, in a catacomb beneath the house, to test a prize cask of amontillado. They descend to the cellar, and as they do the bells on Fortunato's harlequin costume tinkle gaily. On their way, they break open several bottles of wine, and Fortunato flashes a secret Masonic sign. The butt is not a Mason, but in response brings forth a trowel (a Masonic symbol) from the folds of his cloak. "You jest," says Fortunato. "But let us proceed." They descend further. When they come to the lowest reaches of the cellar, the butt suddenly clasps a pair of manacles on his now-drunken rival and binds him to a niche in the wall. The trowel is brought out again and the slow, methodical work of bricking up the wall begins. "An excellent jest," says Fortunato, as the butt continues grimly; and the last thing he hears, the final brick in hand, is the tinkling of the bells. Carnival laughter has taken its revenge upon satiric laughter.

The outstanding feature of the Menippea, according to Bakhtin, is slum naturalism, the *nostalgie de la boue*, in which debased behavior is held up as normal. In Lucian, Petronius, and Apuleius as well as in Rabelais, de Sade, and Alfred Jarry, we encounter the most extreme forms of depravity and vulgarity. This is egalitarianism, of a sort. But it celebrates an equality of degradation, in which every evil is ascribed to each of us, and all pretensions to morality and culture are cynically and cruelly mocked.

Menippean and carnival laughter are not without butts. To the extent that they are egalitarian, they are antihierarchical and delight in poking fun at religious and civic authorities. The ritual laughter of primitive people explicitly mocked the deity, while modern secular feasts such as the Bavarian Fastnacht developed in opposition to sacred celebrations. The holiest religious institutions—the mass, prayers, and sacraments—all were parodied in an age that had a short way with heresy.[9] The result was a bifurcated world, in which laughter was banished from the high seriousness of throne and altar, but over which a radically free and ruthless laughter prevailed during popular and profane feasts.

Carnival laughter is a critique of hypocritical or overexacting social norms. Carnival-goers assert the superiority of the pleasure-loving life over the narrow rules of ostensible superiors that would deprive them of human joys. "Their superiority is false," they claim; "ours is genuine." Carnival laughter is therefore consistent with the Positive thesis. Such laughter might be dark and ugly, of course, but the Positive thesis does not require that one who laughs *be* superior. Instead, it requires only that he believe himself to be superior. And the mocker never does see himself as inferior. He might be an inferior brute, but he can never think himself so when he laughs.

Innocent Laughter

Darwin suggested that laughter is primarily an expression of mere joy or happiness, like that of a child.[10] If so, this is a critique of the superiority thesis, since an infant's laughter does not make comparisons with a butt. But is an adult's laughter like that of a child? Darwin thought that adult laughter begins with a smile that graduates into laughter through sheer exuberance. The muscles employed in a gentle laugh and a broad smile are very nearly the same, with no abrupt line of demarcation between faint smiles and violent laughter.

Nevertheless, physiological explanations only go so far. Suppose that our bodies produced the same enzyme during both laughter and pain. On being told this, would we wish to reconsider our pleasant memories of laughter or our aversion to pain? Clearly not, since our consciousness of pleasure and pain cannot be second-guessed by the physical changes that correlate with reports of our emotions. Suppose again that a comatose patient is strapped to a gurney and injected with a drug. His whole body is "thrown backwards and shakes, or is almost convulsed; the respiration is much disturbed; the head and face become gorged with blood, with the veins distended; and the orbicular muscles are spasmodically contracted," just as we are when convulsed with laughter.[11] Yet the unconscious patient does not laugh.

Adult laughter might thus be different from the child's innocent explosion of joy, even if the physiological changes are similar. My daughter laughed the first time she saw another infant: Great, she thought, finally someone my size! The infant must grow slightly older before he can laugh as we do. How long? Just as long as it takes him to find someone smaller and clumsier than himself. Children may even laugh more heartily than adults, thought Freud, because they have yet to learn to repress their ego's demands or feel guilt when they sense their superiority over another.[12]

Adult laughter is more conscious of sin and thus less innocent than infantile laughter. Nevertheless, the shared mirth establishes a bond of warmth and even affection between wit and listener, and the failure to take account of the tripartite relationship of laughter has led to misleading attacks on the superiority thesis. Stephen Leacock argued that the superiority thesis must be mistaken because laughter expresses sympathy.[13] Similarly, Dorothy Parker said, "I don't think that the superiority idea is true at all. The funny people you like best are the people you laugh *with*."[14] But as they refer to different people, the sociability and superiority explanations are not inconsistent. The relationship between wit and listener is built on sociability; while together they signal superiority over the butt.

Some forms of humor retain their innocence at the expense of their mirth. Mere nonsense is never risible, but may amuse where it surreptitiously mocks some target. Thus Lewis Carroll's nonsense verse might seem droll as a parody of Middle English verse ("'Twas brillig, and the slithy toves"), and the court scene in *Alice in Wonderland* amuses as a satire of unfair judicial procedure. But in less skilled hands nonsense humor is cloying and tiresome, like the adult who thinks it cute to speak in baby talk. Such humor appeals to a retarded personality, in which the proprieties are accorded too great a weight and the comic sense cannot mature. And this was how the nursery humor of the Victorians found its audience in the nineteenth century. Satire was too adult a taste for such people, but they could laugh at *David Copperfield*'s Mr. Dick and at those who acted insane in a childish way.

For most adults, the most innocent kind of laughter occurs at the conclusion of comedies of integration. Here the theme is the transformation and regeneration of society, in which obstacles to the fulfillment of normal, healthy desires are confronted and removed. Typically, two lovers seek to marry, but are opposed by established authorities (the father in Plautus' *Pot of Gold*) or societal conventions (Lady Bracknell in *The Importance of Being Earnest*). The young rebel against an elder—the *senex*—and we always take the former's side. However, the tension between constraint and regeneration is necessary, for we cannot do without either. The impediment usefully restrains chaotic impulses; yet a society without a principle of rebirth has lost the power of transmission to future generations. At the end of the play, the opposition is removed, often through a wedding in which the generations are reconciled.

Comedies of this kind emphasize the element of sociability in laughter, in the bond between wit and listener, or between playwright and audience. The playwright takes us into his confidence and invites us to laugh at the butts on stage. "Good gentlemen," Harpagon whispers to us, "my thief, is he hidden in the pit amongst you?"* The resolution of the comedy seems to come from the side of the audience.[15] *Plaudite, comedia finita est* (Applaud, the comedy is over) was the invocation at the end of

---

*"Messieurs, mon voleur, n'est-il point caché là parmi vous?" *L'Avare.*

the Roman comedy, as though the integration was incomplete unless the audience applauded the rebirth of civil society. *Plaudite, spectatores, et valete.*

But even here, in Arcadia, there is also a butt. Comedy celebrates the transfer of authority from one generation to another, from the tyrannical and comic *senex* to the young lovers. What makes the play a comedy is not the change in power relations, but the reintegration of the defeated parent into the new society. Otherwise, we would have the tragedy of *King Lear.*

The Absurd and Postmodernism

Absurdities are sometimes risible, and when this is so they resemble a paradox. We follow a flight of thought only to see it disappear in a cloud of nonsense. In a master satirist, like Stephen Leacock, this is often a highly effective tool of ridicule. The bumbling provincial (*My Financial Career*) places all his money in a bank and is so rattled when this is seen to be a trivial amount that he clumsily withdraws all of it and never banks again.

There was a time, however, after World War II and before the New Left, when "The Absurd" meant something different and altogether more serious. It was then a grand name for the sense that life lacked purpose and meaning. The term gave its name to a generation *Growing Up Absurd* (as described in Paul Goodman's rambling book) and to a Theater of the Absurd. It was wonderfully suited to photographs in *Life* (a lonely philosopher pictured on an ice floe), but as an intellectual movement scarcely outlived that magazine. An Internet search of libraries reveals few books on the Absurd written after 1970.[16]

Absurdist drama was at times amusing when it mocked a butt, like the ridiculously proper English couples in Ionesco's *La cantatrice chauve*. But where a butt could not be found, the Theater of the Absurd was a grim affair. The characters were mysterious, their actions incomprehensible, and the plays were anticomedies. Traditional comedies begin with tension (the lovers' frustration) and end with integration (marriage or a feast or both). The comic hero is blocked by restrictions (want of money, social prejudice) that he overcomes to establish a new society. Bitter enemies are reconciled, said Aristotle, and walk off the stage as friends (*Poetics* 1453a). The villains are converted from pompous seriousness to comedy, or else (like the melancholy Jaques in *As You Like It*) dismissed as sore losers and spoilsports. By contrast, absurdist drama stressed a disintegration in which meanings, values, and personalities were subverted. In theory one might laugh, with irrationalities exposed and anxieties laid bare; but few spectators did so. Instead the mood was somber. Modern man stood "alone, afraid, and condemned to [his] freedom; victim of a nameless anxiety, dread, anguish, and guilt."[17] Those who had retained some fundamental beliefs—in family and religion—were shaken; those who had already abandoned them wondered what all the fuss was about.

What killed the Theater of the Absurd was the rejection of normative values. Laughter supposes a sense of superiority, and superiority entails normative distinctions. A theater that denies the existence of a normative order cannot amuse, on the Positive thesis. Nor did it.

Postmodern accounts of laughter face a similar difficulty. While postmodernism means several different things, the dominant North American strain adopts a radically skeptical epistemology. One of the founders of the movement, Jacques Derrida, sought to "deconstruct" meaning through literary analysis. Deconstructionism asserts that we experience the world directly through our senses but understand it only through our language. Our senses give us fleeting glimpses of the world; our language interprets these experiences and gives content to them. Each word leads to another word, in an endless circle, without ever coming to rest in reality or a determinate meaning. Language can only be understood in opposition to other words, and never as referring to some thing or person. Every meaning, moreover, is arbitrary, and for every interpretation there is an equal and opposite counterinterpretation.[18]

Derrida's predecessor, Georges Bataille, saw laughter as a response to dogmatism that reveals the limits of rational calculation. This resembles Bergson's theory of laughter, but unlike Bergson, Bataille did not think that laughter prefers one set of (intuitive) norms to another set of (rational) ones. Instead, laughter dissolves all ties and limits, exposing the fragility of established truth. Bataille's philosophical laughter is associated with anguish and agony, and is distinctly unhappy. "There's an indefinable gaping in laughter, something mortally wounded."[19]

Theories that deny our knowledge of the world might be deeply troubling and perhaps even infuriating. But whatever else they might be, they are not funny. And the same is true of theories that deny the validity of our norms. Laughter assumes a code of comic virtue from which the butt has deviated, and a theory that seeks to subvert all virtues will never raise a laugh. To the extent that such ideas are taken seriously, the more likely reaction is an anxiety that banishes laughter.

At most, one might see the ironist's faint smile of superiority. The postmodern ironist is not without a sense of superiority over those who have not read their Derrida and naively cling to obsolete values. Such people will not understand the double meaning upon which irony depends. Were we all to share the deconstructionist's belief in the contingency and indeterminacy of values, the occasion for irony would therefore disappear. But that is just what liberal ironists such as Richard Rorty would not want, since public laughter at moral codes or liberal ideals would be a threat to good government. The laughter must therefore be suppressed and replaced by a wholly interior sense of irony. We are left with private skepticism and public liberalism, and for Rorty the contrast gives the intellectual a perspective from which to be alienated and to look down upon nonintellectuals with the superior smile of irony.[20]

There is a good deal of self-congratulatory crowing about postmodern laughter, but little by way of wit, humor, or anything that might make one laugh. Hélène Cixous's *Laugh of the Medusa* is typical of this literature. Cixous argues that feminism can "shatter the framework of institutions [and] break up the 'truth' with laughter."[21] This resembles the Kantian analysis of laughter as incongruity, and if a mere incongruity is not risible neither is a celebration of meaninglessness. At most, this is the triumphant laughter that feasts over the defeat of a hated (male) oppressor, and to that extent it is consistent with the Positive thesis.

Self-Deprecatory Humor

Laughter is normally directed outward, toward other people. Indeed, we ordinarily find it easier to recognize small vices in others than large ones in ourselves. "Satyr is a sort of Glass," noted Swift in *The Battle of the Books,* "that wherein Beholders do generally discover everybody's Face but their Own." Yet we sometimes tell jokes on ourselves, and this provides the fifth and final objection to the superiority thesis. How can laughter require a sense of superiority if self-deprecatory humor is amusing? How can I triumph over myself without simultaneously losing points with others?

When looked at closely, however, one finds that self-deprecatory humor seldom amounts to an acknowledgment of inferiority. In fact, there are at least five different ways in which the joke told on oneself might reveal a hidden superiority or even a hostility to the listener.

1. The joke might misrepresent the facts: I suggest a weakness, but in fact am strong. I boast that "I used to talk in clichés but now avoid them like the plague." If you take this as anything other than a joke, then the joke is on you.

2. I might joke about a handicap, but at least I can joke about it. Since you apparently can't, I infer that the subject is more embarrassing to you and that I am superior to you. We all have weaknesses, after all; only the most powerful can joke about them. Was Pope a bit of a sycophant? Who isn't?

> I am his Highness' Dog at *Kew,*
> Pray tell me Sir, whose Dog are you?

3. The weakness is a trivial one. I joke of such matters to show how little I care about them. Of his tin ear in music, Ulysses S. Grant said "I know only two songs. The first is Yankee Doodle. The second isn't."

4. I reveal a weakness to show my disdain for you. I do not reveal weaknesses to people I respect. But by condescending to you, I show that I think you inferior. This is why Socrates stood up from his seat when he found himself lampooned in *The Clouds.* He wanted the audience to see how little he thought of Aristophanes.

5. I have the wit to tell a joke and you do not. By telling one about myself, in a battle of wits, I reveal my contempt for your wit. Recall Cyrano's jokes about his nose, told to show his scorn for his adversaries' opinions and the dullness of their wit. "You think that's witty? Let me show you how to ridicule a deformity!"

In addition, the self-deprecatory joke is sometimes a preemptive strike against harsher criticism from others. Sir Isaiah Berlin cheerfully mocked his own scholarship, but was greatly offended when anyone else did so.[22] Such jokes seem to represent us in an unfavorable light, but their purpose is very different. We dodge the blow because we laugh, and laugh all the more because we have done so.

The self-deprecatory joke might also reveal a former self's weakness. "Once I had a comic vice. Now that I have overcome it, I can joke about it. I wonder if you can do the same?" This kind of joke is more like a boast than a confession and does not cast serious doubt on the superiority thesis. We discover, said Lamennais, an interior person whom we distinguish from ourselves and over whom we triumph. We project ourselves above the weaknesses hidden in some fold of our heart; we see past them and take pride in our clarity of vision. Through self-deprecation, we step agilely above ourselves, leaving those who are more rigid behind.*

The most triumphantly self-deprecatory pose is the ironist's mask of ignorance, displayed in deadpan fashion. Aristotle's *eirōn* (or self-deprecator) pretends to a weakness but hides a secret strength, thereby tricking his audience to undervalue him The supreme example is Socrates, who punctured the vanity of his pompous interlocutors by first inviting their scorn and then trouncing them in discussion. "The only thing I know," he said, "is that I know nothing." He would begin a dialogue by posing an ostensibly simple question: What does beauty or friendship or justice mean? Listeners would confidently offer up a definition, only to be exposed as more ignorant than Socrates.

In this way, said Alcibiades, Socrates spent all his life joking (*Symposium* 216e). At his trial, he brought on his sentence of death by mocking his prosecutors. He had been found guilty of corrupting the youth of Athens and when asked to speak to sentencing proposed that he be maintained for free at the state's expense. One can almost hear the crowd's roar of laughter, repeated again when he suggested the smallest possible fine. "Yes, I think that I just might be able to manage that."

Like Socrates, the ironist is a risk-taker: he speaks on two levels and might not be sure that his audience will see the double meaning. If it sees one level only, it might fail to recognize that the ironist is on its side and take offense. Daniel Defoe's *Shortest Way with Dissenters* mocked the Anglican establishment by facetiously proposing violent measures against low church dissenters, but earned its author a stay in the pillory when the dissenters missed the irony. The jokes might also fall flat, like those of Mark Twain's *Pudd'nhead Wilson,* whose irony sailed over the heads of the eponymous lawyer's back-country neighbors. "I'd like to buy

---

*"On rit de soi-même, il est vrai, c'est qu'alors le moi qui découvre le ridicule en quelqu'une des régions inférieures de l'être, se sépare de ce dont il rit, s'en distingue, et jouit intérieurement d'une sagacité qui l'élève dans sa propre estime. Ainsi l'orgueil se nourrit de la vue même de certaines faiblesses cachées dans les replis du cœur, et qu'il a su y discerner. On n'est pas dupe de soi, comme on le dit, et on s'admire en cela même." Félicité de Lamennais, *Esquisse d'une philosophie* (Troyes: Cardon, 1840), III.9.II, 370–71.

half that dog," says Wilson, of a barking cur. Why only half, he is asked? "Because I'd kill my half." The wit is feeble, but leave that aside. Wilson is thought to be simple and his legal career is blighted. "Irony was not for those people. . . . They . . . decided without hesitation that if there had ever been any doubt that Dave Wilson was a pudd'nhead—which there hadn't—this revelation removed that doubt for good and all."[23] At the novel's end Wilson triumphs by cleverly winning an acquittal in a capital case, but until then he is undervalued by his neighbors.

Because he speaks on two levels, the ironist runs the risk that he will be misunderstood and ridiculed. This is not to say that ironic humor is inconsistent with the Positive thesis, since the ironist is aware of his superiority over those who lack the wit to catch the double meaning. However, other self-deprecatory jokes do ask the listener to feel contempt for the speaker and pose a more serious difficulty for the Positive thesis. These are like the rituals in which a smaller animal bows to a larger one to signal subservience. Much professional comedy is of this variety: think of the stage Irishman's exaggerated brogue, with the audience paying for the privilege of exhibiting its contempt and the comedian laughing all the way to the bank. Self-ingratiating jokes might also amount to an attempt to extract a benefit through flattery by one who stoops to conquer (the stage-Irishman, offstage). He subordinates himself, it is true, but he might still feel entitled to feel a certain contempt for you if his flattery succeeds. If it doesn't, or if by his smarminess he has sold himself cheap, the listener can scarcely be expected to respect the flatterer, and the laughter will now be directed at (and not with) the wit.

These kinds of jokes are not inconsistent with the superiority thesis, for the laugh identifies an inferior butt. What is different is that the wit and butt are one, and that only the listener laughs. However, this is merely to say that the wit might have a strategic reason to adopt a pose of inferiority. He does not signal his superiority; but as he has volunteered the joke we may presume that he is paid off in other ways. In any event, to the extent that his own laughter is counterfeit this is not a troubling counterexample, since the superiority thesis seeks only to explain genuine laughter.

Such jokes are, however, inconsistent with the sociability thesis, for they place the wit and listener in competition. In some cases the wit signals his superiority to the listener; in others, the positions are reversed. But in both cases the joke weakens rather than strengthens the bonds between the two. This explains why the self-deprecatory joke at times leaves us with a sense of unease.

In sum, superiority is always a necessary element of laughter, as the Positive thesis asserts. Our laughter is never without a butt, even in the ostensible exceptions described in this chapter.

PART TWO

The Normative Thesis

4   Objections to the Normative Thesis

Nothing's more fatuous than a fatuous smile.

Catullus, *Carmina* xxxix

Let us turn from the Positive to the Normative thesis, from the claim that laughter signals the wit's sense of superiority to a butt to the claim that this is a true superiority. We begin, as the Scholastics did, by examining objections to the Normative claim: *videtur quod non*. It seems *not* the case that laughter always signals a real superiority, however much the wit might think himself superior.

This might happen in one of four ways. First, the satirist's contempt for the butt might banish laughter. The satirist might be bitter and even unhappy. If so, how is he superior? I label this objection the Paradox of Satire. Second, laughter might be excessive and over-deter us from harmless behavior. Third, the Hobbesian Paradox suggests that laughter might signal inferiority because a true aristocrat will disdain to laugh. Lastly, laughter might signal inferiority and not superiority if it is more virtuous to abstain from ridicule.

Of these, the first three objections seem weak, and I answer them here. But the last objection is more substantial, and its answer must wait until we examine the content of laughter norms more closely in succeeding chapters.

The Paradox of Satire

Without playfulness, superiority fails to raise a laugh. Laughter may be biting and satire might even be bitter, but a bitter author does not smile himself, nor does the reader if he shares the author's bitterness. The difference between playful and bitter satire may be observed in the shift from the third to the fourth of Gulliver's voyages. The third voyage is Swift at his most amusing, mocking the pedants of the Royal Society. Yet the satire is weaker here than in the fourth voyage to the land of the Houyhnhnms, one of the most caustic attacks on human pretensions ever written, which shocks the reader without amusing him. The more intense the satire, the fewer laughs it raises. The Paradox of Satire is that it asks the reader to share its rancor; and if it succeeds the satire fails.

When it comes to other people's vices, most of us are thick-skinned; but the satirist is a man without a skin. He senses faults before anyone else, and wears a perpetual frown. Most of us encounter grossness, cowardice, and obsequiousness two or three times a day and never give it a second thought. These are the obscene graffiti of life, seen so often that we have become accustomed to them. The satirist's gift is the ability to point out that which we already know, and to provoke a moral or aesthetic response. He does not discover new vices, but uncovers old ones to which we have become inured. He provides no new information, but only reminds us that we already know enough to be shocked, had we not resigned ourselves to a contented indifference.

Bitter satire is Juvenalian. "Was there, at any time," Juvenal asks, a "richer harvest of evil" than in the cruel Rome of Domitian? (*Satire* 1.87). A city where "every street is just full of stern-faced sodomites. How can you lash corruption when *you* are the most notorious furrow among our Socratic fairies?" (*Satire* 2.8–10). In their imitations of Juvenal's *Third Satire,* Boileau and Johnson feigned a mild dislike of Paris and London. Juvenal's denunciation of Rome is altogether different: "The man holds nothing sacred; nothing is safe from his organ, not the lady of the house, nor the virgin daughter, nor even her still unbearded fiancé" (*Satire* 3.109–11). And it gets worse—*Satire 6, Roman Wives,* and *Satire 9, Woes of a Gigolo,* are brutal. Juvenal's blunt denunciation of vice is "shot full of horrible truths,"* said Boileau, and the savage indignation stifles our laughter.

By contrast, Horatian satire is witty, ironic, and detached. "Horace still charms with graceful negligence," said Pope, "and without method talks us into sense" (*Essay on Criticism* 653–54). While Juvenal never speaks of

---

*"Tout pleins d'affreuses vérités." Boileau, *L'art poétique* II.159.

himself, Horace often does so, generally in a self-deprecating tone. Though he mingles with the great, he presents himself as wholly without influence. In the *Voyage to Brundisium,* he describes a trip with his patron Maecenas to a famous summit conference that sought to patch up the quarrel between Octavian and Anthony. Maecenas' purpose, merely hinted at, is to bring peace to the Empire; Horace's purpose, presented in unblushing detail, is to avoid discomfort and get laid. As between Horace and Juvenal, there is no question who is more amusing.

The need for a Horatian playfulness explains why the drollest satires are never entirely bitter, and why the tone of world-weariness and contempt often sounds false. Boileau's *First Satire,* modeled on Juvenal's attack on Rome and urban sophistication, is a set piece by one of the best-connected poets in the court of Louis XIV, full of jibes at his enemies. In *London,* Johnson's take on Juvenal's *Third Satire* is more formulaic still. The man who said "He who is tired of London is tired of life" expresses his desire to abandon the city; the most famous hater of Scotland ("Much may be made of a Scotchman if he be caught young") yearns for a Highland retreat. We do not believe a word of it, nor are we meant to. If we did, the satire would fail to entertain.

As an objection to the Positive thesis, the Paradox of Satire may thus be seen to fail. A bitter satire is simply not amusing. What is missing is not the sense of superiority, but the spirit of playfulness. Superiority is a necessary and not a sufficient condition for laughter, and when the satire is bitter the absence of playfulness may banish laughter. And if the satire is mirthless, the Paradox of Satire is not an objection to the Normative thesis either. Under the Normative thesis, our laughter signals a true superiority; but there is no laughter in bitter satire. In any event, a bitter satire obviously does signal superiority.

Excessive Laughter

Edward de Vere, the seventeenth Earl of Oxford, was one of the ornaments of the Elizabethan court. He was fabulously wealthy, lived in grand style, and was so good a poet that some think him the secret author of Shakespeare's plays. One day, making a low obeisance to the Queen, he happened to fart; and was so ashamed that he immediately left for the Continent. There he stayed for many years, until he was quite sure his humiliation had been forgotten. When he at last returned, the Queen herself welcomed him back. "You have been gone far too long," she grandly announced to her court. "I had quite forgotten the fart."[1]

Excessive laughter was also portrayed in Patrice Leconte's film *Ridicule,* where the court of Louis XVI ignores substantive policy problems and devotes its energy to deftly delivered barbs. A young nobleman arrives at court from the provinces with a worthy plan to drain some marshes tucked under his arm. The plan is filed away, as is every project for improvement. But the nobleman perseveres, after he is given good advice by a courtier: "Be witty, sharp, and malicious and you will succeed." No one gets anywhere without stepping on someone first, and the favorite weapon is wit. A rival may be humiliated by a bon mot, and even driven to suicide, by a court that, six years before the Revolution, literally laughs its head off.

The examples suggest that we might have too much of a good thing, and that the costs of laughter might outweigh its benefits. There is a golden mean of laughter, since the excessive sense of humor of a man who giggles at almost anything can quickly become tiresome. Such people are decidedly inferior, like Aristotle's buffoon (*bōmolochos*), who says things a man of refinement would never say (*Nicomachean Ethics* 1128a34).

How might laughter become excessive? Laughter confers the public benefit of correcting comic vices and the private benefits of increased status. It might then be excessive where the only gains are private ones. Suppose that laughter levels are efficient, in the sense that, with any more effort at ridicule, the costs of wit-work would exceed all signaling gains. Would the mockery cease? Possibly not, since the parties might still have a private incentive to laugh at each other. *Ridicule* described such a world, where value-increasing work is ignored and the courtiers obsess over wasteful status gains. Apart from devoting too much time to wit-work, the courtiers might also worry excessively about being caught out as butts. The impulse to shield oneself from laughter by practicing the comic virtues is normally benign, but might not be so when the laughter is excessive and the courtier sacrifices the joy of originality for a world of dull conformity.

The courtiers in *Ridicule* would have been better off if they could have written an effective agreement to ban the use of wit, in the manner of an arms reduction treaty. No such agreement is possible, of course. Nevertheless, the problem of excessive laughter is likely self-correcting. One party has only to stop joking and wait for his move to be reciprocated.

The tendency to excessive wit might thus be addressed through simple patterns of cooperation, such as the mutual back-scratching that evolutionary biologists call *reciprocal altruism.*[2] As well, one of our most important and least appreciated predispositions—boredom—dampens excessive laughter. We are bored doing nothing, and are bored when we repeat the same act again and again. In particular, we are bored by dull wit and the repetition of stale jokes. Before the jokes become excessive, the audience might become bored and leave, taking the status gains with them.

In addition, we might have too little rather than too much laughter. Laughter resembles a market in which the parties bargain for inclusion in competing coalitions of wits and listeners. No one seeks to be a butt, and joining a wit in laughing at another might be a useful device to deflect laughs at oneself. The selection of butts might thus be seen as a matter of negotiation between wit and listener. The wit proposes a butt for laughter, and this offer may be accepted by the listener through a return of laughter or rejected through silence. In such a laughter exchange, individuals may be seen to trade off butts through implicit agreements about who is risible.

However, this does not explain why anyone would bear the costs to produce a joke. No one might do so because of the free-rider problems that arise when the costs of producing a public good (that confers a benefit on everyone) exceed the benefit any one individual derives from it. James Coleman described the free-riding problem through one of Æsop's fables.[3] The mice were pursued by a cat, and held a council to determine what to do. A wise old mouse stepped up and explained that the solution was very simple. Since the mice could outrun the cat if given advance warning, all they had to do was to find a way to attach a bell to the cat. An elegant solution, with only one drawback: who would bell the cat? What was socially efficient for all the mice as a group was not individually rational for any one mouse, and the cat remained unbelled. In the same way, no one might bear the costs of satirizing folly.

Nevertheless, the free-rider barriers to laughter do not seem high, and the status gains from laughter suggest a way in which they might be overcome. Because of the private benefits of membership in a coalition of laughers and the loss of status that comes from being identified a butt, people will compete for membership in winning (wit-listener) coalitions.[4] That is, the private gains from joke-making might be so great they we need not fear an undersupply of laughter.

This would not happen if a butt could always offer an equal status gain to listeners by cracking his own joke at the first wit's expense. Every winning coalition would then be unstable. Since all status gains would dissipate, no one would have an incentive to bear the cost of wit-work. However, the Normative thesis suggests an answer to this difficulty. Suppose that laughter does signal useful information about comic vices, as Bergson thought, and that some people are natural butts because their character traits are socially undesirable. The game would now have a solution, in the sense that it would produce a single winning coalition and a single butt.[5] The natural butt will never be able to compete listeners away to laugh with and not at him, and the process of coalition formation will promote valuable comic norms.

In addition, the costs of wit-work are usually trivial, since our laughter is usually immediate and unreflective. In theory one might speak of a cost function, but it is more like a by-product of being alive than a computational or physical chore. There was no cost for Shakespeare's Beatrice and Benedict, who took pleasure in mocking each other. "Not write?" asked Pope. "But then I think";

> And for my soul I cannot sleep a wink.
> I nod in company, I wake at night,
> Fools rush into my head, and so I write.
> (*First Satire of the Second Book of Horace Imitated, 12–15*)

Juvenal said the same in his First Satire. *"Semper ego auditor tantum?* Shall I always be only a listener? When a limp eunuch gets wived . . . , or a fellow who was once a barber (I ought to know—he shaved me) grows richer than all the patricians . . . , Then it is difficult NOT to write satire." When the costs disappear, so does the free-rider problem and with it the concern about too little laughter.

The fear of too little laughter is thus as speculative as the fear of too much laughter. There is little reason to pay great attention to theoretical arguments that tug in opposite directions, particularly when each seems self-correcting.

The Hobbesian Paradox

The third way in which the Normative thesis might fail is through the doubts the jester might reveal about his relative status—how he compares with the butt. Relative status depends importantly on laughter for, relative to the butt, we move up a notch when we laugh at him. Nevertheless, as we survey our inferiors, there comes a point when ridicule is infra dig, where we are so confident in our superiority that we refrain from laughing, and then laughter might reveal something less than true superiority.

Hobbes himself noted this difficulty with the superiority thesis. Those most prone to laughter, he suggested, would be insecure people concerned to assert their relative status.

> [Laughter] is incident most to them, that are conspicuous of the fewest abilities in themselves: who are forced to keep themselves in their own favor by observing the imperfections of other men. And therefore much laughter at the defects of others, is a sign of pusillanimity. For of great minds, one of the proper works is, to help and free others from scorn; and compare themselves only with the most able.[6]

This might be called the *Hobbesian Paradox:* we signal our sense of superiority by laughing, but the truly superior do not laugh. The most superior person scorns to rank himself against others. He knows "it is vain glory, and an argument of little worth, to think the infirmity of another, sufficient matter for his triumph."[7] He is therefore indifferent to relative status.

Those who laugh may in fact be inferior, and Hobbes's superior person might scorn to join in. At the limit, he will seek to rise above all laughter, as Lord Chesterfield advised his son:

> I could heartily wish, that you may often be seen to smile, but never heard to laugh while you live. Frequent and loud laughter is the characteristic of folly and ill manners. . . . In my mind there is nothing so illiberal, and so ill-bred as audible laughter. True wit, or sense, never yet made anyone laugh; they are above it . . . I am neither of a melancholy or a cynical disposition . . . but I am sure that, since I have had the full use of my reason, no one has heard me laugh.[8]

In an age of high refinement, the display of emotion was vulgar, and the wit disdained to laugh. At the end of a very long life, Fontenelle reported that he had never done more than smile. He had never made "Ha, ha."[9]

Nevertheless, the Hobbesian Paradox fails to deliver a knockdown blow to the Normative thesis. Any coalition of humorless aristocrats is inherently unstable, since within each group a member may increase his relative status by selecting another member as a butt. A society that seeks to rise above laughter is also laughable itself, for no one draws laughter to himself so effectively as the Lady Bracknells who think it beneath them. We resist all attempts to withdraw from laughter, even vulgar laughter, and for good reason. The underclass laughter that mocks excessive virtue—either as hypocritical or joyless—may offer valuable lessons about life, and those who resist it are often those who need it the most.

Vicious Laughter

The first three objections to the Normative thesis must therefore be discounted. Nevertheless, we might still reject the Normative thesis if laughter is wrongful and the morally superior abstain from ridicule. Laughter may be cruel, and we often feel a twinge of remorse when we laugh. We gorge on our pleasure, but afterward experience what Lamennais called the bitter aftertaste of an amour propre that secretly feasts over some guilty pleasure.[10] In a more sober moment, we see that we have degraded the butt and that laughter's malice banishes any feelings of charity. We have asserted a comic superiority over the butt, to be sure, but in doing so did we reveal a moral inferiority?

Vicious laughter troubled Augustan wits, who sought to distinguish their polished satire from ribald Restoration laughter. Low comedy was especially vulnerable to error, thought Dryden, since it required "much of conversation with the vulgar, and much of ill nature in the observation of their follies."[11] The proper moral message was often quite forgotten. Instead of punishing vice and rewarding virtue, the low comedies of Terence "have often shown a prosperous wickedness and an unhappy piety."[12]

Taking pleasure in the butt's discomfiture often seems a little méchant, particularly when a group settles on a butt to ridicule. Christopher Sykes tells how his great-uncle became the official butt for Edward VII and his cronies. The elder Sykes, a stiff and formal man, was devoted to the Prince of Wales, for whom he laid on lavish dinners. One evening the Prince, "moved by heaven knows what joyous whim," poured a large glass of brandy over Sykes's head. Sykes did not move. He let the liquor trickle down his face, inclined his head to the Prince, and without a trace of annoyance said "As Your Royal Highness pleases." The guests burst out in loud, unbearable laughter. A new game had been invented which, "in the touching way of children," the Prince wanted replayed "again." And "he had it again, he had it unnumbered times, he had it to the end."[13]

Our pleasure in laughing is sometimes mingled with a sense of unease, like that of a governess at a party that threatens to get out of hand. Samuel Johnson felt the ambivalence strongly, for he was both a devout Christian and a rambler who had heard the chimes at midnight. He delighted in the friendship of charming rogues like Richard Savage and could never bring himself to dislike Falstaff. Again and again he warns us away from Falstaff, but then describes anew his charm for Hal and for us. Falstaff "makes himself necessary . . . by the most pleasant of all qualities, perpetual gaiety, by an unfailing power of exciting laughter." Johnson cannot hate him, but sighs with relief when he is killed off. "The moral to be drawn from this representation is, that no man is more dangerous than he that with a will to corrupt hath the power to please."[14]

The impulse to laugh might thus arise from the malicious pleasure of ridiculing another. Our laws ban physical aggression but tolerate most forms of ridicule. With one form of hostility dammed up, our malice is channeled into laughter, which makes ridicule doubly pleasant. This is the sense in which Freud saw laughter as naturally transgressive and Charles Baudelaire thought it devilish.

There will be joy in Heaven, but will there be laughter? No, said Baudelaire, for laughter reveals our impurity. It is man's way of biting, said the *poète maudite,* and those who laugh at others can never be innocent themselves. Innocents would not enjoy asserting their superiority over others, and thus would not laugh. "Neither laughter nor tears may be seen in the paradise of all delights; both are the children of suffering."*

The few examples of laughter in the Bible seldom reflect well on the laugher. The first express mention is when God tells Abraham that Sarah will bear him a son, to be called Isaac (*yitzchak*, or "they [he] will laugh"). "Abraham fell upon his face, and laughed" (Gen. 17:17). A normal

---

*"Le rire et les larmes ne peuvent pas se faire voir dans le paradis de délices. Ils sont également les enfants de la peine." Charles Baudelaire, "De l'essence du rire," in *Œuvres complètes* (Paris: Pléiade, 1976), 2:525, 528.

response, since Abraham was over a hundred and Sarah was in her nineties and infertile all her life. Sarah also laughs to herself when she hears the news, asking, "After I am waxed old shall I have pleasure, my lord being old also?" (Gen. 18:13). God hears her, and asks Abraham why she doubted Him. Brought up short, Sarah denies that she laughed, but God responds, as butts are wont to do, "You did laugh!"

> Then Sarah denied, saying: 'I laughed not': for she was afraid. And He said: 'Nay; but thou didst laugh.' (Gen. 18:15)

In time Isaac is born, and Sarah's joy recalls the name God gave Isaac. "God hath made laughter for me; every one that heareth will laugh on account of me" (Gen. 21:6). At first the laughter seems innocent. Yet two verses later, Sarah observes Ishmael "mocking" (m'tzachek) and has him and his mother Hagar driven into the desert. This is one of the most poignant passages in the Bible, and we struggle to understand Sarah's apparent cruelty. No doubt she recalled Hagar's mockery when she bore Ishmael and the barren Sarah was "despised" in Hagar's eyes (Gen. 16:5). But even then the sentence of banishment is deeply troubling unless we recognize how Ishmael's fate is linked to that of Isaac and laughter. The banishment of Ishmael prefigures the sacrifice of Isaac and represents the choice God makes of his people Israel, a free choice that transcends human standards of justice. God will not forget Ishmael, but his mockery costs him his inheritance as Abraham's firstborn son.

Sarah's laughter (tzchok) was not mockery (m'tzachek), but was still displeasing to God. The two words share a common root, even as Isaac and Ishmael share a common father, and Biblical scholars have suggested that Ishmael's mocking-m'tzachek is an allusion to Isaac-yitzchak.[15] This explains what follows next, the sacrifice of Isaac (laughter). God will show more favor to Isaac than to Ishmael, but not before putting Abraham to the test. "Abraham," God calls. And Abraham answers "Here am I." Take laughter, God commands, "thine only son, whom thou lovest, even laughter," and offer him in sacrifice. God had made laughter but reserved the right to take him away. In the end, laughter is spared, but as Kierkegaard noted the priority of religion and religious imperatives over ethical norms was firmly established. So too, religious norms trump comic ones in the binding of Isaac. From a religious perspective, our first duty is to the Creator, Whose subjects we are. We begin not as Lockean proprietors but as Divine property, and as property we attain our highest state of being not by exercising rights of ownership but by recognizing how, like Isaac, we are bound to God.

Jesus wept, but did he laugh? Lammenais thought not,[16] and Chrysothom agreed. On Calvary, it was the soldiers who laughed. "He saved others; himself He cannot save." Sir Thomas Browne took up the question in his *Pseudodoxia* and concluded that, being human, He must have laughed, at Cana and at a good many other places besides. His mirth was simply too trivial to merit inclusion in the Gospels. G. K. Chesterton suggested another explanation for the *risus absconditus.* Christ must have had a sense of humor, but as His official biographers are silent on the matter, He might have hid His laughter from men. "There is some one thing that was too great for God to show us when He walked upon our earth; and I have sometimes fancied that it was his mirth."[17]

Nevertheless, the Bible affords little comfort to those who love laughter. "Woe to you who laugh now," He said, "for you will mourn and weep" (Luke 6:25). In the Pauline tradition, the world laughs at virtue and Christians have a duty to be "fools for Christ's sake" (1 Cor. 4:10). In praising folly, God mocks the pedant's false sophistication. "God chose what is foolish in the world to shame the wise" (1 Cor. 1:27). "For the wisdom of this world is foolishness with God" (1 Cor. 3:19). The truly virtuous may therefore be willing to court ridicule in accepting what Unamuno called "the foolishness of the Cross."[18] This was the sense in which St. Francis celebrated the foolishness of Holy Poverty, and in which Erasmus praised folly. This was also the laughter that Kierkegaard sought, in "a comic poet à la Cervantes, who will create a counterpart of Don Quixote out of the essentially Christian,"[19] for an age that no longer understands Christian virtue.

5   Comic Virtues and Vices

Inward goes the way, full of mystery.
Novalis

Vicious laughter poses a weighty objection to the Normative thesis, and indeed would be unanswerable if one took it to assert that laughter is always benign and the jester always superior. This version of the thesis must be wrong, since decidedly inferior people laugh. Moreover, the fact that rival groups may trade off laughter against each other must lead us to reject the idea of a universal set of comic norms. If laughter signals were always reliable, we could never have such conflicts. Since we do, laughter signals provide us with too many signals on how to live, and some of these must be wrong.

Yet if we abandon a hard version of the Normative thesis that attributes inerrancy to laughter, we might still defend a soft version in which most laughter offers us valuable lessons on how to live, and I do so in this section.

The Rose-Wreath Crown

Wherever we hear laughter, our attention immediately perks up. We automatically look to the wit, fixing our gaze on him in an unembarrassed way. He possesses the gift of joy, and we look on in the hope of sharing it, or in the secret fear that we are his butt. Our regard for him tells us to attend to laughter signals. How could we esteem the messenger unless we prized the message?

What are the special qualities of the wit that mark him for our attention? More than anything, we admire the wit's mental quickness. The original meaning of *wit* was intellectual agility; cleverness in repartee came later. The same is true in French and German: *esprit* and *Witz* (or *Geistreich*). Our language tells us that there is a connection between wit and mental creativity.[1]

In all primitive societies, folktales celebrate the trickster, whose mental agility permits him to surmount those whose superiority rests on a merely physical advantage. In the very first laughter in Western literature a clumsy artificer is mocked for his want of grace, but later takes revenge through a trick. In Book 1 of the *Iliad,* the lame Hephaistos crafts a set of serving cups and brings them, full of wine, to the gods on Olympus. The bandy-legged god trips, spills the wine over himself, and retires in confusion, to the peals of laughter from the other gods (*Iliad* 1.595–99). But Hephaistos's physical failings are compensated by a superior technical ability. The god of fire and crafts fashions a metal net and with it traps his wife, Aphrodite, in the arms of her lover, Ares. The two cannot escape, and all the other gods troop in to see the guilty pair. And when they catch sight of Hephaistos's clever device a fit of uncontrollable laughter seizes the happy gods (*Odyssey* 8.266–328).

We always prize the wit's intelligence and value the unrehearsed sally over the remembered joke. For spontaneous wit, few exceeded Sydney Smith. Smith was an Anglican cleric who one day found himself attacked by a freethinker. "If I had a son who was an idiot," said the freethinker, "I'd make him a parson." "Very probably," responded Smith, "but I see that your father was of a different mind."[2] In our time there is a story, said not to be apocryphal, of a lady who faced a doctoral examination in Paris, and whom a mischievous professor asked, "Mademoiselle, qu'est-ce que c'est l'amour?" Without missing a beat she answered, "The Amur is the river that separates Russia and China." For which, the story goes, she was immediately granted her degree.

Apart from his intelligence, the wit's insouciance elicits our admiration. The grim and fearful cannot laugh, but the man of humor is courageous. He rides to battle gaily, with a jest on his lips. Where others are tense and nervous, he is detached and sardonic. Of all people, we wish most to be like him. By contrast, the grim agelast is conscious of his inferiority. Like Alfred de Musset's enfant du siècle, like the Generation X'er, he knows that others have lived life to the fullest but that he can never do so. He is a glowering Gladstone matched against a sardonic Disraeli, an earnest Carter before an ebullient Reagan. We can never like him, nor can the gods either.

The wit shows just the right degree of self-assertion and liveliness in conversation. His laughter is light, pleasure-loving, and sure of itself. It does not calculate. Like senior partners in a law firm, it leaves details and trifles for lackeys and subordinates. It smirks at the earnestness and piety of inferiors, and because of this is sometimes thought amoral. But a morality that criticizes laughter must be, in the eyes of laughter, a false morality, for laughter possesses a serene conviction of a life well-lived, to which blame cannot legitimately attach, and signals a sincere belief in the superiority of its norms.

The special affection we feel for those who never lose their sense of humor amidst life's little emergencies may be seen in the career of Lord Hartington, that solid barometer of English sensibilities. Hartington's poise never left him; indeed, he was so composed during his maiden speech in the House of Lords that he was seen to yawn. In *Eminent Victorians,* Lytton Strachey describes why ordinary Englishmen loved him.

> They loved him for his casualness—for his inexactness—for refusing to make life a cut-and-dried business—for ramming an official dispatch into his coat-pocket, and finding it there, still unopened, at Newmarket, several days later. They loved him for his hatred of fine sentiments; they were delighted when they heard that at some function, on a florid speaker's avowing that "this was the proudest moment of his life," Lord Hartington had growled in an undertone "the proudest moment of my life was when my pig won the prize at Skipton Fair."[3]

Because of the natural reverence we feel for lighthearted wit, an air of complete prepossession and a sense of humor may carry one past the most annoying obstacles. "King" Allen was a well-known Regency beau and a good friend of Sir Robert Peel. One day, while Peel was chief secretary for Ireland and the two were traveling in an open carriage near Dublin, they had the misfortune to run over the oldest inhabitant of a village. A large crowd gathered round the dead woman, and Peel was recognized. The Tory government and Peel were very unpopular, and the mood turned ugly. Would they escape the mob's fury? Then, with complete self-assurance, Viscount Allen stood up and called out, "Now, postboy, go on, and don't drive over any more old women." Everyone stepped back, amazed at Allen's aplomb, and the pair continued on their way.[4]

The special quality that such people possess is good humor—the theologian's *hilaritas mentis* or cheerfulness of the heart. They have a serene contentment with their lot. Good humor does not exclude a desire to better oneself, or to enter into competition with others for earthly prizes. Indeed, the good-humored will relish the competition as a game. Whatever the result, they will emerge with equanimity. There is a grace to their laughter which always pleases, and when we share in it we experience the sweetest of epiphanies. The dullness of ordinary life is transfigured; the promised land is in view.

Good humor is a special grace (as well as the name of a mobile ice-cream vendor). It is a gift of intrinsic worth, and as a free gift we have no right to it. Instead we owe thanks (gratia) to Him from whom we received it. The state of Hell, where humor is entirely absent, is the law faculty described in *The Screwtape Letters* by C. S. Lewis:

> We must picture Hell as a state where everyone is perpetually concerned about his own dignity and advancement, where everyone has a grievance, and where everyone lives the deadly serious passions of envy, self-importance and resentment.

In a democratic age, when titled peers no longer command respect, we still pay homage to the nobility of laughter. More than anyone, Nietzsche celebrated laughter as an aristocratic virtue. His hero, Zarathustra, is a dancer and comedian, whose laughter is a badge of superiority. Like Hartington, he pays little attention to society's demand for gravity. "One does not kill by anger but by laughter. Come, let us kill the Spirit of Gravity!"[5] "I am enemy to the Spirit of Gravity," said Nietzsche, "and truly, mortal enemy, arch-enemy, born enemy!"[6] His Zarathustra is prankish, with a talent for joyous irony. He has little time for the nervous, sour people. "I do not like these tense souls, my taste is hostile to all these withdrawn men."[7]

Today Nietzsche is often remembered as a nihilist and held responsible for many of modernity's ills. But he was neither a moral relativist nor a modernist; instead he argued that, as a matter of fact, traditional religious values no longer commanded respect and that the Enlightenment project to replace them with a rational system of values had failed. The nineteenth century was a transitional stage. What would follow, he hoped, was his own positive moral system that celebrated the superior man, Nietzsche's *Übermensch*.[8]

How to recognize the superior man? Through his laughter and gaiety. Laughter demonstrates the superior person's triumph over life's vicissitudes, as well as his contempt for moral theories that kill laughter by demanding gravity and pity for the plight of inferiors. "This laugher's crown, this rose-wreath crown: to you, my brothers, do I throw this crown! I have canonized laughter; you Higher Men, *learn*—to laugh!"9 The true aristocrat triumphs over joyless ethical systems through a life-affirming act of will that announces its nobility and strength through laughter.

The study of laughter is a branch of philosophy—*Lebensphilosophie* or the philosophy of life—that was of great importance in Nietzsche's day but withered thereafter. Only in recent years has philosophy returned to the question of how we might find value in life or endow it with meaning.10 For both Nietzsche and Bergson, laughter provided an answer. Nietzsche employed laughter as a shield against "slave moralities" that interfere with the quest for self-perfection, and Bergson saw laughter as a social signal on how to live well. We need not buy into Nietzsche's rejection of Christianity and commonsense morality or accept Bergson's curious vitalism (the *élan vital*) to regret the abandonment of a foundational question of philosophy and to welcome its return.

The Gay Science

Imagine a man from Mars, come to earth to examine our customs, and for the first time happening upon a man telling a joke to some friends. The smiles, then the explosions of laughter, loud and through bared teeth, with the faces contorted in the peculiar grimace of Hugo's *L'homme qui rit*. Our Martian visitor would be alarmed at first. He would recognize a display of strong emotion, but an emotion of what kind? Anger? No, since it dissipates without consequence. Yet something extraordinary has happened, to judge by the violence of the emotions it released. Over time, the Martian will see the ceremony of the joke repeated, with the same result. He will likely conclude that he has beheld a religious ritual, doubtless a profound one. He has witnessed our homage to Dionysus, the god of the superabundance of life and joy.

The name for the study of joy is the gay science. This is Nietzsche's term, but he did not invent it. The *gaia sciensa* or *gai saber* was poetry—specifically the poetry of Provençal troubadours, the first poets of modern Europe. Troubadours represented a unity of freedom, chivalry, art, and dalliance. Wandering knights, poetry, song, courtly love, romantic passion, what could be more joyous? In his song to the Mistral Wind of Provence, Nietzsche called it "sadness killer, heaven sweeper"—"since I met you, like a tempest roars my joy."[11]

Joy has never received much attention from philosophers. Aristotle distinguished between two kinds of well-being, happiness (*eudaimonia*) and amusement (*paideia*). Neither means quite the same thing as joy. Happiness refers to a successful life that conforms to man's end or function; amusement is simply a light and ephemeral pleasure. The happy life is a virtuous life, and this is necessarily serious.

> Happiness . . . does not lie in amusement; it would, indeed, be strange if the end of life were amusement, and one were to take trouble and suffer hardship all one's life in order to amuse oneself. Now to exert oneself and work for the sake of amusement seems silly and utterly childish.[12]

Amusement is not an end, like happiness, but only a means to an end insofar as it permits us to relax. With relaxation, we are rejuvenated and might thus work harder and more seriously. What a grim choice we are offered! A happiness that is not amusing and an amusement that is not happy.

Aristotle's views on joy (*chara*) were ambivalent. He observed that most people would regard pleasure (*hēdonē*) as an element of *eudaimonia*, which "is why the blessed man (*makarios*) is called by a name derived from a word meaning enjoyment (*chairein*)." Aristotle also employed *makariotēs* (bliss or happiness) as a synonym for *eudaimonia*. However, he regarded joy as a passion, like anger, fear, and pity. These are feelings, he said, and as such they are automatic and can neither be praised or blamed. "We feel anger and fear without choice, but the virtues are modes of choice or involve choice." At most, the student might be trained to take delight in uplifting pleasures (*Nicomachean Ethics* 1152b8, 1099a33, 1106a3, 1179b26).

For a celebration of joy in the ancient world, one must turn from philosophy to comedy or religion. Comedy began with the annual festivals in honor of Dionysus, the patron of poetry, song, and drama. Tragedy preceded comedy at the Dionysia, and according to tradition evolved from choral songs concerning the death and resurrection of Dionysus. The ivy-crowned god was born to Zeus and the mortal Semele, who died when she asked to see Zeus in his glory. I rather think she heard him laugh, the laughter of a god being more than a mortal can bear. Dionysus had not yet been born, and survived only because Hermes rescued him and placed him inside Zeus's thigh. When he grew up, the twice-born Dionysus traveled throughout the Greek world to bring word of the death and resurrection of laughter, through ecstatic festivities and ritual feasts. He is irresistible and imma-nent, and is called the god who comes suddenly. In Hölderlin's *Bread and Wine,* the other gods hang shyly back from us. But one god steps boldly forth, loud-crying, joy-bringing Dionysus. The god who comes— *der kommende Gott*—is the god of epiphanies, who brings ecstasy to his followers and terror to those who resist him.

There are strong parallels between the life of Christ and the cult of Dionysus, and one may also turn to the Gospels for a celebration of joy. The special quality of Heaven is not pleasure or happiness but joy-*chara.* News of the Savior is tidings of great joy (Luke 2.10), and the reward of the faithful servant is entry into the joy of the Lord (Matt. 25.21–23). "And ye now therefore have sorrow: but I will see you again, and your heart shall rejoice, and your joy no man taketh from you" (John 16.22). The joyful vision of Heaven was reaffirmed by Christian theologians and poets. Aquinas described the joy that souls take in the sight of God (*Summa* II.I.Prologue 4), and a "joy which transcends every sweetness" was found in Dante's Heaven (*Paradise* xxx.34).

The earthly experience of joy, even in sensual pleasure, permits a glimpse of higher joys, like the spiritual ecstasy portrayed in Crashaw's *Hymn to St. Teresa.*

> O how oft shall thou complaine
> Of a sweet and subtile pain?
> Of intollerable joyes?
> Of a death in which who dyes
> Loves his death and dyes againe,
> And would for ever so be slaine.

The message about the unity of earthly and Heavenly joy is abundantly clear, even for those who are unaware of the double meaning of *dye.*

> How kindly will thy gentle heart,
> Kiss the sweetly-killing dart:

And close in his embraces keep,
Those delicious wounds that weep
Balsome, to heale themselves with.

The steps to the temple begin here, on earth, where earthly joys reveal deeper ones:

Which who in death would live to see,
Must learne in life to dye like thee.

There is also no mistaking the message in Bernini's sculpture of St. Teresa in Sta. Maria della Vittoria's Cornaro chapel. On viewing the sculpture, in which an angel repeatedly penetrates St. Teresa's side with a flaming golden arrow, a Spanish diplomat observed, "if that is spiritual ecstasy, then I too have known it."

Joy shares one attribute with happiness and pleasure, said C. S. Lewis: experience them once and you want them again.[13] Yet next to joy, mere happiness seems pallid, almost weightless. Happiness lacks ecstasy's bittersweet release, and we would never trade it for joy. Of her rapture, St. Teresa said, "the sweetness caused by this intense pain is so extreme that one cannot possibly wish it to cease, nor is one's soul then content with anything but God."[14]

Even when religious faith is lost, the experience of joy may recall a remembered but outlived spiritual life. Romantic poets and members of the aesthetic movement have contributed to what Charles Taylor calls an "epiphanic" tradition that celebrates a joyous communion with nature or art.[15] For example, James Joyce sought to imbue ordinary life with meaning through the joyous realization of wholeness and beauty. In a Joycean epiphany, the soul of the commonest object seems radiant.[16] Such experiences are always available to us, though we might be dulled to them by the false gods of politics. When this happens, and when the priest cannot reawaken our sense of joy, the artist may bring forth epiphanies by revealing the hidden joys of everyday experience.

—The ways of the Creator are not our ways, Mr Deasy said. All history moves towards one great goal, the manifestation of God.
Stephen jerked his thumb towards the window, saying:
—That is God.
Hooray! Ay! Whrrwhee!

What? Mr Deasy asked.

—A shout in the street, Stephen answered, shrugging his shoulders.[17]

Aristotle thought that happiness was a quality of whole lives and not of single moments (*Nicomachean Ethics* 1098a18). In part, this reflects the uncertainty of what might lie around the bend. "Call no man happy till he be dead," said Solon, and Sophocles said something very similar of Oedipus, whose example suggests that before evaluating a life we need to see how it turns out at the end. Apart from the need for an ex post perspective, there is also an ex ante argument for restricting happiness to whole lives. Aristotle claimed that only the virtuous were happy, and virtue is like a life plan we adopt at the beginning of our lives because it promises the best overall future life. The happy life is happy from the start. Finally, happiness is more a remembrance than an immediate experience. We do not stop to say, "Now I am happy," but years later we might recollect a happy period in our lives.

This is not ordinarily how we think of joy, which more frequently describes a moment of intense experience than a whole life or even a portion of a life. If happiness is remembered, joy is felt at first hand. Yet it does not follow that we cannot speak of joyful and joyless lives. A joyless life might be painful or persistently unhappy. Or it might be a happy life, as that was understood by Aristotle and the Hellenistic philosophers, a contented life that is devoid of harm and fear but also of ecstasy and elation. Epicurus explicitly denied that joy was a necessary component of pleasure, which he identified as the absence of pain and anxiety. Pleasure was our *telos* or end, and this meant being untroubled in body (*aponia*) or soul (*ataraxia*). The ataraxic are unagitated, undisturbed, and above all unexcited. This might be consistent with contentment, but never with joy.

Joy is as different from contentment as a laugh is from a smile. The relief of anxiety, the gratification of an urge, the satisfaction of an appetite might bring us peace, but not heart-cleansing joy. Simple contentment is a minimal goal: it plays it safe; and a life spent in the pursuit of happiness may be banal. But the quest for joy is heroic: it takes risks. It is willing to give offense, to court a rebuff, to play with fire, and has the deepest contempt for those who are too easily satisfied with more tepid pleasures. I feel sorry for you, wrote Baudelaire to a critic, that you are so easily happy.*

---

*"Je vous plains, monsieur, d'être si facilement heureux." Charles Baudelaire, *Œuvres* 2:233 (Paris: Pléiade, 1976).

The way to happiness is broad and straight, the path lit by Norman Vincent Peale and New Age purveyors of feel-good pieties.[18] The way to joy is narrow and rocky, and not always happy. Yet those who choose it, like Pascal, would never exchange it for the flatness of the merely happy life. Pascal's night of joy came on his conversion, between 10:30 and 12:30 on November 23, 1654. Taking out a page of paper, he wrote "FIRE" across the top, and then "Joy, joy, joy, tears of joy." I was separated from You, I fled You, I denied You. But now, renunciation total and sweet. When he had finished, he sewed his Memorial into his coat, where it was found only after his death. The word most frequently used, after *God* and *Jesus Christ,* is *joy.*

The most authentic encounters with God must, like joy, offer a sense of life lived with the deepest intensity, with something like Hölderlin's holy drunkenness, in which everyday cares fall away in a frenzied oblivion. With laughter, too, we discard the balance sheets of gains and losses, of injuries given and received, exchanging them for the over-full wine cup and divine madness. Our laughter seals a covenant with the gods, in which we render homage for creation with the sacrifice of worldly concerns. We ascend to an altar to worship a god that gladdens our youth.

Pascal's experience with God will seem wholly foreign to most modern readers, from whom the gods have receded. When this has happened, when the sense of the divine has been lost, how might it be recovered? We can scarcely sense the gods, who themselves draw back from us. In *Blood and Wine,* they stand about diffidently, almost embarrassed to present themselves to men who no longer have need of them.

> Unperceived at first they come, and only the children
> Surge towards them, too bright, dazzling, this joy enters in,
> So that men are afraid, a demigod can hardly tell yet
> Who they are, and name those who approach him with gifts.
> *(ll. 77–80)*

Once before the gods withdrew. During the reign of Tiberius, sophisticated Romans and Greeks began to notice that the oracles no longer spoke to them. This was the cause of much wonder, until at last the gods sent a messenger to explain their silence. They chose an obscure sailor named Thamus, who is remembered only in Plutarch's "On the Failure of the Oracles." Thamus was piloting a ship near Paxi in the Ionian Sea, when a loud voice was heard from the island. "Thamus, Thamus,

Thamus," it called, "The Great God Pan is dead." Bring the message to the island of Palodes, he was told. And when he did, when he said the words as he had heard them, even before the last word crossed his lips, "there arose from the island a great cry of grief not of one person but of many, mingled with expressions of dismay."

If we heard that the divine had withdrawn from the world, which could never again afford us joy, we too would lament in just the same way. For this reason, Christianity did not abandon the world, but instead insisted that the divine might find a home within it, through a God who became man and through bread and wine that became God. These are mysteries, and in the great theological debates of the fourth and fifth centuries it was always the intellectuals who spurned the world to insist on a God who was wholly removed from man. Arianism, Nestorianism, and Monophysitism had a good deal going for them. As compared to orthodox teachings, they were rational and clean, and supported by the very best people. But in every case the Church took the side of the peasant against the intellectual, and left us with a theology that is embedded in the world. A church that glorifies and venerates relics, that cherishes holy places and blesses holy water, is one that welcomes the joys of the world.

In its intense physicality, laughter is also rooted in the world, like bread and wine. It partakes of the divine without losing its human nature. For those who laugh, there is no abandonment, no distance from God. Our laughter also erases distances between people, in the communion between teller and listener, and we cannot imagine true companionship without laughter. The morality of laughter is necessarily sociable, particularly when compared to the Aristotelian and Hellenistic morality of happiness. In describing the superiority of the contemplative life, Aristotle praised its self-sufficiency (*autarkeia*) (*Nicomachean Ethics* 1177a28). When external goods and friends are taken from one, the contemplative man still has his inner resources and is thus on safer ground. While this recalls the Depression mentality, one cannot deny that there is something to it, for pollsters report that people were as happy in less prosperous times as they are today. Evidently, there are private substitutes for the external material goods that a strong economy provides. But a norm of self-sufficiency that draws trade barriers around one's heart, that asks us to withdraw into ourselves and bids us not to invest much emotion in other people, is joyless and wholly opposed to the morality of laughter. The purely self-sufficient do not laugh.

Few joys are as deep as the sudden recognition of radical innocence when an efficacious absolution wipes away sin. Nietzsche's Gay Science expressly excluded fresh starts, but the original *gaia sciensa,* with its trouvères and courtly love, celebrated forgiveness. In particular, the cult of the Virgin held out the possibility that grace might be extended to the most worthless sinner, so long as he served his Lady faithfully. In her legends, Mary's favorites were the knight and peasant, for a warm heart especially pleased her. She was imperious with suitors, jealous of rivals, and anything but priggish. She was not timorous or nice, but followed the knight into battle and wiped the death sweat from the peasant's brow. What she did not care for was the calculating merchant and crafty banker. And when her favorites were judged for their all-too-human faults, she could intercede for them, as a mother to her Son, and still the voice of justice.[19]

The medieval world of sin and forgiveness is another country. We still believe in the incredible, but no longer hunger for grace and forgiveness, having lost a sense of personal sin. There are institutional ills, like poverty and racism, but not personal faults. And as only the latter may be forgiven, we live uneasily in a world of diffuse responsibility, without personal guilt but also without the joy of forgiveness.

Like the Gay Science, laughter celebrates forgiveness. Comedy is staged in a world of play and freedom, a world of possibility where anything might happen. By contrast, tragedy takes place in the Republic of Necessity, a world of finitude that circumscribes our desires and our freedom. "Elle s'appelle Antigone," said Anouilh, "et il va falloir qu'elle joue son rôle jusqu'au bout."* Tragedy is a divine comedy, where human choices have already been made and we wait for God's choice. *Les jeux sont faits.* But in the human comedy, where laughter is heard, we remain free to choose, and it is never too late for repentance.

Comic Norms

Laughter helps us answer the question that Plato thought the most fundamental problem of philosophy: how ought one to live (*Republic* 352d). Today the question is seen narrowly, as one for moral philosophers. As

---

*"She is called Antigone, and must play her role to the very end."

Roger Crisp notes, "Moderns tend immediately to interpret the question 'How should one live?' as 'How—*morally speaking*—should one live.'"[20] Moreover, most modern moral philosophers give a restricted answer to the question, since moral duties are thought to be owed only to others. Provided we do not impose harm on third parties, we are each free to choose any path we wish. But this is a very thin answer, if the question is what we are to make of our lives. We can avoid harm to others without shaping our lives as we should. We might comply with all other-directed duties and still fail to exploit personal opportunities for joy. For self-directed moral imperatives, we must turn from the morality of the moderns to that of the ancients, to Plato and Aristotle. Or else we might turn to the morality of laughter.

Let us play with our ideas of the comic for clues about how to live. Forget, for the moment, the moral virtues that silence laughter, and turn instead to the comic norms that instruct us in right behavior. If we but listen, laughter will teach us the virtues that stamp a person as too superior to be risible as well as the vices that mark out the butt for ridicule. We cannot help admiring those who have risen above laughter. We might know that, *sub specie aeternitatis*, what counts is the Kingdom of God. And yet, taking a pratfall on the way to the communion rail, we cringe when we realize that people are laughing at us. Kant announced that the voice of Heaven should be ignored if it is not on the side of justice; but the voice of laughter can never be stilled.

The emphasis on the moral point of view can blind us to what Charles Taylor calls the "diversity of goods."[21] In listing the qualities we admire in a person, moral excellence is not the only thing that counts. Aesthetic taste and beauty are not moral virtues, but those who possess them have nonetheless a power to please. Those who cannot appreciate Bach might be paragons of virtue but they still seem flawed. Similarly, our laughter signals our disapproval of Bergson's machine man, whatever his moral qualities.

What the machine man has forgotten is how complicated a thing it is to plan one's life, and how misleading an overly simple code of conduct might be. For major sins, and minor ones too, the Commandments will suffice. But society expects something more than this, since we might follow all of the Commandments and still be dull, priggish, and pretentious. We might observe all of the laws and still be vulgar, clumsy, and thick. "Society requires something more: it is not satisfied with living, but wants us to live *well*."* And living well means more than being moral and innocent of crime.

Comic norms would be unnecessary if other sanctions—criminal, religious, and moral—were perfect substitutes. However, none of them does quite what laughter norms do. Laughter is out of place where other sanctions are better able to do the job, and there are things that laughter can do that other sanctions cannot. For their pretentiousness, Molière's *précieuses ridicules* do not merit hard time in Purgatory, nor do they commit a crime. But still they deserve the sting of ridicule. Comedy sports with human foibles, not with crimes. For different transgressions, a different set of penalties.

Comic norms have six features that distinguish them from the more somber injunctions of legal, religious, and moral norms. Comic virtues are (1) intuitive, (2) self-directed, (3) extensive, (4) nonperfectionist, (5) directed to a golden mean of behavior, and (6) joyous.

Intuitionism

On rational schemes of ethics, moral requirements may be discovered through deliberation about rights or ends. Even the rights and ends themselves might be specified through intellectual analysis. There is, however, another tradition in moral philosophy—intuitionism—which holds that we know right from wrong directly without reflection. "I stumbled when I saw," said Lear, and we too might see more clearly when we rely on our intuitions and emotions in addition to our unguided reason.

The intuitionist strain in Western thought may be observed in David Hume, Adam Smith, and Edmund Burke, in addition to Pascal and Bergson. In the eighteenth century "moral sense" philosophers such as Shaftesbury argued that our instincts about the good, though capable of corruption, nevertheless provide a reliable guide to conduct. More recently, some Natural Lawyers, such as Robert P. George, who base their theories of ethics upon a conception of human nature, suggest that we may understand our nature through direct intuition.[22]

Comic norms are also intuitive. Before they can be norms, they must be comic, and there cannot be a rational theory of comedy. We could

---

*"La société demande autre chose encore. Il ne lui suffit pas de vivre; elle tient à vivre *bien*." Henri Bergson, *Le rire,* 14.

never explain why a joke *ought* to be funny: either it amuses or it doesn't. Indeed, to offer a rational analysis of a joke is to make a joke about the limits of rationality. Our laughter must be sudden and unreflective, not studied and thoughtful. Deliberation drains it, debate kills it. "Look on her well," said Sheridan of the comic muse. "Does she seem formed to teach? / Should you expect to hear the Lady—preach?"[23]

As creatures of intuition, comic norms are very different from the rules provided by rationalist theories of behavior or politics. This insight underlay all of Bergson's thought. Our most basic sense of life comes from the idea of duration, he said, and that can only be understood through direct intuition. Duration may be measured mechanically, by a clock, but a mechanistic conception of time is different in kind from the real sensation of flow that we intuit as we live life. From this distinction Bergson derived his antimechanistic view of all aspects of life, including laughter.

The parallels between Bergson's intuitionism and that of Pascal are striking.[24] Pascal explained the difference between intuitive and rational norms by distinguishing between the *esprit de finesse* and the *esprit de géométrie*. Rational rules of moral geometry, which aspire to a Cartesian exactitude, are powerless to explain how we should live. What that requires is not geometry but finesse, not rules of reason but intuitions of the heart.

> Mere geometers lack finesse because they do not see what is in front of them, and being used to the precise and distinct statements of geometry, and not reasoning till they have fully examined and arranged their premises, they are lost in practical life, where the premises do not admit of such arrangement, being scarcely seen, and felt rather than seen, and there is great difficulty in teaching another to feel them if he does not already do so. . . . One has to see the thing all at once, with a single glance, and not by a process of reasoning, at least up to a certain degree.*

---

*"Ce qui fait que des géomètres ne sont pas fins, c'est qu'ils ne voient pas ce qui est devant eux, et qu'étant accoutumés aux principes nets et grossiers de géométrie, et à ne raissoner qu'après avoir bien vu et manié leurs principes, ils se perdent dans les choses de finesse, où les principes ne se laissent pas ainsi manier. On les voit à peine, on les sent plutôt qu'on ne les voit, on a des peines infinies à les faire sentir à ceux qui ne les sentent pas d'eux-mêmes. . . . Il faut tout d'un coup voir la chose, d'un seul regard, et non pas par progrès de raisonnement, au moins jusqu'à un certain degré." Blaise Pascal, *Pensées*, in *Œuvres complètes* (Paris: Pléiade, 2000), 2:743 [466].

Intuitive norms cannot be discovered through rational deliberation and might thus be labeled irrational. However, that label confuses more than it clarifies, since a norm that is discovered in a nonrational manner may nevertheless be consistent with a rational life plan. It is highly rational to follow one's instincts or emotions when these seem a better guide than ratiocination. Suppose that, because of judgment biases, we can be expected to guess wrongly in certain cases. Suppose further that in these same cases we might have recourse to a reliable guide (a parent or priest, for example) who can direct us to our best possible choice. In such cases we are better off if we defer to our external guide, since we would end up worse off if we trusted our reason alone. Now, our emotions or passions may be likened to the external guide, since they shape our behavior and are not entirely amenable to our control. And like the guide they might override an impoverished reason.

In Goya's celebrated drawing, the sleep of reason brings forth monsters. But the sleep of passion may also be murderous. Political theorists like John Rawls who seek to explain why we should pursue justice cannot persuade us that we should first care about other people. That is left for tragedy and comedy. By awakening pity, tragedy teaches us that sympathy and love are prior to justice and desert. "O reason not the need," groans Lear, when Goneril and Regan bargain down the number of his retainers. Lacking love, they will break their promises to him, for reason can always find a justification for injustice. Goneril and Regan promised the most extravagant love for their father; Cordelia promised only to love "according to her bond." But her promise was credible, since her natural attachment was sincere. So too, we would not enforce laughter's comic norms unless we first took an interest in the butt. Otherwise he would be no more risible than a machine.

While comic norms are intuitive, they are nevertheless capable of analysis, and we may usefully search for insights about how we should live by deliberating over what makes us laugh.

Self-Directedness

The goal of criminal, religious, and moral norms is the protection of other people. We impose criminal penalties when innocent third parties have been or (in the case of attempted crimes) might have been injured. Similarly, sins are transgressions that injure third parties or betray God, and moral faults are ordinarily concerned with third-party wrongs. In

John Stuart Mill's *On Liberty,* the principal statement of liberal theories of justice, state interference with individual choice is condemned if the sole beneficiary of the interference is the individual himself. Harm-to-others is what matters, not harm-to-oneself. Mill does argue, in *Utilitarianism,* that pleasures may differ in quality, and that a life spent in search of low pleasure is less than rewarding. But this is a counsel of prudence: no one has a duty to exploit high-quality pleasures if he is the only one hurt from not doing so.

As a transgressor, however, the comic butt generally injures only himself. If he seriously injured others, our sympathy for them might stifle our laughter. Comic vices impose real costs, to be sure, but these are the opportunity costs of failing to enjoy life to the fullest. The difference between crime, sin, and moral wrong (on the one hand) and comic defects (on the other) is that between imposing a cost on others and failing to exploit a personal gain. So far as one can tell, God is indifferent to unexploited pleasures. God might punish but does not jest, as Einstein noted.

Moral and comic virtues can overlap on premodern theories of ethics. In Aristotle's account of virtue, there is no firm distinction between avoiding harm to others (which is the goal of modern moral virtues) and self-development (which is the goal of the comic virtues). Aristotle's chief goal, in his lectures on morality, is to instruct sensible young men on how to make a success of their lives (*Nicomachean Ethics* 1095a15). Success in this life requires virtue, he thought, since only the virtuous life is happy. But Aristotle's happiness or *eudaimonia* has the sense of "fortunate," the kind of life blessed by a good *daimon,* and Aristotle's eudaimonistic virtues at times are morally neutral. For example, one of the correlative vices for his virtue of temperance is *anaisthēsia*—the defect of one who does not enjoy food, drink, or sex as much as he should.

Nevertheless, the morality of laughter differs from Aristotelian virtue. Aristotle did not especially prize laughter's lightness, and his great-souled man is an admirable but not particularly cheerful figure:

> Honor and dishonor . . . are the objects with which the great-souled man is especially concerned. . . . He is fond of conferring benefits but ashamed to receive them. . . . He is not prone to admiration since nothing is great to him. . . . Other traits generally attributed to the great-souled man are a slow gait, a deep voice, and a deliberate utterance. (*Nicomachean Ethics* 1124a4–1125a13)

The gentlemanly wit (Aristotle's *eutrapelos*) might jest in good taste but without exceeding the bounds of decorum. He will observe a certain propriety in what he says and what he allows others to say of him. And he will shun the buffoon (*bōmolochos*) who fails to observe the niceties and whose ridicule is excessive (*Nicomachean Ethics* 1128a5).

The recognition that a set of comic norms might be derived from our laughter poses the question whether the virtues are unitary or several. Is there one set of virtues or many? If there is one set, then comic and moral norms may be unified at some higher stage through overarching principles that arbitrate among the commands of different sets of norms. For example, the comic voice might be stilled when third-party harms become significant, and the requirement of playfulness in laughter might be seen as an emotional constraint that enforces this metaprinciple. What is needed is something like the rules of private international law that determine which law governs when the effects of a contract are felt in more than one jurisdiction.

Moral and comic virtues would be unitary if there were one highest good, like the utilitarian's greatest happiness principle. Aristotle may be read as saying that such a good exists, and that it is *eudaimonia* or happiness. In that case, the virtues might perhaps be graded according to their ability to produce the greatest good, so that the conflict between the virtues disappears. Such a view has much to commend it, for why would we want to have a virtue that made us miserable? However, other passages in Aristotle suggest that his more mature view was that the happy life is one in which we pursue several different independently valued ends.[25] Our notions of honor and wisdom are different and distinct, he noted, and the good may not correspond to a single idea. This is what our common experience would seem to tell us. Othello was brave but not entirely wise; Lear was generous but not a little foolish. And (thinking of academics) Edith Sitwell noted that the Graces are but rarely on terms of acquaintance with the Muses. There is no one overarching virtue that reconciles these differences and unlocks the puzzle of how we should act. And this is particularly so when the conflict is between comic and other kinds of norms.

One way to resolve the conflict is to assign a lexicographic priority to the good, as defined by moral rules. In that case, morality trumps laughter every time there is a conflict in signals. But there are two reasons why we might refrain from so tempting a solution. First, we might not want moral imperatives to come in first every time, since the costs of comic vices are often substantial. Of course, there is no need for moral rules to discount personal happiness or flourishing, and utilitarian theories would not do so. But there is a second reason why we might sometimes want to subordinate a morality of reason, and why we might even be prepared to tolerate a range of indeterminacy in deciding how to live. The impulse to laugh is instinctive and not rational, and a rational rule that arbitrates between rational moral and instinctive comic norms would appear to privilege the former. And that is just what we might not wish to do, if comic norms offer persuasive lessons on how to live. When a logical train of thought leads us into a risible absurdity, when the philosopher's first principles turn out in the end to be nothing more than ludicrous machine rules, when our laughter identifies a fallacy, then our instincts have trumped our reason, and a rational rule that seeks to resolve a conflict between rules of reason and of instinct cannot extricate us from our error.

Because the conflict between the virtues is inescapable, Aristotle did not attempt to reconcile them in a rule of reason. Instead, he turned to something quite different, which he called *phronēsis*—the quality of prudence or practical judgment that can integrate the imperatives of the different virtues and direct our action in particular circumstances. *Phronēsis* is so crucial to Aristotle's analysis of virtue that he made the surprising claim that, while the virtues are different, we cannot possess one without possessing them all. Othello cannot be brave if he lacks the practical judgment that can avoid the extremes of cowardice and foolhardiness; but if he possesses *phronēsis* as to one virtue he must also possess it for truth-telling and justice and all of the other virtues. To possess one virtue means that one has an integrated and coherent life, and if one has this, one has all the virtues. This seems wrong, but even were it true it would not follow that there is a rational principle that explains how the different virtues might fit together, since *phronēsis* seems to lack any content apart from a prior conception of desirable ends and means. If one has to ask what these ends and means might be, it turns out that one lacks practical judgment. Like the price of a Ferrari, if you need to ask you don't have it.

This is not a standard view of *phronēsis,* for most neo-Aristotelians appear to think that prudence has a positive content. Yet what can its content be, when it is not scientific knowledge (*epistēmē*) and does not appear quantifiable? Some have suggested that it refers to the special art of choosing ends, particularly when these are *agent-relative* and depend in part on each individual's attributes.[26] But how are these chosen, when the criteria for doing so resist rational calculation? Then again, Aristotle may be read to say that prudence refers to the choice of means, not ends. But if we may weigh the costs and benefits of different ends, then why aren't the means a suitable case for cost-benefit analysis? If the ends aren't mysterious, why are the means less accessible? Alternatively, prudence might refer to the quality of self-control necessary to pursue an end.[27] But in all these cases the command "Act prudently!" collapses into "Pursue good ends."

The opposite of scientific reasoning is not practical reasoning: it is not reasoning at all. To say that prudence does not measure costs and benefits is to say that it does not treat life as a matter of rational calculation. Instead, *phronēsis* analogizes the choice of how we should live to aesthetic judgment, and sees life as a fine art. *Phronēsis* might thus be thought a negative concept that marks the limits of rational calculation. In choosing his best life plan, an individual needs a practical judgment that is something more than purely intellectual deliberation. In this respect, *phronēsis* is not unlike Keats's "negative capability," which the poet defined as the ability to live in "uncertainties, Mysteries, doubts, without any irritable reaching after fact & reason."[28] This, said Keats, was a necessary attribute for great poets, who must keep themselves open to impressions from nature. So too, the choice of a best life plan for Bergson requires a suppleness that is open to impressions from nature or laughter, and that rejects the rigidity of rationalist planning.

A Bergsonian spin to *phronēsis,* under which something more than a rational principle is needed to arbitrate among different virtues or varieties of virtues, is very attractive. We are offered a choice between moral, religious, and comic norms, and in cases of conflict the need for something like *phronēsis* expresses the complexity of the choice and the uncertainty the individual will face.

Extensiveness

The forgone pleasures of comic defects are more remote and difficult to measure than the costs of crime. A mild eccentricity might represent the best possible life-plan for someone with idiosyncratic, harmless preferences. But when the foible becomes an obsession and shuts out avenues of greater pleasure, laughter usefully points this out to the butt. Criminal sanctions are entirely inappropriate here, and as they are reserved for more serious offenses must be limited in scope.

Comic norms may therefore be more extensive and nuanced than legal or moral rules could ever hope to be. In Truffaut's *Jules et Jim,* for example, the over-serious and naive Jules is held up to mild ridicule by the more sophisticated Jim. In the movie, Jules welcomes Jim to his cottage after the war. Surrounded by his wife (Catherine) and their daughter, Jules rhapsodizes about married life.

> JULES: An angel is passing.
> *Jim pauses, examines his watch, and at length says:*
> JIM: No big deal. It's 1:20. Angels always pass by at twenty past.
> JULES *(solemnly):* I didn't know that.
> CATHERINE: Me either.
> *Another silence.*
> JIM: Twenty after and also twenty to.*

Jim's gentle mockery communicates more than he could have formulated in words. Had Jules paid closer attention to the signal he might better have understood the fragility of his marriage.

To say that comic norms are more extensive than legal and moral rules is not to say that laughter provides a detailed set of rules. Comic norms are standards, not rules of behavior. Unlike rules, standards offer only a general guide to right conduct, like the duty to take the care of a "reasonable man" in tort law. The idea that we might extract a set of rules of behavior from our laughter is a piece of machine thought, and deserving of ridicule. To see this, imagine that one were asked to provide a set of "rules" for good art, since comic virtues aspire to the condition of art. We seek to uphold artistic standards, but artistic rules can produce only machine art.

Nonperfectionism

While Aristotle's *eudaimonia* is usually translated as happiness, he gave the term a special significance, and many recent scholars think "flour-

---

*Jules. Un ange passe. *Jim finit par sortir sa montre, et, après un temps: Jim:* C'est normal, il est une heure vingt. Les anges passent toujours à vingt de chaque heure. *Jules.* Je ne le savais pas. *Catherine.* Moi non plus. *Un nouveau silence. Jim:* A vingt et aussi à moins vingt. François Truffaut, *Jules et Jim* (Paris: Seuil, 1971), 62.

ishing" a better translation. *Eudaimonia* was not a subjective good but the exercise of a man's soul in accordance with excellence or virtue, and in this sense Aristotle's moral theory was perfectionist. It saw the moral end as the perfection of the total nature of man, with full happiness achieved through the realization of his capacities.

The theologian's supererogatory virtues are perfectionist in a different way, for they ask us to act beyond the call of duty and do more than keep all the Commandments. The rich young man of St. Matthew's Gospel did not murder, steal, commit adultery, or bear false witness, and still his heart was troubled. "What lack I yet?" he asked. "If thou wilt be perfect," Christ answered, "go and sell all thou hast, and give to the poor, . . . and come and follow me." The young man turned sadly away, since he was very rich, and as he left Christ told his disciples the eye-of-the-needle parable (Matthew 19:16–24).

Because comic norms are thick with rules about self-fulfillment, they resemble Aristotle's perfectionist ethics. The morality of laughter is teleological and assumes universal standards in which butts are naturally risible. Moreover, like supererogatory virtue, comic laughter is unsatisfied with adherence to the negative injunctions of simple commandments. Like the rich young man, it seeks something more. It calls on us to immunize ourselves from laughter by adopting a superior life.

Nevertheless, comic norms are not perfectionist. Perfectionism can be thought to require adherence to a common life plan by all individuals, with each person striving to emulate Aristotle's great-souled man or a saint. However, comic norms do not bid us to abandon our individuality. To say that there are comic vices that are always risible and comic virtues that are always admirable is not the same thing as saying that we should all aspire to develop our virtues in the same way. Comic norms assume that we have ends, but it does not follow that each of us has the same set of ends. Norms may be agent-relative without being wholly subjective and relativist.[29] It is necessary to draw this distinction, since a comic relativism which asserts that one life plan is as good as another is wholly destructive of laughter.

There is another sense in which comic norms are nonperfectionist. Laughter and laughter norms are human, and as George Orwell noted, "the essence of being human is that one does not seek perfection. . . . No doubt alcohol, tobacco and so forth are things that a saint must avoid, but sainthood is also a thing that human beings must avoid."[30] While sainthood and supererogatory virtue entail extremes of behavior, comic norms represent a golden mean.

Comic Virtue as a Mean

Aristotle defined virtue as a middle way between extremes of behavior.[31] For example, the virtue of courage strikes a mean between rashness (excess) and cowardice (insufficiency), and the virtue of liberality strikes a mean between prodigality (excess) and meanness (insufficiency).

For each comic virtue, there are as in Aristotle two correlative vices that represent opposing deviations from the norm's golden mean. Laughter strikes a balance between two extremes, one an insufficiency and the other an excess of a comic virtue. "The sensible man would be called a fool, the moral immoral," said Horace, "if he followed Goodness herself beyond the proper limit!" (*Epistles* I.6.15–16).

Describing virtue as a mean involves several notorious difficulties. Must the virtuous man be a Milquetoast? Surely not, for the virtuous man might be extremely angry when the occasion calls for passion. But he cannot be passionate all the time or none of the time without tumbling into vice. Then again, some evils seem bad per se. What is the moderate virtue of which mass murder is the vice? Only a few murders? Obviously not. Instead, these are cases where "some things are names with their worthlessness included" (*Nicomachean Ethics* 1107a10). Murder is always wrong, because it is always an extreme. Aristotle's point is that for each vice there is a virtue that strikes a balance between self- and other-regarding behavior or between self-defeating extremes. The coward is too attached to self; the foolhardy insufficiently so. The envious are too covetous; but those who are indifferent to the competition of life may be sluggards, since a concern for relative status is a spur to activity.

While virtue is a mean, there must be one good we seek without moderation, and for Aristotle this is *eudaimonia*. When it comes to happiness, more is always better. And the same is true of joy, in the morality of laughter. The Paradox of the Mean is that the ultimate good is sought through moderation, but the mean itself is wholly desirable. As between the great- and the small-souled man, we should not wish to be moderate-souled. Similarly, the comic norms ask us to seek a middle way between comic vices, not between comic virtue and risibility, and not between joy and joylessness.

Joyfulness

Because they are expressed through the joyful medium of laughter, comic norms enthrone joy. The medium shapes the message, for our laughter bids us to treasure joy. But if laughter is joyful it is not extreme. This has the appearance of a paradox, since joy is not associated with moderate behavior. "The golden mean is an uninteresting doctrine," said Bertrand Russell in *The Conquest of Happiness,* "and I can remember when I was young rejecting it with scorn and indignation, since in those days it was heroic extremes that I admired." On closer inspection, however, the sense of paradox disappears. The *experience* of laughter is entirely joyful, but the content of the norm is moderate and our laughter signals the discovery of a risible extremism. The fallacy is in thinking that extreme behavior is productive of joy. The immoderate might be cowardly, graceless, and pedantic, and these are not joyful accomplishments. More moderate people who possess the balanced comic virtues of fortitude, grace, and happy learning are more likely to be joyful.

If the comic norms are Aristotelian, they are distinctly not Nietzschean. Nietzsche's ethic of passionate experience and self-fulfillment canonized laughter, but less wisely rejected Aristotelian moderation. "The secret for harvesting from existence the greatest fruitfulness and the greatest enjoyment is—to *live dangerously!* Build your cities on the slopes of Vesuvius!"[32] This is an ethic that, in evaluating a prospect, ignores every payoff except the highest. In business, it bets the firm's pension fund at Las Vegas. In life, it is a call to imprudence and immoderate vice. This is not a prescription for joy, and we do well to ridicule comic extremes for that reason.

The single-minded pursuit of joyous experience, like Walter Pater's invocation in *The Renaissance* "to burn always with this hard, gem-like flame, to maintain this ecstasy," will usually turn out to be self-defeating. Joy is too ephemeral to be grasped in that manner. Pater's extreme aestheticism is not a recipe for a joyful life, nor are we tempted by Baudelaire's paean to intoxification.

> One must always be drunk. That's the whole thing; the only question.
> So as not to feel the horrible burden of Time breaking down on your
> shoulders and bending you to the earth, you must get drunk without

respite. Drunk with what? With wine, with poetry, or with virtue, as you please. But get drunk.*

While joy is a fundamental good, success in life requires something other than an unrelenting pursuit of ecstatic experience. We are more joyful when we do not pursue joy every waking moment, and laugh better when we do not laugh all the time. The hothouse quality of high aestheticism suggests a want of health and true joy, and to signal this Eugene O'Neill placed Baudelaire's homage to drunkenness in the mouth of a dying consumptive in *A Long Day's Journey into Night.*

In a highly risk-averse society, however, the Nietzschean call to live dangerously might not seem inconsistent with Aristotelian virtue. When we are excessively risk averse and worry obsessively about personal safety, the injunction to take risks might usefully tilt us in the direction of the mean of courage. And that was Nietzsche's point, in describing what he called the Last Man. Through a want of courage, he said, modern man has forgotten his heroic past and is evolving toward a state of ignominious degradation. The evolutionary decline will end with the Last Man, who is contented with his mediocrity, who risks nothing, "who makes everything small." Such people are well balanced, and if there are few epiphanies in their lives they at least have mastered Benjamin Franklin's rules for success. "They have their little pleasures for the day and their little pleasures for the night: but they respect health."[33] From today's perspective, the similarities between the superman and the great-souled man might seem more striking than their differences.

Nevertheless, the differences remain, and they are important. Nietzsche celebrated joy but proved a most unhelpful guide to those who seek it. Aristotle provided more useful counsel, but if there is one quality that the great-souled man conspicuously lacks it is joyfulness. Like Darcy in *Pride and Prejudice,* Aristotle's hero is always conscious of his dignity and of the respect to which he is due, and these are not characteristics we normally associate with joy. In Nietzsche's terminology, this suggests the need for a balance between the Dionysian and the Apollonian impulse, "that measured restraint, that freedom from the wilder emo-

---

*"Il faut toujours être ivre. Tout est là: c'est l'unique question. Pour ne pas sentir l'horrible fardeau du Temps qui brise vos épaules et vous penche vers la terre, il faut vous enivrer sans trêve. Mais de quoi? De vin, de poèsie ou de vertu, à votre guise. Mais enivrer vous." Charles Baudelaire, *Paris Spleen* xxxiii in *Œuvres complètes* (Paris: Pléiade, 1975), 337.

tions, that calm of the sculptor god."[34] In *The Birth of Tragedy,* Nietzsche spoke of the "Dionysian-Apollonian genius" and saw the two impulses as mutually reinforcing and necessary for a healthy and integrated life.[35] In art, the Apollonian impulse reveals itself in harmony and balance, while the Dionysian expresses itself in passion and ecstasy. The morality of happiness teaches that the best of lives, like the best of art, combines both impulses, and that a Dionysian joy cannot be achieved without Apollonian moderation.

We seem poised for a revival of Aristotelian ethics. The renewed philosophic interest in how we should live, and the growing fascination with evolutionary psychology, both point toward the rediscovery of man. The twentieth-century focus on politics and society seems to have played itself out, and we must expect attention to shift from questions of justice and the righting of this or that grievance to the narrower examination of man's ends. After the moral and political failure of communism and the intellectual failures of feminism and deconstruction, the new quests will be inward, and Aristotle will be an indispensable guide. With him we might avoid the banal and narcissistic essays of self-discovery thrown up by the 1970s. Yet something more than Aristotle will be needed, since the inward movement must also reach our yearning for a transcendent sanctity and joy. What we await is a concept of human flourishing that unites ethical norms with our religious and aesthetic impulses and with the morality of laughter.

Transcendence is a theological term that refers to our distance from God, in contrast to immanence. The immanent is before us and can be grasped in its entirety, like tables, chairs, and rules of justice. The transcendent is mysterious and cannot be cast up by a hook of human manufacture. Like God's grace, it is not to be judged by the reasonable and readily accessible standards of human ethics. Before the seventeenth century most Christian theologians spoke of God in transcendental terms, but from Descartes onward God's radical otherness has been de-emphasized.

There are two religions, which cut across denominational lines. One is a therapeutic religion of immanence and politics, which seeks to heal social ills that do not ascend to the level of sins. The other is a redemptive religion of transcendence, a religion of saints and sinners, whose goal is personal salvation. One is a religion of happiness and the other of joy. At its worst, the religion of immanence is casuistic and emotionally flat; at its best, in Tolstoy's later stories, it celebrates solidarity and ministers to corporal needs. At its worst, the religion of transcendence is dismissive of purely human concerns; at its best, it answers to spiritual needs that are elsewhere ignored. A humanistic theology must harmonize both impulses.

The joy of laughter is both immanent and transcendent. It is immediate and unreflective, but reveals a deeper mystery that is at the same time present and absent. Laughter is immanent in the sense that it is directly experienced through intuitive comic norms and unites jester and listener in a bond of solidarity. But laughter is also an experience of conversion that reveals a hidden reality and gives us a new way of looking at the world. We are put in touch with secret and forgotten sources of joy, and what was previously great now seems unimportant. And that was how Bakhtin found his faith, deep in Stalinist Russia. "The carnival sense of the world possesses a mighty life-creating and transforming power, and indestructible vitality."[36] We are swept into the pageant, like the wit and listener who erupt into laughter over a joke. The great god Pan yet lives.

6 The Social Virtues

> Only the evil man is alone.
> Diderot

While we laugh at very different things, some defects seem naturally comic, and they provide us with a list of comic vices and virtues. By playing with our intuitions of the risible we may derive a thick set of comic norms whose intrinsic appeal tells us to attend to laughter's message of the good life.

In this and the next chapter, I offer a taxonomy of the comic vices and virtues, like the moral vices and virtues cataloged by St. Thomas Aquinas. In place of the four cardinal virtues I suggest laughter's four *social virtues:* integrity, moderation, fortitude, and temperance; and in place of the three theological virtues, I propose the three *charismatic virtues* of comedy: grace, taste, and learning.

This chapter examines the social virtues, which are the traits of good character that are acquired when virtuous acts are repeated until they become habitual. They are integrity, moderation, fortitude, and temperance. The correlative social vices, resulting from an insufficiency or excess of the virtue, are hypocrisy and misanthropy (integrity); moral sloth and priggishness (moderation); cowardice and foolhardiness (fortitude); and greed and excessive humility (temperance).

The Social Virtues

Comic Vice: Insufficiency	Comic Virtue	Comic Vice: Excess
Hypocrisy	Integrity	Misanthropy
Moral sloth	Moderation	Priggishness
Cowardice	Fortitude	Foolhardiness
Greed	Temperance	Excessive humility

Integrity is the queen of the comic virtues, and hypocrisy the principal comic vice. Integrity removes the sting from a multitude of lesser offenses, and laughter is never so fierce as when it mocks the hypocrite. Misanthropy, the excessive honesty of the antihypocrite, is also a deeply fascinating vice, and almost the satirist's occupational hazard.

Integrity

Integrity is an adherence to a consistent and rational life plan, one that was reasonably chosen in pursuit of sensible ends. As a comic norm, integrity has both a public and private dimension. To the outside world, the well-integrated person presents a single face, and never betrays himself with actions that are inconsistent with his public principles. Nor does his integrity impose a private burden, for he is at ease with his life plan. It reflects his deepest and most complete desires, and offers him the greatest happiness of which he is capable. Such people give off an aura: they are comfortable in their own skins.

Integrity helps to explain the distinction between the charismatic and social virtues. We laugh at the clumsy, vulgar, and ignorant whether or not they have integrity. For the social vices, however, integrity is a talisman that seems to transform the risible vice into a mildly amusing foible. The coward is sympathetic when he confesses his vice, and might even invite us to laugh with him. About to go under the surgeon's knife, Oscar Wilde (no coward in real life) prayed, "Lord, spare me physical anguish. As for moral anguish, I can handle that myself." Similarly, the moral sluggard (like Falstaff) who cheerfully admits his sins might be a cad and a reprobate, but we smile along with him too.

When we employ the virtue of integrity to justify behavior, we appeal to what Charles Taylor (and Heidegger before him) called an ethic of authenticity.[1] Now, authenticity has three meanings, and the first is very like the comic virtue of integrity. Here authenticity is defined in contradistinction to what it is not: A person is authentic when he is not false, pretentious, or hypocritical. This is the meaning that Taylor ascribes to authenticity, in his effort to rescue the norm from its critics. However, there are two further senses of authenticity that are very different from integrity, and which may be risible. I shall call the first of these *romantic authenticity,* for it assumes a Rousseauian, innate goodness that prevents the person who is true to himself from doing evil. The second, which might be called *postmodern authenticity*, abandons the naive belief in a benign human nature (or in any human nature that is not a social construct). Instead, authenticity serves as a shield against blame even when our actions depart sharply from commonsense morality. On this view, each of us has an original way of being human that others cannot properly condemn.

The second and third kinds of authenticity were memorably satirized by Diderot in *Rameau's Nephew*. The nephew, who has none of his uncle's musical genius, represents an Enlightenment that has abandoned all of the ancien régime's prejudices and speaks the new language of nature, openness, and honesty. Wonderful stuff, thought Diderot. The only difficulty is that romantic authenticity leads to a wholly amoral postmodern authenticity. With his cynical indifference to respectable opinion, the nephew is a moral monster. He prides himself on his smarminess and secret opportunism, and performs despicable acts without a twinge of conscience. What does all that matter, asks the nephew. I am true to my nature and report my private thoughts honestly, whatever they may be. I at least am authentic. But while the nephew holds society in contempt, he is himself contemptible; ridiculing others, he is himself ridiculous. In a letter to Schiller, Goethe described the novel as a bomb that exploded in the middle of French literature.[2] The reverberations continue to be felt, for the ethic of postmodern authenticity is stronger than ever today.

Like integrity, authenticity denotes a consistent life, all of whose parts fit together to form a uniform whole. Postmodern authenticity does not distinguish among life plans, however. Any goal will do, so long as it is pursued in a coherent manner. By contrast, the comic virtue of integrity excludes wholly unworthy life plans. The thief and con-artist may be authentic, but we would not commend their integrity. Yet integrity is not excessively prim either. Less serious sins, like those of the honest rake, may be forgiven when they are frankly admitted. What integrity will not excuse is the complete immoralist, someone like Diderot's butt.

In his novel, Diderot meant to satirize the romantics in general and Rousseau in particular.[3] However, the modern cult of authenticity has blunted Diderot's moral message, for today's reader is unlikely to condemn the nephew and might even find his plea of scrupulous honesty appealing. He is, after all, Meursault in *L'Etranger*, the hero of every college freshman. Camus's novel describes the vapid interior world of a feckless office worker, who recounts striking events—his mother's death, an affair with a girlfriend—in the flattest tones. He falls in with a pimp and in a sun-induced trance kills an Arab. Convicted of murder, he awaits his execution at the end of the novel. Roger Shattuck argues that Camus first conceived of Mersault as a rotter, devoid of culture, self-awareness, and any ethical impulses. However, Camus revised this judgment thirteen years later in an introduction to the American edition of the book. The second Meursault has "a passion for the absolute and for the truth," and in his integrity is "the only Christ that we deserve."[4]

Freud recognized the limits of authenticity, for he fled from Germany in 1938 to a less authentic but more civilized England. While he was thought a radical in his day he is a conservative in ours, since he had no illusions about primitive innocence and argued that civilization required the repression of individual desires. Like Diderot, he was dismissive of the Rousseauian belief in a benign human nature and would have found modern pop psychology utterly naive. Civilization does not promote self-expression so much as repress it, he thought, by restraining the ego's sexual and aggressive impulses.[5]

Laughter rests on a normative foundation, and also restrains unbridled self-expression. Humor flourishes in civilized communities, and is banished by the modern cult of authenticity. When the only vice is inauthenticity, comic vices are obscured and the comic muse is silenced. The comic norm of integrity is therefore very different from authenticity, for integrity preserves laughter whilst authenticity dissolves it. Integrity offers a degree of immunity for minor comic vices, but not the major ones that the modern ethic of authenticity purports to excuse. Rameau's nephew no longer offends, but still remains a figure of amusement, as Diderot intended him to be.

Integrity resembles Aristotle's virtue of truthfulness, which describes the man who represents himself accurately to others (*Eudemian Ethics* 1221a). The truthful man does not claim virtues he lacks, like the boastful impostor (*alazōn*); nor does he sell himself short, like the ironic, self-deprecating man (*eirōn*).

Integrity and Truthfulness

Vice: Insufficiency	Virtue	Vice: Excess
Hypocrisy	Comic virtue of integrity	Misanthropy
False bragging (the *alazōn*)	Aristotelian virtue of truthfulness	Self-deprecation (the *eirōn*)

The correlative vices that represent deviations from the golden means of truthfulness and integrity may also differ from each other. For an insufficiency, the vices are similar. The hypocrite who lacks integrity resembles the impostor who claims a virtue he does not possess. But in the other deviation from the mean, the vices are different. The excess of integrity is misanthropy, not self-deprecation; and only the former is comic.

The self-deprecating *eirōn* might even be the hero of the piece when he takes on an impostor. The Socratic dialogues can be read as comedies in which a self-important braggart is cut down to size by Socrates' pose of ignorance. The *eirōn* may also be the hick (Will Rogers) who shows up the city slicker's false sophistication, or the provincial (Pascal) who punctures the pretensions of learned theologians. The dissembling *eirōn* is sometimes an ambiguous figure, however. He stoops to conquer; others simply conquer. Part of the laughter may thus be directed at (and not with) the self-conscious rube who affects a comic role. Aristotle thought that the *eirōn* might even become a buffoon by accepting his role as a butt. When he strains too hard for a laugh, the *eirōn* passes the bounds of decorum and becomes ridiculous himself.

Hypocrisy

Hypocrisy is of cardinal importance in an account of comic norms. Like rules of ethics, laughter schools us in the good life. But the lessons that ethics and laughter teach are not the same, and may conflict when excessive virtue is mocked. The laughter is particularly strong when the moralist's personal lapse provides onlookers with a sudden release from repressive norms. Then laughter crows over morality. We do not smile when the reprobate is caught out; but let a television evangelist stray and we laugh with savage joy. When detected, hypocrisy is a permission slip to our morals, telling them to take a holiday.

The hypocrite resembles the bragging *alazōn*. The swaggering soldier—Plautus' Miles Gloriosus and Shakespeare's Pistol—is an impostor when he boasts of fictitious battles, and a hypocrite when he thinks himself ferocious and brave. There is a difference between the impostor and the hypocrite, however. The impostor must through word or deed represent himself falsely to others, claiming virtues or accomplishments he does not possess; while the hypocrite may remain silent and still offend against the norm of integrity when his conduct does not correspond to his private self-image. The man who thinks himself brave but acts in a cowardly fashion is a hypocrite, but he is not an impostor unless he boasts of his bravery. One may be a private hypocrite but not a private impostor. The self-deceiving hypocrite might even be truthful as long as he represents himself accurately to others. Those with an inflated idea of their own worth may offend against the norm of integrity because they are not true to themselves; but they may still be truthful if modest in representing themselves to others. Since most of us overestimate our gifts and attainments, making a conscious effort to be self-deprecating likely promotes truthfulness.[6]

Not every kind of hypocrisy is comic. The butt must be unaware of his comic vice, as we noted in chapter 1. The self-deluding are risible, not the self-aware. Like Callimaco in Machiavelli's *Mandragola,* the self-conscious hypocrite might even be held up for our admiration. Callimaco wishes to seduce the "most honest" Lucrezia, who is married to a wealthy and stupid older man, Nicia. After six years of marriage, Lucrezia remains childless, and Nicia desperately wants an heir. Posing as a doctor, Callimaco announces that he can make a special potion of mandrake root (*mandragola*) that will make Lucrezia fertile. The catch is that the first man to possess her after she drinks the potion will die. Nicia must trick a man to cuckold him, and with Callimaco comes up with a plan to find one. The man, of course, is a heavily disguised Callimaco, who announces his love for Lucrezia when he is admitted to her bedroom. In the end, everyone is happy: Lucrezia has a lusty young lover, Callimaco a fine new mistress, and Nicia will have an heir.

The self-conscious hypocrite might also be the villain, like Molière's Tartuffe. As he knows full well that he is false, Tartuffe is not comic, and the play, which succeeds wonderfully as a melodrama, fails as a comedy. Tartuffe poses as a puritan, but schemes for the naive Orgon's wealth even as he tries to seduce his wife. There is no moment when Tartuffe does not know what he is about. Only Orgon is self-delusional and comic. Returning from a trip he is told that his wife is ill. His mind is elsewhere, however. "Et Tartuffe?" he keeps asking. "Le pauvre homme!"

The self-conscious hypocrite knows that his pose is false, but seeks to pass himself off as that which he is not. Like Tartuffe, he infuriates when he covers up black villainy; but when minor faults are obscured, like a toupee over a bald head, we are merely amused. The minor hypocrite might even demonstrate an enviable suppleness, like that of Blake when encountering an annoying acquaintance.

A petty sneaking knave I knew . . .
'O Mr. Cromek, how do ye do?'[7]

Whether the fault is small or large, self-conscious hypocrisy is the tribute that La Rochefoucauld said vice pays to virtue. It does not subvert our moral sense so much as reinforce it, if the alternative is to flout the code. A compact exists, between saint and hypocrite, that moral rules should be publicly defended. The difference is only at the level of private behavior, and that is not observed.

The hypocrite's vice remains a vice, of course, but there is something commendable about his reticence, as compared to the alternative of an in-your-face flaunting of immorality. By observing the proprieties, the self-conscious hypocrite shows a decent respect for his colleagues and neighbors, and perhaps a greater humanity for his victims. Those who parade their sins compound the injury by expressing their contempt for their victims, who might find this even more heartless than the actual wrong.

By contrast, the self-deluding hypocrisy of the villain who thinks himself moral is of greater psychological interest and stands in greater need of ridicule. *Le Tartuffe* was a satire on the Jansenist religious revival that condemned lax morals at the court of Molière's regal patron. Ironically, one of the most amusing satires of self-deluding hypocrisy came from the pen of a devout Jansenist, only eight years before Molière's comedy. In his *Provincial Letters,* Pascal ridiculed the Jesuits as purveyors of cheap grace and easy absolution for their noble patrons. Pascal's friend, the Jansenist Antoine Arnauld, had been charged with heresy in an ecclesiastical court for his views on grace, at the insistence of the Jesuits. Adopting the pose of an ingenuous provincial, Pascal's letters reported on his efforts to understand the charge and the curious doctrines of Arnauld's accusers. When Pascal described the Jesuit doctrine of "sufficient grace" as a grace that does not suffice, a court that could not understand theological disputes did know enough to laugh. What delighted was the pinprick to the intellectual and moral pretensions of a scholarly and spiritually proud order, observed in the act of pandering for political gain, by a single, anonymous author.

In his fourth letter, Pascal turned to the attack. "There is nothing like the Jesuits," he begins. First, their Father Bauny, who excuses sins not committed in the belief that God condemns them. Pascal's comment: Here's a new sort of redemption! Or the Jesuit Father Annat, who gives us a pass for acts committed in ignorance of God and His laws. Wonderful stuff, said Pascal. "I can see more people saved by ignorance and forgetfulness of God than by grace and the sacraments."* Pascal described a contest between the subtle and powerful Jesuits and the austere and friendless Jansenist solitaries of Port-Royal. "I thought that one might be damned for bad thoughts, but that one might be damned for thinking that others did not have good thoughts, truly that I never knew."† Near the end of his life, Pascal was asked why he employed an ironic tone in the Provinciales. "Had I written in a dogmatic style," he answered, "only scholars would have read the letters, and they did not need them."[8]

The ability to sin and think well of oneself is, of all sins, the greatest. I once asked a colleague to do something which, while a little inconvenient, would have been a great kindness. It was to help another colleague organize a paper he was writing. He was a great friend of hers, a gentle and sweet-hearted person, but of modest analytical skill. Several of us were pitching in. Would she help? "I will give it prayerful consideration," she answered sincerely. And of course she never did help him.

Such people provide a reason for the existence of Hell, since they would otherwise escape punishment. That was the point of Graham Greene's *Brighton Rock*, which described a punk who dies in a state of mortal sin. Greene's challenge was to show how a self-pitying wretch deserved eternal damnation, and in succeeding he clarified the Church's teaching on Confession and moral desert (almost as much as he confused them in *The Heart of the Matter*).

In recent fiction, the outstanding example of a self-deluding hypocrite is Howard Kirk, in Malcolm Bradbury's *The History Man*. Kirk is a tenured radical at a redbrick university, utterly self-absorbed and infinitely capable of rationalizing self-promotion and motiveless malignity. Bradbury came as close as anyone to capturing the evil will perfectly satisfied with itself. Near the end of the book, Kirk's double-dealing is exposed, and the reader is led to expect that, like Tartuffe, Kirk will be punished. He is wholly without empathy and behaves despicably to everyone close to him. He scapegoats the innocent for the same reason that James Carville's dog licks himself: because he can do it. Formerly Kirk

---

*"Je vois . . . plus de gens justifiés par cette ignorance et cet oubli de Dieu que par la grâce et les sacrements." Blaise Pascal, *Les provinciales* (Paris: Pléiade, 1987), 73.

†"Je croyais bien qu'on fût damné pour n'avoir pas de bonnes pensées, mais qu'on le soit pour ne pas croire que tout le monde en a, vraiment je ne le pensais pas." Blaise Pascal, *Les provinciales*, 75.

would have been unmasked and disgraced. But times have changed: hypocrisy no longer offends, and Kirk goes on to an earthly triumph. Which is to say that, like *Brighton Rock,* the theme of the book is the necessity of Hell (the satirist's proof of the existence of God). All the more reason, then, why we should laugh at comic hypocrisy, to economize on more drastic forms of deterrence.

Hypocrisy is the Queen of the comic vices, and few things are as pleasureful as the delight we take in mocking the hypocrite. We desperately need such laughter, for no vice is quite so beguiling. We always see the mote in another's eye, ignoring the beam in our own. How could it be otherwise, *cher hypocrite, mon semblable,* when our self-love is so strong? Who could bear to know what others think of one, or (what is worse) how seldom they think of one? Our capacity to delude ourselves is infinite, and is never so strong as when we think we at last have achieved self-knowledge. We see our lives as a drama in which we are the hero. In the moments before sleep, we give ourselves all the best lines, like Vernon in Ian McEwan's *Amsterdam,* "resonant lines of sad reasonableness whose indictments [are] all the more severe and unanswerable for their compression and emotional restraint."9

We are all a little like Usbek, in Montesquieu's *Persian Letters.* In his letters home to Persia Usbek recounts the extraordinary customs of Europeans and their hypocrisy. They ban slavery in Europe but tolerate it in their colonies; they laud justice but act in a self-interested manner; they support religion but in private are atheists. These are the letters of an intelligent, moderate, and liberal man, but they are accompanied by another set of letters that reveal him to be a cruel tyrant who is easily manipulated by his wives and eunuchs. No doubt we are all self-delusional when it comes to our own faults, which is why our laughter at hypocrisy is so very benign.

Misanthropy

If an insufficiency of integrity is hypocrisy, an excess is misanthropy, the man who sets his standards so high that no one can possibly meet them. The two comic vices are intimately related, for nothing annoys the misanthrope more than insincerity. True merit (his own) goes unrewarded, while a gullible society that prefers false smiles to gruff integrity promotes the fawning hypocrite. For his part, the hypocrite regards the misanthrope with the same delight that the opportunist takes in the patsy.

The misanthrope is the man with a "Kick Me" sign on his backside, just waiting to be exploited by the hypocrite.

The ur-misanthrope is Umbricius in Juvenal's *Third Satire*, seen again in the imitations the satire fathered: Boileau's *First Satire*, Pope's *Imitation of Juvenal*, and Johnson's *London*. The misanthrope is also Jonathan Swift, whose King of Brobdingnag exclaims to Gulliver, "I cannot but conclude the Bulk of your natives, to be the most pernicious Race of little odious Vermin that nature ever suffered to crawl upon the Surface of the Earth."[10] Most famously, the misanthrope is Molière's Alceste, the protagonist of *Le Misanthrope*.

If misanthropy is the satirist's besetting sin, then *Le Misanthrope* is a satire upon satire. Written during a black period, after Molière discovered his wife's infidelity, the play describes a modern Umbricius who seeks to quit the French court and his flirtatious lover. Unlike Boileau's and Johnson's misanthropes, however, Alceste's ire is wildly excessive. Were the court as false as Boileau made out, or London as noxious as Johnson claimed, one would reasonably wish to leave it. But Molière's court is merely polite, and the courtiers are no more duplicitous or empty-headed than people generally. In the debate over misanthropy and polite manners, it is always his friends and never Alceste who speak for good sense. To Philintre's reasonable observation that

> Quand on est du monde, il faut bien qu'on rende
> Quelques dehors civils que l'usage demande.

Alceste angrily responds:

> Non, vous dis-je, on devrait châtier sans pitié,
> Ce commerce honteux de semblants d'amitié.*

Alceste's lover, Célimène, is a sprightly and witty young lady, with a taste for coquetry and gossip. She is Millamant in Congreve's *Way of the World* and Scarlett O'Hara in *Gone with the Wind*. Alceste's rejection of her at the play's end is maddeningly perverse, since it is deeply painful

---

* *Philintre:* But in polite society, custom decrees / That we show certain outward courtesies. *Alceste:* Ah, no! we should condemn with all our force / Such false and artificial intercourse. Molière, *The Misanthrope* (trans. Richard Wilbur) (San Diego: Harcourt, Brace, 1965).

and wholly unnecessary. His rivals withdraw, and Célimène consents to marry him:

> Si le don de ma main peut contenter vos vœux,
> Je pourrai me résoudre à serrer des tels nœuds.*

A normal person would accept, and the play would end as a conventional comedy with the double marriage of Alceste to Célimène and Philintre to Eliante. But Alceste with both hands destroys his chance for happiness. He will marry, but only if Célimène agrees to an impossible condition.

> Oui, je veux bien, perfide, oublier vos forfaits;
> J'en saurai, dans mon âme excuser tous les traits . . .
> Pourvu que votre cœur veuille donner les mains
> Au dessein que j'ai fait de fuir tous les humains,
> Et que dans mon désert, où j'ai fait vœu de vivre,
> Vous soyez, sans tarder, résolue à me suivre.

Let her come to the desert to expiate her sins! Célimène's response is the only possible one:

> Moi, renoncer au monde avant de veillir,
> Et dans votre désert aller m'ensevelir!†

A woman of spirit, which Célimène happily possesses in abundance, could never agree to a life of constant humiliation. Through his accidie, his inability to experience joy, Alceste becomes the principal victim of his vice. No doubt, it is always like that, for those who turn their backs on the world seldom find that the world takes much note of their absence.

It is a tribute to Molière's self-awareness that, married to a true cocotte, he recognized the dangers of surrendering to a bitter and self-indulgent misanthropy. However, the contest is drawn so finely that we

---

*If my hand in marriage will content you / Why, there's a plan I might well consent to.

†*Alceste:* Woman, I'm willing to forget your shame / And clothe your treacheries in a sweeter name . . . / My only condition is that you agree / To share my chosen fate and fly with me / To that wild, trackless, solitary place / In which I shall forget the human race. *Célimène:* What! I renounce the world at my young age, / And die of boredom in some hermitage?

secretly sympathize with Alceste. Otherwise the play would not succeed nearly so well. We recognize just how delicious bile can taste and why it is so essential that we resist the dark urge to chastise. With Stephen Crane, we eat it because it is bitter and because it is our heart. Yet all along we recognize how costly this is. We would will our emotions to be more tolerant, had we the power to do so. One hundred years ago, Sir Walter Raleigh understood:

> I wish I loved the human race.
> I wish I loved its stupid face.
> And when I stood and talked to one,
> I wish I thought 'What jolly fun!'

If only it did not take a lobotomy to love them, we complain.

Misanthropy is often a pose, however. The man who yearns to be rescued by the person he has walked out on is not a misanthrope but a narcissist. He holds one hand out to keep the world at bay; but with the other hand furtively beckons you to him. "Do not believe me," he pleads. "Come rescue me." Or else, like Alceste, he asks his lover to leave the world with him. In fact, we are not meant to believe that Alceste will carry out his threat. The play ends with his friends seeking to persuade him to change his mind, and we are led to think they will succeed. Alceste will stay at court to rail against it and bring misery to all whose life he touches.[11]

The misanthrope does not hate all mankind, for he does not hate himself. While he may despise others, his self-love does not flag, and the difference makes him a misanthrope. I am a liar and a cheat? Fine. What do I care if others share my vices? Pascal thought that human nature was degraded, but since he thought he was as fallen as everyone else he was not bitter and not a misanthrope. Nor is it enough to think that others are inferior to me. I might react to ordinary knavery with bemused tolerance when I see it as the way of the world. *Così fan tutte*. In any event, forewarned is forearmed. If I know that others are rogues, I can protect myself from them. The secret is deeper, then. It is that the world betrays me. It does not love me, esteem me, worship me, as I deserve to be loved, esteemed, and worshiped. As my mother did, for example. And I will never forgive the world for my psychic wound. The misanthrope's great secret is narcissism.

The misanthrope's assertion of higher integrity is therefore suspect.

Even if (unlike Rousseau) he does adhere to high moral standards, there is a lie at the heart of his soul. His hatred is not what it seems, and his life lacks integrity. Perhaps he is even a bit of a hypocrite, with the two deviations from integrity bending back to touch.

> So that I fear they do but bring
> Extremes to touch, and mean one thing.[12]

With more self-awareness, the misanthrope would care less what others thought of him and might learn forgiveness. Told that he had been libeled, he might say, with Epictetus, "My friend does not know me very well. If he did he would have told you of my more serious faults!"

Molière recognized Alceste's sin, and like Walt Whitman's poetry *Le Misanthrope* is something of a litmus test for narcissism. Those who lack Molière's insight into the perverse forms self-love may take will identify with Alceste. The supreme example is Rousseau, who like Alceste expressed a preference for a simple and natural society over a polite and artificial one, and who like Alceste saw himself betrayed by everyone who sought to help him. In his *Lettre à d'Alembert,* Rousseau argued that the theater (and comedy in particular) should be suppressed since it inevitably corrupts morals. The Encyclopedist d'Alembert had proposed that the prim Republic of Geneva should relax its ban on the theater, and Rousseau saw an opening. He would defend his adopted city and decry the morals of the stage and of the Encyclopedists. Geneva had wisely banned the theater, wrote Rousseau. "Everything in it is evil and pernicious . . . and even the pleasure of comedy is founded on human vice; as a consequence, the more a comedy is pleasant and perfect, the more deleterious its effect for our morals."* Rousseau adored Molière, he said, and *Le Misanthrope* in particular, even though the play perversely sought to make the virtuous Alceste seem ridiculous. Yet it was Rousseau who was risible, and his complaints were those of every misanthrope, who always sees himself betrayed by his unworthy friends and lovers.

The sociable Diderot understood all this. In his *Fils naturel* he wrote, "Only the evil man is alone," and sent a copy to Rousseau, who saw this as a personal attack and thereupon broke with Diderot. Very possibly the

---

*"Tout en est mauvais et pernicieux . . . et le plaisir même du comique étant fondé sur un vice du cœur humain, c'est une suite de ce principe que plus la comédie est agréable et parfaite, plus son effet est funeste aux mœurs." J.-J. Rousseau, *Lettre à M. d'Alembert sur son article Genève* (Paris: Flammarion, 1967 [1758]), 89.

line was directed at Rousseau, who seems to have claimed an exemption from all moral duties. He borrowed freely and never repaid; he gave nothing and abused his benefactors; he preached a cult of youthful innocence and put his children up for adoption. One morning he arrived uninvited on Diderot's doorstep, seeking help in revising a book. For the next two days the two worked incessantly; and when they were finished Diderot asked Rousseau for a favor: would he spend fifteen minutes to help Diderot with a problem that was plaguing him? No, said Rousseau: it's late; I have to leave early tomorrow; I'm going to bed.[13]

Misanthropy is a troubling comic vice, since it is so difficult to recognize, particularly in oneself. We are apt to see something noble in the misanthrope's rejection of the world, for his self-love awakens our own. That is why few things are as healthy as the ability to laugh at misanthropy.

Moderation

The second social virtue, moderation, is related to that of integrity. Moderation is a middle way between extremes of behavior, and in an Aristotelian system of ethics is very nearly the definition of virtue itself. Aristotle's great-souled person is truthful, and speaks not too highly or lowly of himself; he is neither miserly nor prodigal, but generous; he is sensible in his diet and neither abstains from fine food and wine nor overindulges. He takes a reasonable amount of exercise and is neither a sluggard nor a health fanatic.

Integrity comes easily for the moderate person, as there are no embarrassing foibles to hide. He is seldom a hypocrite (unless he is the paradoxical kind, seen in *The Importance of Being Earnest,* that pretends to be wicked and is secretly virtuous all along). Nevertheless, the two comic virtues are not the same, for those who lack moderation, like Othello, may still possess integrity. And a moderate person may be a hypocrite, like the aged trollop who dedicates the remainder of her life to chastity.

Moderation might seem a very tepid virtue. Could it be risible? The conformist is usually a moderate soul, and conformism is faintly ridiculous in an age that prizes authenticity. Conformity might thus be seen as a self-defeating attempt to avoid laughter by eliminating authentic, individual characteristics. It is risible not because the conformist is moderate, but because the moderation is strategic. Moderation is virtuous when the pursuit of balance does not impose psychic costs, but represents a sincere expression of personal desires. What is admirable is the integrated personality that takes pleasure in moderate behavior, and not the conformity that practices moderation while privately hating it. The conformist sacrifices personal happiness for a false ideal and is therefore a figure of fun. He is the stuffy bridegroom at whom we jeer when he is jilted at the altar.

Moderation's correlative vices are the two forms of excess: moral sloth and priggishness (or excessive pleasure-seeking and excessive rectitude). Laughter is ordinarily on the side of pleasure, and moral sloth can only be comic if the search for pleasure is self-defeating. The moral slug overeats, overdrinks, and generally overindulges. The result is not pleasant and is often comic. "Honey, you're a mess," said Marlene Dietrich to Orson Welles in *A Touch of Evil,* as we giggled along. Were his appetites more moderate, the moral sluggard would derive more pleasure from life.

The prig is a more interesting and comic case. The frank sensualist has a certain integrity. We might not admire him, but seldom laugh. At least he is not a hypocrite. What delights is not the man who has smoked pot, but he who smoked and did not inhale. The prig is not a hypocrite either, but we still laugh at his comically inadequate view of life. While the prig is true to his ideals, these are false values that demand too much of one. In promoting virtue, he is tireless—but, oh, how we wish he would tire. He is the butt of Hemingway's *Earnest Liberal's Lament.*

> I know monks masturbate at night
> That pet cats screw
> That some girls bite
> And yet
> What can I do
> To set things right?

No one ever mocked excessive virtue more effectively than Oscar Wilde. In the contest for our affections, the amusing cynic is found to have unsuspected reservoirs of compassion, while the puritan's secret is a lukewarm heart. The comedic catharsis occurs when, forced to choose between excessive virtue and tender generosity, the naive heroine (Lady

Chiltern in *An Ideal Husband*) adopts a human and forgiving moral code. We have been rooting for this all along, of course. With Molière, we prefer a comfortable vice to a fatiguing virtue.*

Fortitude

Fortitude is a principal comic virtue, since one of the best ways to protect oneself from being laughed at is to laugh in the face of adversity. A grim literature seeks to convey the awfulness of war by portraying its unrelieved misery. But the greater the suffering, the more we appreciate the wartime jest. The best account of life in the trenches during World War I was Robert Graves's *Goodbye to All That*. Graves described the mindless slaughter, the frightful bombardments, and pervasive squalor that left him an emotional wreck for years after. At the end of the book he concluded that, such were the horrors of war, he and his companions would never fight again—unless it were against the French.

We have a special fascination for gallows humor, the jest told on the scaffold. Betrayed by Robespierre, Danton met his end with grim amusement at the macabre ceremonies of the guillotine. "You'll show my head to the crowd," he told the executioner. "It's worth it." St. Thomas More's jest, delivered after he stumbled and was helped up by the executioner, is also well-known. "I pray you, Master Lieutenant, see me safe up and, for my coming down, let me shift for myself."[14]

Before one may speak of fortitude, four elements must be present: a grave danger; the recognition of the danger; the self-mastery to quell rational fears; and prudence. Self-mastery is no great virtue when the danger is trivial, and when it is severe a person who sleeps through it does not display courage. But where the danger is real those who place themselves at risk are brave even though they might quake. The Great Turenne could not stop himself from trembling in battle, and as the cannons began to roar he addressed his body contemptuously. "Carcase," he said. "You tremble. Just wait until you see where I take you next!" The self-mastery to overcome such fear is true fortitude, according to Aristotle. By contrast, an Achilles who flings himself into battle to avenge the death of a friend, so overcome with rage that he is not conscious of danger, does not display fortitude but only anger. The highest form of forti-

---

*"J'aime mieux un vice commode / qu'une fatigante vertu." *Amphitryon* 1.4.

tude, said Aristotle, is that of the person who is aware of danger and who places himself in harm's way without self-conscious fuss. After performing a heroic act, he says (and thinks) that he simply did what anyone else would do in his place. His virtues are so much a part of him that he finds it costless to perform virtuous acts. Finally, fortitude requires the prudence that can distinguish between acceptable and foolish risks and shun the latter. Prudence might seem a tepid virtue and not unlike the discretion that Falstaff employed to shield his want of valor. However, true prudence is willing to court danger when the expected gain justifies the risk. What the requirement of prudence does exclude is imprudent risk or foolhardiness, for that is a comic vice and not a virtue.

The comic virtues teach us how to extract joy from life. How then can fortitude, which exposes us to danger, constitute a comic virtue? The answer is that a life spent in the avoidance of danger is not a joyful one. To experience joy we must run risks. We must gamble on ideas, knowing the risk of failure; we must hazard our fortune, knowing the risk of bankruptcy; we must fall in love, knowing the risk of heartbreak. The secret is to take risks and not to abstain from them. The comic virtue of fortitude keeps us from so loving joy that we lose it.

The principal aristocratic virtues are generosity and courage: The higher man is openhearted and brave. He does not stop to check balance sheets or calculate risks. He disdains meanness and strategic behavior. He is Charles Péguy, generous to friend and foe and fearless with both, a Dreyfusard as to Dreyfus and an anti-Dreyfusard as to the Dreyfusards, who died upon the field of honor on the first day of the Battle of the Marne. "In my memoirs," he said, some chapters might be entitled "the memoirs of a blockhead" or "the memoirs of an imbecile." But none could be called "the memoirs of a coward."[15]

The comic vice of insufficient fortitude is cowardice, together with its symptoms of self-pity and whining. Few things are more devastating than the ridicule a cowardly act attracts. During the confused civil war called the Fronde, the youthful La Rochefoucauld sided with the Prince de Condé and sought to assassinate his patron's enemy, Cardinal de Retz, then bishop-coadjutor of Paris. Condé insinuated his men in the Palais de Justice, Retz's stronghold, and at a signal swords flashed out. Retz's men also unsheathed their swords and the two sides faced each other, separated by a sword's-length. No one stirred. Finally, the president of the Parlement arrived and ordered the great hall cleared. The rival leaders bowed and swords were sheathed. However, Retz took alarm at the cluster of enemies and withdrew to another chamber. As he walked through the door, La Rochefoucauld closed it on him, pinning him so he could not escape, and shouted for his friends to stab Retz while he was held fast. But it is not an easy thing to kill a bishop, and no one moved. Retz's partisans arrived; the bishop was freed; and with all the honors of the contest he sailed past La Rochefoucauld, who stood seething with anger, ready to challenge Retz to a duel. "Be calm, my friend," said the prelate. "You are a coward and I am a priest. There will be no duel between us." La Rochefoucauld had been ridiculous, and as the mature cynic later noted in his *Maxims,* ridiculousness dishonors more than dishonor does.

For grown men, crying used to be shameful and not a little risible. A few tears on the hustings cost Edmund Muskie a chance at the presidency in 1972, much like Hilaire Belloc's lachrymose Lord Lundy. Belloc's butt could not cope with simple requests for patronage appointments.

A hint at harmless little jobs
Would shake him with convulsive sobs.

His career languishes, and his grandfather takes charge. Lord Lundy might have been the next prime minister but three, his grandfather expostulates,

But as it is . . . My language fails!
Go out and govern New South Wales!

Laughter often has a nasty edge, and never more so than when it seeks to toughen up the whiner. Yet the nastiness is benign, since fortitude lessens pain. The injured person suffers less himself and passes still less to those around him. When the pain is great, he excites the admiration of those who know of his loss, and teaches them how to bear pain. By contrast, the whiner magnifies his own pain and that of those near him. Listening to sob stories may also sap our own fortitude. Some forms of severe emotional distress appear to be a learned response, where we are taught to feel emotional pain by being told of its existence.[16] A state that inculcates fortitude through its legal regime might thus be a happier one than a state that smirks at fortitude and rewards the whiner. The instinct to laugh at cowards is similarly benign.

Mocking the whiner is delightful because the plea for sympathy imposes a psychic cost on listeners. That is just as it should be, where the victim's pain is real and we ought to respond. But when the demand for sympathy is excessive we begin to grow edgy. We know we are being played with, and resent it. When the demand is outrageous, we might even become angry. Or we might laugh, as Mordecai Richler's alter ego does in *Joshua Then and Now* at an emotionally manipulative production of *The Diary of Anne Frank*. The Nazis burst into the apartment, practice unspeakable barbarities, and then prepare to leave. They cannot find Anne. "Look up the stairs," yells Joshua from the back row.

Our delight in laughing at whiners is so strong that, in bathos, it has its own genre. Bathos is reverse pathos, the quality in a work of art that evokes pity or sympathy. Where the pity is misplaced because the injury is slight, the work is bathetic. When this effect is unintentional, as in *Love Story* (which asks us to pity a Harvard student who is cast off by his parents and forced to drive an old MG-TD) we laugh at the author; when it is intentional and the author is ironic we laugh along with him, as we do with Pope at the dangers Belinda faces in *The Rape of the Lock*.

If cowardice is risible, so too is an excess of courage, or foolhardiness. Indifference to danger might perversely seem heroic, until the satirist points out the folly, as Hugh Kingsmill does in mocking A. E. Housman.

What, still alive at twenty-two,
A clean upstanding lad like you?
Sure, if your throat 'tis hard to slit,
Slit your girl's, and swing for it.

Like enough you won't be glad,
When they come to hang you, lad:
But bacon's not the only thing
That's cured by hanging from a string.

Foolhardiness is the comic vice of the d'Artagnans and Cyranos. Or Mad Jack Mytton, perhaps. Mytton once overturned his carriage upon discovering that his guest had never enjoyed that intoxicating pleasure. "What, never upset in a gig? What a damned slow fellow you must have been all your life." Another time, to cure his hiccups, Mytton set fire to his nightshirt. Severely burned, he retired to bed, but not without a sense of satisfaction. "The hiccup is gone, by God," he announced.

Different deviations from the mean are not always equally risible, and our laughter is always more restrained when we encounter an excess than an insufficiency of courage. We might laugh at the swashbuckling hero, but part of us admires him greatly. This is not surprising, since our self-interest protects us from excessive courage but not from cowardice. Social norms address the problem of asymmetric incentives through asymmetric laughter. Besides, it is sometimes hard to tell whether a Cyrano is rationally or irrationally courageous, since he is an exceptionally skilled swordsman. Where a person is foolishly brave, however, say George C. Scott as General Buck Turgidson in *Dr. Strangelove,* then we do find him funny. Buck yearns for an all-out first strike nuclear attack on the Soviet Union. "I'm not saying we wouldn't get our hair mussed. But I do say no more than ten to twenty million killed, tops. Uh, depending on the breaks."

Temperance

Since extremes of behavior are generally risible, temperance is a cardinal comic virtue. If temperance were defined to exclude all deviations from the mean, however, every comic vice would offend against the norm of temperance. I therefore use temperance in a restricted sense, in contradistinction to excessive and inadequate acquisitiveness. When the goods to be acquired are material things, excessive acquisitiveness is called greed and is risible.

We must be careful here, however, for greed means something more than the simple desire to better oneself financially. Otherwise Ivan Boesky would have been right: greed is good. But greed always implies an excessive acquisitiveness, and is thus a comic vice. The greedy person ignores other, more valuable goods in his pursuit of material rewards. The miser is a special case: he sacrifices joy and does not even enjoy the money he hoards. For example, Molière's *L'Avare* concludes with a double wedding. The happy couples depart, leaving the miser alone with his money.

An excessive desire for nonmaterial goods is vainglory, and is less risible than greed. There is a sense in which Sir Garnet Wolsey is ridiculous, but only when viewed through the prism of Gilbert and Sullivan. Otherwise, we would not think of laughing. Once again, this is because we have every private incentive to seek wealth, but less so to seek fame, particularly when this might entail physical danger. We therefore have less need to laugh at people like Wolsey, General Gordon, Kitchener, or the pantheon of Imperial heros. Nevertheless, the search for reputational advantage might still be taken to comic lengths. Consider Lord Cardigan, the dim-witted cavalry commander who led the Charge of the Light Brigade. To make a splash, he dressed his troopers in flamboyant uniforms and posted them strategically along Piccadilly so that they might salute him as he passed.

The costs that a butt imposes are normally borne by himself (see chap. 5). When it comes to inadequate acquisitiveness, however, the costs are ordinarily borne by third parties. We might find the hobo or spendthrift pathetic, but their want of ambition is seldom comic unless it imposes costs on third parties, notably their children. Mrs. Jellyby's telescopic attachment to the African poor in Dickens's *Bleak House* is risible because she lets her own children go hungry. Similarly, in Tom Wolfe's *A Man in Full*, a hardworking son comes to realize the hypocrisy of his hippie parents' injunction to go with the flow. "It didn't take a genius to figure out that this phrase . . . was supposed to place a mystical aura around being a weak sloven and giving in to your lowest animal appetites."

7   The Charismatic Virtues

Why should our virtues be grave?
We like ours nimble-footed.

Nietzsche, *The Gay Science*

The social virtues are acquired when virtuous acts are repeated until they become habitual. By contrast, the charismatic virtues are not a matter of repetition or stable preferences. Instead, they describe the attributes of what used to be known as a "man of parts." The gentlemanly *charieis* was graceful, elegant, and clever, favored of the gods and skilled at taking *chara* or joy from life or turning a *charisma* or witty saying. He possessed, as a gift from the gods, physical finesse or *grace;* aesthetic sense and appreciation or *taste;* and the intellectual attainments of *learning.*

Grace

A child first laughs like an adult when he encounters a graceless and clumsy person. An adult finds the pratfall less funny, but sees other kinds of clumsiness as more risible. He must pick his way past an immense variety of complicated social events in addition to the occasional ice patch, and if he stumbles anywhere he is risible. His clumsiness might take

The Charismatic Virtues

Comic Vice: Insufficiency	Comic Virtue	Comic Vice: Excess
Clumsiness or gaucherie	Grace	Excessive finesse
Vulgarity	Taste	Preciousness or camp
False pedantry	Learning	True pedantry

many different forms: the man who cuts himself shaving; the speaker who forgets to check his fly; or the professor of municipal law who, observing a large-breasted student in the front row, begins to discuss the "Titties and Towns Act."

Sexual clumsiness—the faux pas—is a special kind of gaucherie. A colleague of mine once stopped on his way down a very public staircase to whisper something into the ear of a secretary, for which she promptly slapped him. Hard. Nothing daunted, he continued down the stairs to the receptionist, who told him he had a telephone call. He took it, rang off, and handed the telephone back to the receptionist. She held it in her left hand, like a wizened and disgusting object, and with her right reached for a can of disinfectant, which she sprayed over the mouthpiece. A very effective display of contempt all around, and a wonderful source of laughter.

While grace is not one of the social virtues, there is still something distinctly social about it. Grace is best displayed in close contact with others, as on the dance floor. Consider the Manhattan pedestrian, who navigates his way through a crowd without bumping into other people. Like him, we can walk toward each other and, aided by some mysterious antenna, veer off at the last moment, scarcely aware of the near-miss. This requires a shared rhythm of walking, in which all parties have the same avoidance patterns. There is no such thing as private grace, any more than there is a private language. Rather, grace requires an adherence to common patterns of behavior.

So regarded, grace is a solution to a coordination game. In such games, the parties are best off when they hit on the same strategy, whatever this might be. It does not matter whether the rules of the road prescribe that one veers left or veers right before an oncoming person, so long as all people break the same way. Coordination gains are not restricted to the sidewalk or highway, but may be observed in every field where we interact with one another. In particular, communication requires the coordination that knows when it is one's turn to speak and when to keep silent, when to signal and when to receive—skills academics possess in short supply.

There is such a thing as an optimum amount of grace, that gets us through life's little corners with agility and without bruised elbows. It follows that there is also such a thing as excessive finesse, where the nimbleness of the dance floor is exhibited at the food court. He who minces through the construction site, who sashays through the battlefield, who tiptoes through the tulips, shows an excess of grace and is risible. A well-known photograph from thirty years ago wonderfully portrays this comic vice. At a dinner for Commonwealth prime ministers at Buckingham Palace, the politicians file into the dining room from a photo-op. Left behind, a youthful Pierre Trudeau performs a pirouette for the photographers, parodying the formality and elegance of his surroundings.

Since an excess of grace is risible, Bergson's account of laughter must be thought incomplete. Excessive grace is not rigidity but the opposite, the other deviation from the mean. Both are amusing, though it is easy to see how Bergson might have overlooked excessive grace, since very few people need to be laughed out of it. Unless it is meant as parody, as in Trudeau's little dance, excessive grace is seldom encountered.

Taste

There is also an optimum quantity of taste, with an insufficiency of taste turning into vulgarity and an excess into preciousness. The precious are particularly vulnerable to ridicule, since they depend so much on the esteem of others. When Molière mocked the *précieuses ridicules,* with their absurdly poetic speech, they immediately withdrew, leaving scarcely a trace beyond his comedy. Today, they seem to belong to another and quite distant world, to *Brideshead Revisited*'s Anthony Blanche, reciting *The Waste Land* through a megaphone to an Oxford Quad; or to the high aestheticism of Oscar Wilde and the *Yellow Book.* Earlier still, they are Beau Brummell and his circle, leaning out from the bay window of White's club to mock the neckcloths of passersby.

How did the Beau himself arrive at the pinnacle of neckcloth perfection?

> The first *coup d'archet* was made with the shirt collar, which he folded down to its proper size; and then, standing before the looking-glass, with his chin poked up towards the ceiling, by the gentle and gradual declension of his lower jaw he creased the cravat to reasonable dimensions.[1]

A friend called on Brummell one day and saw his valet emerge with an armful of flowing white cravats. "These, sir, are our failures," announced the Beau grandly. The Beau's friend, Lord Petersham, was the arbiter elegentiae of snuffboxes; a light blue Sèvres box, he thought, was "a nice summer box, but it would not do for winter wear."[2] All such dandies have gone the way of Brummell himself, broken and penniless in Caen, obliged to beg for his single luxury, a biscuit and a cup of coffee. When will you pay me, asked the confectioner? "A la pleine lune, Madame," answered the Beau with a bow. "A la pleine lune."[3]

Excessive taste is seldom encountered except as parody, where taste turns into camp and mocks itself. Camp is over-the-top irony, where an ostensible devotion to a genre mocks the genre itself. Thus the absurd Buck Rogers movies, with their hokey spaceships and stilted dialogue that thrilled children in the 1930s, acquired a camp following in the 1960s. During that decade, camp represented both a denial of objective aesthetic standards and the triumph of the aesthetic over the moral and political. Camp subordinated high to popular art and elevated questions of style over all others. In Mel Brooks's *The Producers*, it was camp that turned "Springtime for Hitler" into a Broadway hit. The movement flourished for a while, but today its message that art trumps politics is as dated as the aesthetic movement.

An excessive style is easily policed by laughter. But the vulgar, with their inadequacy of style, are more robust and may return the jest. "We're not vulgar; they're simply precious," say the Roseannes and the Jerrys. The question, after all, is where the golden mean might be, and by lowering the bar several notches vulgar laughter might effectively silence the aristocratic laughter that mocks it. While laughter informs us about desirable standards of taste, these standards are contestable and contested through rival forms of laughter.

Learning

Learning also has its excesses and deficiencies, and like taste there is often some dispute about where the mean might lie. At a minimum, one should be able to employ the tools of one's trade. One reliable figure of fun is the tyro—the dude at the ranch, Patrick O'Brian's Stephen Maturin aboard ship. However, mere ignorance is seldom risible in itself. Those who openly confess their lack of education do not provoke our laughter. Instead, what is hilarious is the false pedantry of the ignorant who pretend to be learned—the *Dottore* in the *commedia dell'arte* or Sganarelle in Molière's *Le médecin malgré lui*. When a patient timidly objects that the heart is on the left, not the right side, the impostor blandly carries on. "Yes, it used to be there. But we've changed all that, and now we use modern methods."*

These are the glory days of false pedantry, where the overreaching academic wonderfully entertains us. What takes the prize is Thomas Kuhn's *The Structure of Scientific Revolutions,* and even more those who cite it. Kuhn argued that scientific change is not incremental, but occurs through revolutionary "paradigm shifts" in which the conceptual structure of past learning is razed and rebuilt from the ground up. A simple enough message, and one with limited explanatory power, since few refinements, scientific or otherwise, junk all prior learning. Nevertheless, the Kuhn book has a special appeal for the pedant who feels that he is observing and (why be modest) sparking an intellectual revolution himself. My very own paradigm shift!

I have a special fondness for the gratuitous reference to Hegel, and surely the prize here must go to Harvard's Duncan Kennedy. Footnote 2 in his *Structure of Blackstone's Commentaries* begins, "The works that have most influenced me are G. Hegel, *The Philosophy of Right* (T. Knox trans. 1952); G. Hegel, *The Phenomenology of Mind* (J. Baillie trans. 1967)," and then goes on to cite Lévi-Strauss and Marcuse, among others.[4] What gives the footnote its special charm is that none of these authors are cited elsewhere in the 174-page article, nor does anything in the text suggest a familiarity with them.

Descending a level takes us to middlebrow learning. This is the false pedantry of the intellectual demimonde that takes seriously John Updike as a novelist and Stephen Sondheim as a composer. Their parents read Tennessee Williams and looked to Harvey Cox for spiritual guidance; their grandparents read H. G. Wells and quoted George Bernard Shaw. Their thoughts are shallow, secondhand, and expressed with the subtlety of the teenage atheist. They were memorably parodied in Lionel Trilling's *The Middle of the Journey:* The local Protestant clergyman, well-meaning and dim, espouses a fashionable leftism before visitors from New York, without recognizing that one of them (Maxim as Whittaker Chambers) has just broken with the Communist Party.

---

*"Oui, cela était autrefois ainsi; mais nous avons changé tout cela, et nous faisons maintenant la médecine d'une méthode toute nouvelle."

"The Research Magnificent, I call it. Do you know that book by H.G. Wells?" And when Maxim nodded economically, Mr. Gurney went on to say that in some ways religion could be said to be an effort for social justice.

Maxim said, "In short, you do not believe in God."

"It depends on what you mean by God, Mr. Maxim. If you mean a Being who may be understood as some divine purpose in the world, or some principle that is at bottom good—"

"Suppose we say that God is the Being to whom things are rendered that are not rendered to Caesar."[5]

The middlebrow pedant perfectly expresses the most fatuous sentiments of the day in an ostensibly learned manner, so that the poverty of thought is obscured to the bien-pensant. The great satirist of middlebrow learning was Flaubert, who mocked the inane clichés that substitute for intellectual conversation. Does it not seem to you, Madame Bovary asks her lover, that the contemplation of the sea elevates the soul, gives ideas of the infinite, the ideal? With a more discriminating circle of friends, her adolescent daydreams and cheap sentiments might be ridiculed away, but she lives in a world of thirdhand "smartness." Over three decades, Flaubert assembled a dictionary of middlebrow flatulence, the *Dictionnaire des idées reçues*.

> *Actresses.* Destroy our sons. Of a horrible sensuousness, give themselves up to orgies, waste millions, end up diseased. Oh! I'm sorry! Some of them make very good mothers!
> *English gardens.* Much more natural than French gardens.
> *Rhyme.* Never agrees with reason.*

Bad poetry is the ne plus ultra of middlebrow pedantry, since it pretends to a most demanding intellectual skill. It seldom gets worse than William McGonagall's *Tay Bridge Disaster,* which begins:

---

*Actrices.—La perte des fils de famille. Sont d'une lubricité effrayante, se livrent à des orgies, avalent des millions, finissent à l'hôpital. Pardon! Il y a en qui sont bonnes mères de famille! *Jardins anglais.*—Plus naturels que les jardins à la française. *Rime.*—Ne s'accord jamais avec la raison.

Beautiful Railway Bridge of the Silv'ry Tay!
Alas! I am very sorry to say
That ninety lives have been taken away
On the last Sabbath day of 1879,
Which will be remember'd for a very long time.

Bummer. But let's not forget that it was a lovely bridge, and a very fine river too. Like McGonagall, the bad poet overreaches and tumbles into absurdity. A dreadful event—the train disaster—is insipidly conjoined with commonplace and cheap sentiments. Alternatively, a trivial subject is handled in a ludicrously solemn manner. G. K. Chesterton, who wondered at the mysterious absence of cheese poetry, could not have heard of James McIntyre, the Ontario Cheese Poet. McIntyre's *Ode on the Mammoth Cheese Weighing Over 7,000 Pounds* is very likely the worst poem ever written (at least by an undertaker).

We have seen thee, queen of cheese,
Lying quietly at your ease,
Gently fanned by evening breeze,
Thy fair form no flies dare seize.

All gaily dressed soon you'll go
To the great Provincial show,
To be admired by many a beau
In the city of Toronto. . . .

We'rt thou suspended from balloon,
You'd cast a shade even at noon,
Folks would think it was the moon
About to fall and crush them soon.

False pedantry is a species of hypocrisy. In pretending to a learning he does not possess, the false pedant is also an impostor who offends against the Aristotelian virtue of truth-telling. These are familiar vices, and the pedantry of the truly learned is therefore a more interesting comic vice. But when is learning risible in itself?

We would not think to laugh at a scholar who balances a love of learning with other attainments, even if he fails to reach the pinnacle of Sir Thomas Urquhart's never-too-much-to-be-extolled Admirable Crichton. James Crichton entered St. Andrews University in 1570 at the age of ten;

he received his B.A. at twelve and his M.A. two years later. After a few more years of study, he arrived in Paris where he posted notices challenging the scholars of the Sorbonne to dispute with him on

> any science, liberal art, discipline or faculty, practical or theoretick, not excluding the theological nor jurisprudential habits, and in any of these twelve languages: Hebrew, Syriac, Arabick, Greek, Latin, Spanish, French, Italian, English, Dutch, Flemish and Sclavonian, in either verse or prose, at the discretion of the disputant.

An extraordinary offer. Yet when

> all the choicest and most profound philosophers, mathematicians, naturalists, mediciners, alchymists, apothecaries, surgeons, doctors of both civil and canon law and divines both for controversies and positive doctrines, together with all the primest grammarians, rhetoricians, and logicians

put their heads together they were unable to best the paragon of learning; who, while they prepared for the academic battle, relaxed with

> hawking, hunting, tilting, vaulting, riding of well-managed horses, tossing of the pike, handling of the musket, flourishing of colours, dancing, fencing, swimming, jumping, throwing of the bar, playing at the tennis, baloon or long catch; and sometimes at the house games of dice, cards, playing at the chess, billiards, trou-madam and other suchlike chamber-sports, singing, playing at the lute and other musical instruments, masking, balling, [and] reveling.

Not to mention enjoying "the courting of handsome ladyes and a jovial cup in the company of bacchanalian blades."[6] Crichton disputed with the nimble-witted doctors from nine in the morning to six at night, and was then declared the winner. The next day, to unwind, he gave an exhibition of horsemanship at the Louvre, where he picked off the ring with his lance fifteen times in succession.

Some scholars have wondered whether such a monster of perfection really existed. Apart from Urquhart, there is little record of the ever-renowned Crichton's existence. And Urquhart, for whom the story was a digression in a book advertising the virtues of his universal language ("for while others have but five or six [cases], it hath ten besides the nominative"),[7] had a regrettable tendency to exaggerate. Noble-born though he was, we might be disposed to doubt his claim that he could trace his lineage through 153 generations, back to Adam. Yet as an ideal of happy learning, the Admirable Crichton lives on for every academic.

Nor would we laugh if, like Belloc's regal dons, the scholar simply delights in the pursuit of obscure learning.

> Dons English, worthy of the land;
> Dons rooted; Dons that understand.
> *(Lines to a Don)*

Dons like Dr. Porson, whose love of learning sometimes took the form of chasing ill-prepared students about the classroom with a poker. Dons:

> Who shout and bang and roar and bawl
> The Absolute across the hall.

Dons not particularly attentive to their personal decoration, but whose pulse quickens when they think, with Sir Thomas Browne, that "what Song the *Syrens* sung, or what name *Achilles* assumed when he hid himself among women, though puzzling Questions, are not beyond all conjecture."[8]

No, learning is never risible in itself. The scholar who delights in obscure learning is after all enjoying himself. He is Aristotle's contemplative man, whose life possesses the highest degree of virtue and happiness. Such people are more admirable than the student whose pursuit of learning is purely instrumental, and designed to advance some personal interest. The strategic scholar misses the point of learning, for his scholarship is mechanical and joyless. Marlowe's Faustus is the very type of such scholars. Faustus is entirely without a thirst for knowledge, remarked C. S. Lewis. "It is not truth he wants from his devils, but gold and guns and girls."[9] Worse still is what Julien Benda called the *trahison des clercs*—the flashy pedant who sacrifices the joy of intellectual pursuits for partisan politics, and thereby renders unto Caesar what is meant for a higher Authority.

The true pedant might nevertheless become ridiculous through his vanity, when he seeks to prove that his organ is bigger than that of his colleagues. No love is greater than that of the vain mind for its own idea, or blinder either. Jeremy Bentham comes to mind here. The father of utilitarianism thought it a waste to have himself buried after death, when, stuffed and mounted in a glass case, he might provide inspiration for generations of scholars to come.[10] The subject obsessed him, like every subject he thought on, nor were social conventions or nice questions of decorum allowed to intrude. What he proposed was that, after death, his body be turned into an "auto-icon" according to the science of taxidermy, so that future generations might have the chance to see him and the other great men of the past. Auto-icons should be mounted in a great park, he proposed, lined up in a row like statues at Versailles and alternating with mighty trees, as a spur to ambition for future scholars.

But then a wonderful thought intruded. Suppose that auto-icons were given the powers of motion and speech, through mechanical devices; and imagine, asked Bentham, the Bentham auto-icon brought forward and introduced to Cicero, St. Paul, Confucius, and Justinian. All would applaud him. Bacon and Locke would congratulate Bentham on his greatest-happiness principle, and discuss how it supplemented the lacunae in their work.

A lesser scholar might have betrayed a scintilla of self-doubt about the project or his personal worthiness, but such emotions were entirely foreign to Bentham. And so his body may be viewed today in University College, London (the "Godless Institution on Gower Street"), protected from nonutilitarian student pranksters by a glass cage. Thanks to the Internet, we can view the body through a web-cam, which, if less exciting than other spy-cams that come to mind, nevertheless celebrates scholarship in a most striking manner. Nor is the web-cam entirely devoid of action. Once a year, in accordance with Bentham's wishes, the auto-icon is wheeled from its case to a meeting of University College's Board of Trustees, where it is recorded as "present, but not voting."

Apart from his narcissism, the true pedant becomes risible when he sacrifices more useful lessons upon the altar of his dry-as-dust specialty. His ostentatious display of scholarship signals a crabbed life that has sacrificed joy for the false pleasure of displaying excessive learning. Such a person was given several talents and buried all but one. "The pedant, with his general maxims, almost always misses the mark in life," said Schopenhauer. "In art, in which concepts are unfruitful, he produces lifeless, stiff, abortive mannerisms. Even with regard to ethics, the purpose to act rightly or nobly cannot always be carried out in accordance with abstract maxims."[11] Such people possess a single hammer and see everything as a nail. Every question of art, music, literature, and history is examined from the same perspective, be it deconstructionism or the greatest-happiness principle. A vexed issue that demands the most sensitive insight is contemptuously dismissed with the same curt formula that the pedant applies to every single problem. The result is machine scholarship, and that is always risible.

True pedantry is particularly risible when an excessive reliance on reason obscures the intuitive lessons of the comic norms, when Pascal's *esprit de finesse* is forgotten and life is lived in an *esprit de géometrie*. This was the Schoolman's error that Thomas à Kempis gently mocked in *The Imitation of Christ:* "It is better to feel contrition than know the definition thereof." Academic silliness of this kind does not come naturally: it must be taught, since an ordinary person would never believe what the academic placidly accepts. "To the learned it is given to be learnedly foolish," said Hobbes. Dennis Prager tells of a person who called up his radio show after he had described a brutal rape of a young girl. What the caller wanted to know was what in the rapist's childhood might have led him to do such a thing. "Right away," said Prager, "I knew I was talking to someone with a post-graduate degree." The French have a term for this. Professional training is called *formation professionelle;* and the pedant's excessive reliance on reason is lampooned as a *déformation professionelle.*

In the following chapters, we observe the results of true pedantry at close hand.

8 Machine Law

> We can never be despised
> according to our full desert.
> Montaigne

Several years back I met a lawyer friend who had recently returned from Russia. He had been brought there, along with a good many other experts, to teach the Russians about the legal system that won the cold war. My friend had been asked to draft a new Russian corporations code. Over lunch, he explained the problem to us. "How do you introduce Western corporations law to a country that lacks a stable court system?" he asked. There was silence around the table. Give nuclear weapons to the Russian Supreme Court, we wondered? Au contraire. "Cumulative voting!" he announced triumphantly—rules that give minority shareholders a seat on the board of directors.

It is easy enough to put this down to the fatuous naïveté of the innocent abroad. But there is something more at work, of greater interest to the student of laughter. By absurdly extending a simple idea into places it did not belong, my friend had proposed machine law and become Bergson's machine man.

Chapters 6 and 7 examined how an individual might become risible by tumbling into comic vice. This chapter extends the analysis from individuals to ideas, from comic vices to risible law, and asks how law is made more efficient when machine law is lampooned. In the following chapters I examine the benefits to scholarship of a sense of humor and the aesthetic costs we bear when we forget to laugh at ugliness.

Risible Law

Judges seldom show any signs of appreciating how risible American law may be. There are exceptions, to be sure. Judge Scalia once began an opinion with "I join the opinion of the Court except that portion which takes seriously, and thus encourages in the future, an argument that should be laughed out of court."[1] Several other members of the bench, such as Judges Alex Kozinski, Frank Easterbrook, and Danny Boggs, are true wits as well.

There is much to be said for a sober-minded bench. The effort to seem witty might easily become tiresome, when the case is serious and the sally is issued from on high. Yet much of the law is highly amusing, and the failure to notice its comedic possibilities sometimes leaves us the poorer. Not only do we miss the diversion of comedy, but nonsensical legal doctrines survive because we have lost the knack of laughter.

There is a great store of harmless nonsense in the common law, to one who knows how to extract it. A. P. Herbert's satires were master-pieces of the genre. Herbert wrote up mock accounts of court decisions, recounting the efforts of an obstreperous layman, Alfred Haddock, to exercise an Englishman's rights and privileges just as often as he could. In *R. v. Haddock*, the accused was charged with leading "a large white cow of malevolent aspect" through the City of London to the offices of the Collector of Taxes. In his defense, Haddock argued that the cow was ten-dered as delivery of his taxes, since he had signed the cow and endorsed it "Pay to the Collector of Taxes, who is no gentleman, or Order, the sum of fifty-seven pounds (and may he rot!)." The court held that the per-sonal comments were simply an honest man's understandable reaction to paying taxes, and did not deprive the cow of its status as an uncondi-tional promise of payment, as required by the Bills of Exchange Act. The method of payment was somewhat unconventional, to be sure, but noth-ing in the statute required promissory notes to be written on paper. The charge was therefore dismissed, since the accused had lawfully paid his taxes with a negotiable cow.[2]

My introduction to statutory interpretation came in the form of an apocryphal case, *R. v. Bird,* a parody written by Toronto lawyer Hart Pomerantz, which Canadian law students passed around in samizdat fashion. The case, a decision of Mr. Justice Blue, turned on whether a defense for cattle trespass (the tort of letting one's cattle stray across a neighbor's field) lay under the Migratory Birds Convention. After due consideration of the legislation and the mischief it sought to prevent, Blue J. concluded that, for the purposes of the statute, a cow was a bird.

Such satires succeed because they contain a kernel of truth. Let us therefore look for the risible amongst real, not imagined, decisions, where the joke is unintentional.

1. An administrative agency regulates springs in one's backyard under a grant of authority derived from a statute that deals with navigable waters and adjacent wetlands.[3]

2. An FBI agent was fired for embezzling $2,000 from the government to feed his gambling habit. He was reinstated after a court ruled that his passion for gambling was a "handicap" and that the government had wrongly discriminated against him.[4]

3. Drew P. was a child in rural Georgia who suffered from infantile autism and severe mental retardation. The school board offered Drew an extensive educational program, including an expert on autism, but his parents were dissatisfied. They wanted a special school out of town, and a court agreed with them. The out-of-town school happened to be in Tokyo.[5]

4. Chaya Amiad brought her dog to a Seattle clothing store and was asked to leave. Amiad was not blind, but afterward claimed that she had an emotional dependence on the dog and sued under the Americans with Disabilities Act. A psychologist treating Amiad for depression said the dog was a mental health service animal. The Seattle Office of Civil Rights agreed, ordering the storekeeper to pay Amiad $250 and attend sensitivity training.[6]

5. As a final case, consider *Wickard v. Filburn*,[7] which so expanded the scope of Washington's power over the states that American federalism began to look like a legal fiction. For many years, Filburn owned and operated a small farm on which he kept a herd of dairy cattle and some poultry. To feed his animals, he also raised winter wheat. Any wheat left over one year was used in the following year for reseeding. In planting and harvesting his wheat he exceeded the acreage limits of the Agricultural Adjustment Act of 1938, arguing that, under the interstate commerce power, the federal restrictions were inapplicable since the wheat never left his farm. However, the Supreme Court upheld the restriction: If Filburn had not

grown his own wheat, he would have purchased it on the market, and such wheat might have come from out-of-state.

Now, how is it that such cases have escaped our laughter? They are not parodies, like *R. v. Bird,* but that should not matter. The best laughter is often reserved for the unintentionally comic. Yet we do not laugh. The expansion of victim rights and the extensions of federal power are defended by liberals and opposed by conservatives with the same heavy seriousness. But in throwing away the self-correcting powers of laughter, they have conspired to produce the most comic jurisprudence.

Kreimer v. Morristown

Consider that most Swiftian of decisions, *Kreimer v. Town of Morristown.* Kreimer was sympathetically described by Judge Lee Sarokin as one "whose access to showers and laundry facilities [was] severely curtailed by his homeless status."[8] It was more than a matter of personal hygiene, however. "Dressed in soiled and sweat-soaked clothes, the homeless man spent his days stalking, staring down, and speaking loudly and belligerently to library staff and patrons. Kreimer's foul smell and anti-social behavior literally drove people from the facility, a fact many witnesses observed."[9] The lack of access to showers no doubt explains his nickname: Smelly Bum. And so the library patrons of Morristown, N.J., complained when he chose to spend much of his day in their company. The library responded with a set of admission guidelines which, not surprisingly, excluded Kreimer. His thirst for knowledge denied, Kreimer sued, the American Civil Liberties Union harrumphed, and the library policies were struck down at trial as unconstitutionally vague and restrictive.[10] That might bother some people, wrote Judge Sarokin, but *tant pis.*

> No one can dispute that matters of personal appearance and hygiene can reach a point where they interfere with the enjoyment of the facility by others. But one person's hay-fever is another person's ambrosia.[11]

Is this a deliberate satire? The giveaways are all there, in the clever parody of official legalese: the strident tone that dwindles to nothing ("No one can dispute"), the preference for the Romance word over the Germanic ("interfere with the enjoyment" instead of "bother"), the false opposition between hay-fever and ambrosia. Surely all doubt is removed when we come to the high flatulence of the peroration:

> No matter how laudable and understandable the goals of the library may be, we cannot—we dare not—cross the threshold of barring persons from entering because of how they appear based upon the unfettered discretion of another.

No, no, a thousand times no! And finally the bathetic conclusion, its author laughing up his sleeve.

> The greatness of our country lies in tolerating speech with which we do not agree; that same toleration must extend to people, particularly where the cause of revulsion may be of our own making.

The learned judge compares public policy analysis to excrement, and criticizes those who prefer one to the other! Did Gulliver ever visit a place so mad? Was there really a judge named Sarokin? Or was the name a pseudonym behind which a clever conservative hid his identity and exposed his savage indignation? A growing number of academics now believe that the opinion's true author is Judge Alex Kozinski, who lampoons the civil liberties invented last week in California as the "MTV Constitution." Say farewell to the Founders, and hello to trendy slogans and mushy, feel-good liberalism. Never mind the loss of property rights, says Judge Kozinski. Think instead of what you will gain when courts uphold euthanasia: the Right to Die!

Judge Kozinski's satire succeeded beyond his expectations, however, when gullible White House staffers had a "Judge Lee Sarokin" appointed to the Third Circuit Court of Appeals. Wholly lacking a sense of irony, they read the decision and thought they had found just the man for their employer. In every law school, academics wagered that the wittiest of judges had at last overstepped the bounds. But when the time came for him to be sworn in, a heavily disguised "Judge Sarokin" took his place with the other judges. For almost a year the farce continued, and Kozinski-Sarokin commuted back and forth between California and the East Coast, until an exhausted "Judge Sarokin" took early retirement, bringing an end to the most successful imposture since Gladstone adopted a false beard to bowl for England as "W.G. Grace."[12] (Judge Kozinski denies all this—but that is just what would one expect him to do.)

The Sick Chickens Case

In the past, a case as ridiculous as *Kreimer* would never have seen the light of day, for then the wit (more than Shelley's poet) was the unacknowledged legislator of the world. He could repeal a ridiculous law through laughter, and that is just what happened in the "Sick Chickens" case—*Schechter v. U.S.*[13]—which struck down a National Recovery Administration code as an unconstitutional attempt by Congress to regulate intrastate commerce. The National Industrial Recovery Act, a piece of extravagant socialism, had authorized the president to approve "codes of fair competition" that trade associations or groups had submitted to him. The codes sought to reduce "cutthroat" competition through highly detailed restrictions on industry practices. This harmed consumers by stifling competition, and for this reason industry groups supported the codes: they permitted merchants to organize a cartel and sell their goods at monopolistic prices.

One such code was New York's "Live Poultry Code," which regulated the poultry business in mind-numbing detail. For example, it mandated "straight killing," under which customers were barred from choosing the chickens they bought, and instead had to accept the luck of the draw. Otherwise, consumers would pick the best chickens and leave over the scrawny chickens that were worth less than the inflated monopolistic price. Merchants would then be stuck with unsold inventory unless they lowered their prices. The example wonderfully shows how difficult it is to police cartel-breaking, and how the grant of a monopoly means little unless every possibility of defection is bricked up. The only effective form of state capitalism is a Peronism that stifles the economy by prescribing rules through and through and absolutely.

Now, in the Sick Chickens case, the defendants operated a kosher poultry slaughterhouse in Brooklyn, where they purchased live poultry from commission men for slaughter and resale to retail poultry dealers and butchers. They were rule breakers, who sought to attract clients by chipping away at the Live Poultry Code. Their competitors took notice, and in due course they were charged and convicted with a variety of offenses under the code, including "selective killing," under which customers were permitted to pick their chickens, in violation of "straight killing" requirements.

On its facts, the case was trivial in the extreme. Yet the fate of the First Roosevelt New Deal hung in the balance, and when the case reached the Supreme Court local counsel had been elbowed aside by more eminent litigators. Solicitor-General (subsequently Justice) Stanley Reed argued that the nation's economic recovery would be jeopardized if the impugned legislation was not upheld. Selective killing would shake up the price structure by depressing the price for good poultry rejected by the earliest purchasers. In reply, a distinguished New York lawyer, Frederick Wood, argued that the chickens had left the stream of interstate commerce after their sale to a New York commission man and before their purchase by the defendants, and that the federal government lacked the constitutional authority to pass the National Recovery Act. Given the court's previous rulings, however, the issue was a toss-up, and what won the case for the defendants was an exchange during the oral argument by Joseph Heller, the defendant's less than tony, original lawyer.

In the midst of Heller's rambling argument, Justice McReynolds asked for a definition of "straight-killing." The learned judge was one of the "Four Horsemen" (with Justices Butler, Sutherland, and Van Devanter), a group of conservative jurists who opposed early New Deal legislation so effectively that liberals saw Apocalyptic parallels. He could therefore be expected to sympathize with the defendant, but Heller wasn't biting.

MR. JUSTICE MCREYNOLDS: What do you understand that provision amounts to?

MR. HELLER: Which provision is that? (*Hunh?*)

MR. JUSTICE MCREYNOLDS: The one that you are just speaking of, the "straight-killing" provision.

Heller was obviously confused. The Supreme Court wanted to be instructed on the selection of chickens?

MR. HELLER: The straight-killing provision is in this Code.

But the learned justice was not put off so easily.

> MR. JUSTICE MCREYNOLDS: Yes. But the practice, what is it?
>
> MR. HELLER (*stalling now*): That is, of the "straight-killing"?
>
> MR. JUSTICE MCREYNOLDS: Yes.
>
> MR. HELLER: Do you want me to explain "straight-killing"? (*Amazing! You never know with these people.*)
>
> MR. JUSTICE MCREYNOLDS (*despairing*): Well, never mind.

For a moment it seemed that the Court had lost interest in Brooklyn chicken-buying habits. But now another of the Four Horsemen began to smell blood.

> MR. JUSTICE VAN DEVANTER: Explain what the clause requires.
>
> MR. HELLER (*stubbornly*): It is set out in the Code.
>
> MR. JUSTICE MCREYNOLDS (*catching on at last*): If I understand this correctly, these chickens are brought into New York by the carload, and then they are taken out and put in coops?
>
> MR. HELLER: Yes, sir. They are put in coops by the commission merchant. (*Have these guys ever bought a chicken?*)
>
> MR. JUSTICE MCREYNOLDS: How many are there in a coop?
>
> MR. HELLER: From 30 to 40, according to their size. (*Or fought over one in Brooklyn?*)
>
> MR. JUSTICE MCREYNOLDS: Then, when the commission man delivers them to the slaughterhouse, they are in coops?
>
> MR. HELLER: They are in coops.
>
> MR. JUSTICE MCREYNOLDS: And, if he undertakes to sell them, he must have straight-killing?
>
> MR. HELLER: He must have straight-killing. (*But now the penny finally drops.*) In other words, his customer is not permitted to select the ones he wants. He must put his hand into the coop when he buys from the slaughterhouse and take the first chicken that comes to hand. He has to take that.

At this point, the transcript notes that most deadly of responses:

[Laughter.]

Now, why was there laughter? Heller was not a wit. He was more than a little plodding. But, prodded by Mr. Justice McReynolds, he had brought home the absurd reach of the impugned regulations. The tension and ennui of economic crisis and *arcana juridica* were forgotten, as justices and spectators pictured a crowded, jostling butcher shop, and a regulator saying "Madam! Unhand that chicken!" After all the fine oratory, the statute and NRA codes were simply machine law, and ridiculous.

> MR. JUSTICE MCREYNOLDS: Irrespective of the quality of the chicken? [Laughter.]
>
> MR. HELLER: Irrespective of the quality or the price of the chicken.
>
> MR. JUSTICE MCREYNOLDS (*warming to his audience*): Suppose it is a sick chicken?
>
> MR. HELLER: Well, he could reject a sick chicken.
>
> MR. JUSTICE MCREYNOLDS: Now can he break up those coops and sell them, half a dozen chickens to one man, and half a dozen to another man?
>
> MR. HELLER (*gleefully*): He cannot. He can sell a whole coop, or one-half of a coop.
>
> MR. JUSTICE MCREYNOLDS: And that is all?
>
> MR. HELLER: That is all. And when he sells five, or six, or two, or three, he cannot permit the purchaser any selection of the chickens in the coop.

Now the laughter becomes general, and everyone wants in.

> MR. JUSTICE STONE: Do you mean there cannot be a selection if he buys one-half of the coop?
>
> MR. HELLER: No. You just break the box into two halves.
> [Laughter.]
>
> MR. HELLER: There is no selection in the case.
>
> MR. JUSTICE SUTHERLAND: Well suppose, however, that all the chickens have gone over to one end of the coop?
> [Laughter.][14]

When the laughter had died away, President Roosevelt's first New Deal was dead.

What are the special characteristics of risible law? Of all the theories of comedy, Bergson's best explains which laws attract our laughter. We laugh at machine law, as we do at the machine man. We laugh at rigid laws, sensible enough when their scope is limited, but ridiculous when unbounded and seen as ends in themselves. Bergson gives an example of such a law, in the customs inspector who narrowly saves the shipwrecked passenger from drowning and then asks if he has anything to declare. In the same way, constitutional liberties are risible when high-sounding mobility rights are employed to permit a vagrant to smell up a library, when a regulation is absurdly overextended, and when a whiner is awarded millions for bruised feelings.

What machine law lacks is the complexity and suppleness of a human legal system. Machine law absurdly takes a simple and modest rule to be a supreme and overriding principle, and thereby parodies itself. It sacrifices human happiness to no useful or admirable end, and forgets that the Sabbath was made for man and not man for the Sabbath. It is like the man who elevates economy into avarice, temperance into abstemiousness, prudence into cowardice. What it lacks, more than anything, is a sense of humanity, of what it means to live well, and of the kind of life to which we should aspire.

The result is risible law, when we possess the detachment to ignore the human costs of nonsensical rules. With a stronger sense of pathos, the result is anything but comic, and this was the message of one the best legal books in the last ten years. Philip Howard's *The Death of Common Sense* described in human terms the blight of wasteful rules, such as those which prevented Mother Teresa from opening a homeless shelter in South Bronx. The nuns spent two years in navigating bureaucratic regulations, which mandated household appliances their order had banned. Given their vows of poverty, the nuns did not want a washing machine—they preferred to wash clothes by hand, as they did in India. In the end they were defeated by a requirement that a $100,000 elevator be built in their four-story building. This was simply too much. The nuns thought that the money could be better spent on the poor in their other missions. They left New York, but not before sending a polite letter to the city expressing their regrets and noting that they had learned a useful lesson about the law and its many complexities. Howard described the absurd extension of rights, the explosion of litigation, and the mind-numbing regulations. The book had an enormous impact on the lay reader. So far as the legal profession was concerned, however, it might have fallen stillborn from the press. Evidently, what was needed was ridicule.

9   Machine Scholarship

My aim is to teach you to pass from a piece
of disguised nonsense to something that is
patent nonsense.

Ludwig Wittgenstein

The satire of philosophic nonsense is one of the oldest literary forms. Aristophanes mocked Socrates' otherworldly views by portraying him suspended in the air and worshiping *The Clouds*. Voltaire's *Candide* is an ironic comment on optimistic rationalism and Leibnitz's jargon of "sufficient reasons" and "pre-established harmonies." Not so long ago, Tom Stoppard parodied the self-referential world of analytical philosophy in *Jumpers*. "That was the year of 'The Concept of Knowledge,' your masterpiece, and the last decent title left after Ryle bagged 'The Concept of Mind' and Archie bagged 'The Problem of Mind' and Ayer bagged 'The Problem of Knowledge.'"[1]

Analytical Philosophy

What I should like to examine, however, is how philosophers themselves have used ridicule to deliver a knockdown blow to nonsensical theories. How is philosophy different when the philosopher employs a sense of humor?

Few fragments remain of Democritus, alas. The "laughing philosopher" never left home without a mocking look on his face, trying with "all the powers of irony and laughter to reclaim . . . the vilest and most profligate town in all Thrace," as Sterne put it. However, in the 1920s and 1930s a school of philosophy arose that proclaimed that most prior philosophizing was nonsense in the best sense of that term. The movement was called logical positivism, and took a very narrow view of what counts as a meaningful utterance. A sequence of words is meaningless unless it is either a definition ("'Red' is a primary color") or an empirical statement about the world ("This pen is red"). Definitions teach one a language, but if one already speaks it (knowing the definition of "primary color," for example) they tell one nothing. That leaves empirical statements, which to be meaningful must be testable or verifiable, at least in the weak sense that we can imagine a state of the world in which the statement is either true or false. Under this *verification principle,* metaphysics, ethics, and aesthetics are all bogus disciplines. They appear to be saying something, but on closer examination are seen to be composed of pseudostatements that, being unverifiable, are entirely devoid of meaning.

To illustrate how the verification principle excludes pseudostatements, a leading logical positivist, Rudolf Carnap, examined a passage from Heidegger's *What Is Metaphysics?*

> What is to be investigated is being only and—*nothing* else; being alone and further—*nothing;* solely being, and beyond being—*nothing. What about this Nothing? . . . Does the Nothing exist only because the Not, i.e., the Negation, exists?* Or is it the other way around? *Does Negation and the Not exist only because the Nothing exists? . . .* We assert: *the Nothing is prior to the Not and the Negation . . .* Where do we seek the Nothing? *Anxiety reveals the Nothing . . .* That for which and because of which we were anxious, was "really"—nothing . . . Indeed: the Nothing itself—as such—was present . . . *What about this Nothing?—The Nothing itself nothings.*[2]

Not only did Heidegger write all this, but the italics are in the original. For sheer lunacy it is hard to beat, and Carnap no doubt recognized that he was onto some(noth)ing. For what can we say about nothing? The layman might think there is *nothing* to worry about, but for the metaphysician that is just the problem. To whom shall we turn for an answer? Is *no one* able to define nothing? Then surely *he* can—but where shall we find him?[3] Carnap's wit lay in recognizing the possibility of laughter when words lose their meanings and a sentence in proper grammatical form is shown on analysis to be devoid of meaning. What Heidegger said wasn't true, of course; worse still, it wasn't even false. Even when he "nothed." We might as well try to find the meaning of a piece of music. Or as Carnap put it, "metaphysicians are musicians without musical ability."[4]

Logical positivism originated in Vienna, but was brought to England by A. J. Ayer in the 1930s. After graduating from Oxford in 1932, Ayer traveled to Austria, where he met Carnap and his fellow members of the Vienna Circle. Returning to England six months later, Ayer wrote *Language, Truth and Logic*, which launched his career and made logical positivism accessible to an English-speaking audience. Even more than Carnap, Ayer emphasized the nonsensical quality of traditional philosophy. The metaphysicians "show how easy it is to write sentences which are literally nonsensical without seeing that they are nonsensical"; "all utterances about the nature of God are nonsensical"; "those philosophers who fill their books with assertions that they intuitively 'know' this or that moral . . . truth are merely providing material for the psycho-analyst."[5]

As his early book showed, Ayer had a great deal of panache, which age did not wither. When he was seventy-seven he observed Mike Tyson forcing himself upon an unwilling Naomi Campbell and asked the boxer to stop. "Do you know who the f—— I am?" demanded Tyson. "I am the heavyweight champion of the world!" "And I," replied Ayer imperturbably, "am the Wykeham Professor of Logic."[6] Early in his career, however, the self-assertion was less appreciated, for there is something about a young man who tells you that your life's work is nonsense that is not wholly pleasing. Nor did it help that Ayer lived in London, hobnobbed with playwrights, and was seen as a member of a left-wing establishment. When another philosopher, J. L. Austin, began looking for nonsense in Ayer, therefore, traditional philosophers could not have been more delighted.

Austin is little-known, but he was one of the most influential philosophers in the last century. He taught at Oxford, and more than anyone else embodied the "ordinary language" philosophy that identified the meaning of a word with the way it was used in ordinary conversation. Austin had an extraordinary ability to deflate philosophic puffery through ridicule, as when he dismissed the metaphysician's *ivresse des grandes profondeurs*—the intoxification that comes from diving too deeply into the philosophic depths.[7] In his lifetime Austin published little. Nevertheless, his fearsome analytical abilities and mordant wit deterred some of his colleagues from publishing anything at all, lest Austin take them apart. His method was to ask the simplest and deadliest of questions, one that made his colleagues tremble: "What does this *mean?*"

Ved Mehta has given us a fascinating account of Austin's lectures. "He was a tall and thin man," wrote the blind author, "a sort of parody of the desiccated don." Austin would read a portion of Ayer's *The Problem of Knowledge* and then ask "What does he mean by this?" "I was told that Austin performed like this day after day, mocking, ridiculing, caricaturing, exaggerating, never flagging in the work of demolition, while the skeptical undergraduates watched, amused and bemused, for behind his performance—the legend—there was the voice of distilled intelligence."[8]

What Mehta had witnessed was one of the lectures that were posthumously published as *Sense and Sensibilia*. Austin's target was Ayer, then riding high. In *The Foundations of Empirical Knowledge*, Ayer had contrasted the layman's naive view of empirical knowledge with the more sophisticated understanding of professional philosophers such as himself.

> It does not normally occur to us that there is any need for us to justify our belief in the existence of material things. At the present moment, for example, I have no doubt that I really am perceiving the familiar objects, the chairs and table . . . with which my room is furnished. . . . When, however, one turns to the writings of those philosophers who have recently concerned themselves with the subject of perception, one may begin to wonder whether this matter is quite so simple. . . . [These philosophers] are not, for the most part, prepared to admit that such objects as pens and cigarettes are ever directly perceived. What, in their opinion, we directly perceive is always an object of a different kind from these; one to which it is now customary to give the name of "sense-datum."[9]

The passage invites ridicule, both for the put-down of the naive layman and for the pompous manner in which Ayer identified his views with those of the right-thinking logical positivists who had "recently" written of sense data and who "for the most part" agreed with him. But what does all this *mean*, asked Austin? Ayer implied that the ordinary man believes that he perceives material things. Yet the ordinary man would never say anything of the sort. He does not "perceive" the pen in front of him—he sees it. And he would not speak of "material things" either. What had happened, said Austin, is that Ayer had snuck in philosophical terms as stalking-horses for "sense data." There's the pen I see and here's the sense datum I perceive (as though those were two different experiences).

Now, why would it ever make sense to speak of seeing in such an abstract manner? Ayer's answer (which Austin called the Argument from

Illusion) is that the same thing may show up as very different kinds of sense data. In refraction, a stick that looks straight when held in the air looks bent when dipped into water. The stick does not change its shape—only the sense datum does. What we directly perceive, then, is not a stick but a sense datum. But is this really an illusion, asked Austin? Is the ordinary man really fooled? A stick in the water does not look like a bent stick—it looks like a stick in the water. Similarly, a mirage does not really look like a body of water and a movie does not really look like real life. At most, an illusion might fool an ordinary person the first time around, but not thereafter. What Ayer seemed to have had in mind, thought Austin, were not illusions but delusions, like the madman's belief that he is seeing pink rats. The point, however, is that ordinary people are not madmen, even though Ayer's argument assumes that they are. Had he paid more attention to ordinary language, Ayer would have noted that words like *look* and *reality* are much more complicated than he took them to be.

Ayer's mistake was a species of nonsense in its own right: in ascribing a nonstandard meaning to words such as *reality* and *material things*, he himself had committed metaphysics. But his greatest sin was his failure to observe the complexity of our language. In rejecting any statements that failed to satisfy the verification principle, Ayer had subscribed to a machine theory and become ridiculous.

The greatest modern analytical philosopher, Ludwig Wittgenstein, was acutely aware of how laughter might assist in philosophical analysis. He once suggested that a serious and good philosophical work might consist entirely of jokes.[10] As an example, Norman Malcolm tells how, on a walk in a park, Wittgenstein mocked the legal concept of ownership by offering Malcolm property rights to a tree, on the condition that he not use it in any way or interfere with anyone else's use of it.[11] Like philosophers, lawyers also speak nonsense when they ascribe special meanings to words that are divorced from real-world applications or real-world usage.

Throughout his life Wittgenstein wondered how language could represent the world. At first he wondered whether it could ever do so; later he thought it could, in the same way that a picture represents its subject, but that it could do nothing else; later still he amended his picture theory to ascribe meaning to statements that do not purport to represent the world at all. Bertrand Russell laughed him out of his earliest theory that all statements about the world are meaningless. "This was in a lecture room," wrote Russell, "and I invited him to consider the proposition

'There are no elephants in this room at present.' When he refused to believe this I looked under all the desks without finding one."[12] Later Wittgenstein asked Russell, "Will you please tell me whether I am a complete idiot or not?" Taken aback, Russell asked him what he meant. If he were a complete idiot, Wittgenstein said, he would become an aeronaut; otherwise he would become a philosopher. Russell asked Wittgenstein to write a paper for him. After reading only one sentence, Russell told him, "No, you must not become an aeronaut."[13]

Wittgenstein set forth his second theory in the *Tractatus Logico-Philosophicus,* which he wrote in an Italian prisoner of war camp during World War I. The *Tractatus* saw propositions as meaningful to the extent that they offered a picture of the world. Since statements about metaphysics, religion, and ethics do not do so, they lack meaning. As the *Tractatus'* famous seventh proposition put it, "Whereof we cannot speak, thereof we must be silent."

Since he thought that he had solved all the problems of philosophy, Wittgenstein logically abandoned it to teach elementary school in a small Austrian village. After several years, however, he became unsatisfied with the *Tractatus* and returned to philosophy and to Cambridge. The *Tractatus* had identified one species of nonsense—metaphysics—but now he saw that it had a ridiculously narrow view of how language is used itself. The *Tractatus* described a certain kind of language—but "a language more primitive than ours."[14] Language did more than represent pictures: it also gave orders, made promises, speculated, told stories, and joked. There is a charming story that recounts how Wittgenstein realized this while riding on a train with an Italian economist, Piero Sraffa. Wittgenstein had said that every meaningful proposition must have the same logical form as that which it describes, and Sraffa ridiculed this by making a Neapolitan gesture. "What is the logical form of that?" asked Sraffa, as he brushed the underside of his chin with his fingers.[15] When the train ride was over, the mechanistic linguistic analysis of the *Tractatus* was buried, and modern British analytical philosophy was born. All because of a simple gibe.

Zombies as Machine Men

Dualists like Descartes posit that human beings are a union of two distinct things: a mind and a body. The mind (or soul) is a thinking substance, while the body is a mechanical system. Dualism is distinguished from monism, the belief that everything is composed of one substance, whether spirit or matter. Today philosophers no longer speak of the conscious mind as a spiritual *substance,* after this view was trenchantly criticized by Gilbert Ryle in *The Concept of Mind.* This kind of dualism, Ryle argued, commits what he called a "category mistake" in which something is taken to belong to a different category from its true one. Bodies have weight, dimension, and the rest of it; consciousness doesn't. Or if it did, then this would collapse into monism. The argument was elegant and (as far as it went) persuasive. For most students, however, what stuck was not the close analysis but the phrase Ryle used to lampoon the dualist's nonmaterial explanation of human behavior: the "ghost in the machine."

The ultimate ghost in the machine is the sophisticated computer that is said to possess the ability to think. Imagine a supercomputer, like IBM's Deep Blue, programmed to act like a person in every conceivable case. Now imagine the computer given bodily form and the power of movement, as Bentham hoped might happen with his auto-icon. Slight it and it sighs; prick it and it bleeds. Proponents of artificial intelligence (AI) would say that the machine can feel, think, and intend every bit as much as a person can.

AI theories that ascribe personal qualities to a machine commit Ryle's category mistake in reverse. If the naive dualist mistakenly likens consciousness to a thing, the AI theorist mistakenly credits things with consciousness. Few laymen would make this mistake; nevertheless, most contemporary philosophers would. AI theories have powerful advocates in philosophers such as Daniel Dennett, who has advanced a particularly hard version of AI. Weak AI theories assimilate computers to men by crediting both with consciousness. But Dennett's hard AI theory assimilates men to computers by denying consciousness to both. "The net effect," says philosopher John Searle, "is a performance of *Hamlet* without the Prince of Denmark."[16]

Searle's ridicule has done much to debunk the machine man of AI. In *Consciousness Explained,* Dennett had responded to critics who argued that he would ascribe consciousness to zombies: a construct that exhibits every human characteristic but is not conscious at all. (In Haiti, where the term originates, a zombie is a dead person who is magically given humanlike powers, so that the term might fairly apply to Bentham's mechanized auto-icon.) A powerful objection, but Dennett rose to the challenge. "Since that is all we ever get to see of our friends and neighbors, *some of your best friends may be zombies.*"[17] The remark was ironic, but Dennett's true views were curiouser still. As Searle notes, Dennett did not argue that some of us are zombies and some not, or that all zombies are conscious, but rather that no one, zombie or human, is conscious. "His claim is in fact that *we are zombies,* that there is no difference between us and machines that lack conscious states."[18] What is behind this intellectual pathology, argues Searle, is a crude form of logical positivism, which insists that we should dispense with mental events such as consciousness since we cannot verify their existence in other people. But even the logical positivist can verify the existence of *his* feelings. All he need do, notes Searle, is pinch himself.

By mistaking a machine for a man, AI theorists become the very type of machine men whom Bergson mocked. Like the machine lawyer, the machine philosopher becomes ludicrous when his theories ridiculously fail to account for the richness and complexity of human experience. Through laughter, we are recalled to common sense.

Machine Political Theory

Edmund Burke's defense of the British constitution and his attack on the machine politics of the Jacobins are well-known. What is little appreciated, in an age that mistrusts laughter, is how Burke employed ridicule to make his point. Burke's rejection of Jacobin metaphysics was prescient in 1790. With the benefit of hindsight it seems less so. But even today how many people recognize the humor in Burke's *Reflections on the French Revolution?*

Burke wrote the *Reflections* after the fall of the Bastille and the kidnaping of Louis XVI at Versailles, but before the flight to Varennes, the execution of the King and Queen, and the days of the Terror. The Revolution had yet to eat its children—Danton, Desmoulins, Robespierre. The high lunacy of the ten-day week and the renamed months were still in the future, along with the Feast of Reason. Burke's Whiggish friends could still rhapsodize over the Fall of the Bastille. "How much the greatest event it is that ever happened in the world!" burbled Charles James Fox. "And how much the best!" But Burke foresaw the sanguinary course the Revolution would take and hastened to warn his countrymen, even though this meant a break with his closest friends and political allies.

Burke is the great philosopher of conservatism, and one of the most profound English political thinkers. However, he is little read on the Continent, where political philosophy is a very serious affair, and where Burke's elegance, passion, and wit are taken to signal a frivolous thinker. And yet Burke's use of humor was as logical as any piece of Continental rationalism, for he believed that we are motivated to act by our passions as much as by reason. The English, he said, "are generally men of untaught feelings," so that "instead of casting away all our old prejudices, we cherish them to a considerable degree, and, to take more shame to ourselves, we cherish them because they are prejudices." This was an older use of the word *prejudice,* synonymous with sentiment or passion as opposed to reason. As a motive to action, prejudice offers a surer guide than reason, said Burke.

> We are afraid to put men to live and trade each on his own private stock of reason; because we suspect that this stock in each man is small, and that the individuals would be better to avail themselves of the general bank and capital of nations, and of ages. Many of our men of speculation, instead of exploding general prejudices, employ their sagacity to discover the general wisdom which prevails in them.[19]

With a political philosophy that rests on sentiment, what is more logical than an appeal to sentiment? And so Burke movingly described the fall of Marie Antoinette, proving the primacy of sentiment by evoking the reader's sympathy and anger at the loss of the "chastity of honour, which felt a stain like a wound, . . . which ennobled whatever it touched, and under which vice itself lost half its evil by losing all its grossness."[20] If the appeal to our emotions still succeeds, it supports Burke's deeper point that our traditions and sentiments are more reliable guides to action than abstract rationalism is.

The appeal to prejudice was a thumb in the eye to English political rationalists such as Dr. Richard Price, the dissenting minister whose sermon in support of the French Revolution led Burke to write the *Reflections.* Burke contrasted Price's didactic sermon with the theater, which must move our emotions to succeed, and which he thought must therefore afford more reliable moral instruction. "No theatric audience in Athens would bear what has been borne" by Dr. Price's friends.[21] In this sense, our emotions are wiser than our reason. Our sense of pity for the victims of the Revolution told us of horrors to which reason was blind. So too, our sense of humor identifies nonsense more clearly than any political geometry.[22]

Considered as a satire, the principal comic vice that the *Reflections* attacks is hypocrisy: the hypocrisy of the pettifogging lawyers who made up the Tiers État and who claimed a political virtue they did not possess; and the hypocrisy of a revolution that proposed to rid France of a tyranny but replaced it with one infinitely worse. "Amidst assassinations, massacre and confiscation, perpetrated or meditated, they are forming plans for the good order of future society." And what have they brought France? Not riches, surely, for "France has bought poverty by crime!"[23]

More generally, Burke satirized the "mechanic philosophy" of machine theorists, with their comically inadequate views of life. "The pretended rights of these theorists are all extremes; and in proportion as they are metaphysically true, they are morally and politically false." They promised a more humane society. But is that what we should expect, when the "decent drapery of life" is torn away? "On this scheme of things, a king is but a man; a queen is but a woman; a woman is but an animal; and an animal not of the highest order." The king of France was brought back to Paris by a mob ("excuse that term, it is still in use here"). He had not yet been killed. "The age has not yet the compleat benefit of that diffusion of knowledge that has undermined suspicion and error"[24]—but it could only be a matter of time.

As a guide for politics, said Burke, we should trust our passions more than our reason. And amongst the passions Burke did not scorn our sense of humor. Why did he oppose Dr. Price, he asked himself? Because it was *natural* for him to do so. Even as it is natural to laugh at machine theories. Burke is read today not for his politics—his opposition to democracy, for example—but for his understanding of the wisdom that is coded in our sentiments: our sense of pathos and our sense of humor. The book touches us so closely that we cannot doubt its message. Burke's butts are not simply risible, we sense; they are risible as a matter of natural law.

Baby Selling

While few laymen would seek amusement in a book on price theory, economists often are witty. Stephen Leacock was an economist, after all, and a University of Chicago Ph.D. at that. Leacock is said to have invented the ur-economist joke when, wandering home one evening after a merry evening at Montreal's University Club, he lost his keys in the snow on Côte-des-Neiges. A policeman found him on his knees near a lamppost, looking for the keys. "Where did you drop them?" asked the policeman. "Over there," pointed Leacock, to a spot about fifty yards away. "Then why are you looking over here?" asked the puzzled policeman. "There's more light here," was the answer. The joke is told to explain the empiricist's preference for questions that are easily researched and trivially important.

Nor is economics the dour profession that laymen take it to be. "The dismal science," Carlyle called it, and generations of innumerate English majors were taught to sneer at supply curves. But Carlyle's complaint was that the economist worried too much about the plight of slaves, and no one would take his side today on that issue. Carlyle was even wrong about the dismal part. Economics is about growth, and growth is anything but dismal. What is dismal is economic waste of the kind created by machine rules.

Nevertheless, our theory tells us that there ought to be such a thing as machine economics, and it tells us moreover where to find it. Principles of economics that treat people like machines are always risible, and socialist economies, with their Five-Year Plans and mile-long queues, were a wonderful source of humor. Closer to home, the free-market economist is also a natural butt when he treats a person as a thing. And that is just what happened when Richard Posner wondered whether adoption shortages might be cured through a market for babies. The academic left reacted with anger to the extension of free markets, but the anger was stilled when everyone recognized how closely the article read like a parody.

> Part I of this paper develops a model of the supply and demand for babies for adoption under the existing pattern of regulation and shows (1) how that regulation has created a baby shortage (and, as a result, a black market) by preventing a free market from equilibrating the demand and supply of babies for adoption, and (2) how it has contributed to a glut of unadopted children maintained in foster homes at public expense.[25]

On close analysis, Posner and his coauthor found most of the objections to baby selling unfounded. There was no reason to think that prices would be high were baby selling legalized. "On the contrary, prices for children of *equivalent quality* would be much lower."[26] What the ban does is suppress the market-clearing functions of efficient markets. "In a legal and competitive baby market, prices would be equated to the marginal costs of producing and selling for adoption babies of a given quality." Indeed, a move to free markets could be expected to increase baby quality by reducing the likelihood of product defects. "It is contended, for example, that the health of the child or the child's mother is regularly misrepresented. . . . Such abuses are probably largely the result of the fact that the market is an illegal one." With better warranty protection, buyers might get better goods at the same price. "The same price would buy a higher-quality package of rights." Lastly, there is little reason to fear that the purchaser would buy a baby in order to abuse it. "Few people buy a car or a television set in order to smash it."[27]

A law student recently recognized the article's potential for parody when he posted an advertisement on eBay, the online auction house. The student offered for sale a baby that was the product of two University of Chicago law students, and named Richard Posner as arbitrator in case of warranty claims for product defects. Before the hoax was revealed, the bids had topped $100,000.

Three hundred years ago Jonathan Swift examined the incentive effects of a similar proposal.

> I have been assured by a very knowing American of my acquaintance in London, that a young, healthy child well nursed is a most delicious, nourishing, and wholesome food, whether stewed, roasted, baked, or boiled; and I make no doubt that it will equally serve in a fricassee or a ragout.

Swift's *Modest Proposal*, which satirized English policies that kept Ireland in poverty, outlined other advantages of a market for babies that Richard Posner had ignored. The scheme

> would increase the care and tenderness of mothers toward their children, when they were sure of a settlement for life to the poor babes, provided in some sort by the public, to their annual profit or expense. We should see an honest emulation among the married women, which of them could bring the fattest child to the market. Men would become fond of their wives during the time of their pregnancy as they now are of their mares in foal, their cows in calf, their sows when they

are ready to farrow; nor offer to beat them or to kick them (as is too frequent a practice) for fear of miscarriage.[28]

The incentive effects are very similar to those of baby selling. More children would be brought to market were both schemes legalized, and they would be of a higher quality. But Swift had sense enough to realize that his proposal was ridiculous and Posner did not, and the difference made Posner a butt.[29]

The risibility of machine economics illustrates the political neutrality of laughter. This is a useful lesson, for laughter often seems directed at the modern liberal, so much so that, with Quintilian, the conservative might almost say *Satura tota nostra est:* satire is all our own. The most acidic satires have come from the pens of deeply conservative writers: Juvenal, Butler, Dryden, Pope, Swift, Johnson, Chesterton, Belloc, Wyndham Lewis, Roy Campbell, Evelyn Waugh, Kingsley Amis, Mordecai Richler, Florence King, Tom Wolfe, Joseph Epstein, John Cleese, P. J. O'Rourke, James Hynes, Michael Kelly, and Mark Steyn. A Walter Olson or Dave Barry simply reports upon a piece of fatuous liberalism and exclaims "I'm not making this up!" The link to conservatism comes from the comic norms on which laughter depends. The conservative accepts the norms, while the life-style liberal rejects them and the laughter that goes with them.

Nevertheless, conservatives such as Posner become risible when their policies rest on a comically inadequate view of our humanity. Bergson's explanation of the risible is not confined to a single political perspective. What is risible is not liberal politics but machine politics, left and right.

The machine theorist is generally a rationalist who reduces politics down to One Big Idea. In an essay on *Rationalism in Politics,* Michael Oakeshott noted that the rationalist "stands (he always stands) for independence of mind on all occasions, for thought free from any authority save the authority of 'reason.'" He believes that his solutions are obvious to all men of goodwill, and that disagreement is a sign of bad faith. "His mind has no atmosphere, no changes of season and temperature; his intellectual processes, so far as possible, are insulated from all external influences and go on in the void."[30]

I do not know whether Oakeshott had read *Le rire,* but his rationalist is a perfect Bergsonian butt and a purveyor of machine theory. No doubt such people are more likely to be political liberals than conservatives. A machine theory must be a theory, and conservatives resist theories. In particular, the Tory perspective of Burke and Oakeshott is not a theory so much as a rejection of theorizing. Nevertheless, a rationalist theory, right or left, might be a splendid source of humor.

While American libertarianism is theoretical and rationalist, there is a prudential and antirationalist libertarianism whose roots extend back to Burke and Pascal's *esprit de finesse*. Bergson's explanation of laughter was in this tradition. *Le rire* is entirely consistent with Bergson's political views, as expressed in *Two Sources of Morality and Religion*, which celebrated the freedom of an open society. For Bergson (as for Sir Karl Popper), an open society is mobile, organic, and fluid; and a closed society, like an ant colony, is unchanging, mechanical, and stratified. Open societies do not impose top-down order; instead, they let the individual choose his best life plan. Closed societies demand an unthinking allegiance and unalterable duties. They are shot through with mechanistic rules that leave little room for private choices and therefore invite our laughter.

Machine Art and Machine Cities

10

> The madman is not the man who has lost
> his reason. The madman is the man who
> has lost everything except his reason.
>
> G. K. Chesterton

Strolling down the Via Marguta in Rome one evening, looking idly at art galleries full of ink-blot paintings, I came across something that stopped me in my tracks—a Virgin from the fourteenth century, in the style of Lorinzetti or Martini. A closer look revealed a poster from Siena, pasted onto another ink-blot painting, like a *papier collé*. Still, I hung about the gallery and chatted with its owner. I told him where I was from and where I taught, and he exclaimed, "But I know someone from your school!" Small world. But then not such a coincidence either, since my colleague was a Roman and a serious art collector. He had designed his house around an inner gallery and had filled it with modern art, including, it appeared, some work by PosterMan. The gallery owner told me that my friend had even helped to arrange an exhibition of PosterMan's art in America. Later, back home, my friend told me about the artist. And as he spoke, his eyes narrowed and his voice fell to a reverential hush. "He's cutting-edge," my friend said.

I thought no more of it until the exhibition was over, ten months later, when my friend told me what had happened. He had gone to the airport to pick up PosterMan, who had—surprise!—also brought his wife and two children. Not a problem, thought my friend, as he has a large house and a most generous disposition. He needed this, as PosterMan had a habit of sneaking into my friend's wine cabinet at ten in the morning to drink his Brunello de Montalcino. Still, my friend thought, it's only for a

143

week. Two days before the exhibition the gallery called, threatening to cancel the show if they weren't reimbursed for some advertising bills. PosterMan had promised to do so, but had frittered away a $25,000 grant and had no money left. So my friend paid the gallery $800. Fine, said the gallery. Now where are the paintings? They had never received them. And so my friend tracked them down at the airport and paid for the customs broker. But there was another problem. The theme of the exhibition was capital punishment, and PosterMan had made an exact replica of an electric chair. The waybill said "Electric Chair." The customs inspector, not unnaturally, wanted to know what the chair was for. "Will you be using it for medical purposes?" he asked. At last the art cleared customs. My friend rented an enormous truck and brought it to the gallery. But there was another problem. There was not enough of Poster-Man's art to fill up the gallery. Would my friend lend some of his paintings by PosterMan for the show? He did so, but during the show several people offered to buy them. PosterMan said, "Why don't you sell them. I'll pay you back when I return to Italy. I need the money to get home."

My friend is a very patient man, but this had gone a bit too far. He told PosterMan that, alas, he was too attached to the paintings to sell them and that, as his parents were arriving shortly, PosterMan and family would have to move from his house. The sensitive artist exploded. "What do *you* care about art!" he spat.

The example illustrates two ways in which artists may be risible. First, the pose of sincerity, the aristocratic pretension that he is above getting and spending, is hypocritical when the artist is merely a sponger, particularly when he asserts the right to abuse his patron at the same time. This can be a great source of fun, and indeed Karen Finley became a national laughingstock when she squawked about losing a National Endowment for the Arts grant in 1990. Finley, a "performance artist," smears chocolate (meant to symbolize excrement) over her nude body, and when her grant was taken away the chocolate hit the fan.[1] There is no end to this kind of hypocrisy, but I will focus on the second way in which the artist is risible, as a maker of machine art.

Machine Art

Any study of risible modern art must begin by paying homage to Tom Wolfe, whose *The Painted Word* devastated New York art critics when it appeared in 1975. The book was prompted, oddly enough, by an article cultural conservative Hilton Kramer had written. Kramer had been to an exhibition of Photo-realism, and found it wanting in one crucial respect: it lacked a theory. In this comment, Wolfe saw all that was wrong with modern art. The antagonists were at cross-purposes, however, since a theory that explains what motivated the artist or shaped his vision, like John Ruskin's study of Gothic architecture, may indeed assist the viewer. In any event, nothing is easier to come by than a theory.

No, theories are not the problem. Instead, the butt that Wolfe had identified was art forms that are *all* theory and nothing else: Cubism, Concrete Painting, Abstract Expressionism, Conceptual Art, splotches, rectangles and circles, sculptures of bicycle parts, toilet fixtures, Finley's performance art, and PosterMan's Old Sparky. Let us suppose that some originality is required before each new movement is launched. The problem is that, when the art is all concept and painterly skill is not needed, the art can be easily reproduced by an assiduous ape. "Paint a canvas pure black and sell it for $10,000? Yes, I think I can manage that." The result is machine art, and that is risible.

There is the appearance of a paradox here. How is it that machine art, the art of twentieth-century modernism, is also an art that celebrates the "action painter," the heroic artist, critic Clement Greenberg's Jackson Pollock? The answer is that, when skill goes out the window, when only innovation counts, the artist must see himself as a pure innovator and preen with the vacuous self-consciousness of a Hemingway hero. Like Cooper's Leatherstocking he sets off alone for the frontier, for the painter-hero never creates a genre: his innovation dies with him. One man, one movement. Hence the profusion of modernist genres and the importance of brand name on art markets: one pays a premium for a Jackson Pollock, but not for the best abstract impressionist from Minneapolis.

Modernism has had a remarkable run. The paint-splattered tarpaulins that Pollock placed on his studio floor to keep it clean have sold at an enormous price: they were Pollocks, after all, and who could tell the difference between them and his paintings? Similarly, the paintings of de Kooning's old age, after he succumbed to Alzheimer's disease, commanded the same high prices as before. (Remarkable, said the critics: his brain is gone and his creative ability is undiminished!) But in the end the bubble must burst. In truth, the layman never cared for the modernist's machine art. Instead, it was representational art—Realism—that brought visitors to a museum and collectors to the gallery. Realism is the opposite of machine art, since fidelity to the discipline of the line requires skill. And, paradoxically, only Realism can represent the mystery of the world and the pathos of life.

At the National Gallery of Art, one of the most successful recent exhibitions was on the art of Victorian England, from Turner and the Pre-Raphaelites to the high Olympus of Lord Leighton and Alma-Tadema. The organizer had cleverly placed side-by-side two paintings that had figured in the 1878 decision that destroyed John Ruskin's career as an art critic. Ruskin had attacked Whistler's dark and impressionistic "nocturnes" ("I have seen, and heard, much of cockney impudence before now; but never expected to hear a coxcomb ask two hundred guineas for flinging a pot of paint in the public's face"), and Whistler successfully sued for libel. Ruskin argued, in essence, that the nocturnes were machine art, knocked off quickly and without finish. This was excessive, of course. Even at the time, critics recognized the similarity between Whistler and Ruskin's hero, Turner. Still, Ruskin's counsel did win the valuable admission that Whistler could paint a nocturne quickly. How long did it take him to paint *Nocturne in Black and Gold?* he was asked. A couple of days, Whistler answered nonchalantly. Ruskin's counsel exploded: "The labour of two days is that for which you ask 200 guineas?" "No," said Whistler. "I ask it for the knowledge I have gained in the work of a lifetime." (Ouch!) In his defense, Ruskin brought along several famous artists as expert witnesses, including William Frith, whose sprawling and incoherent *Derby Day* is a realistic portrait of Victorian high and low life.

And here they were at the National Gallery in Washington, *Derby Day* next to *Nocturne in Black and Gold,* the first alive with color and movement, the second an austere array of murky hues, the first pointing backward to the storytelling art of Copley and Carpaccio, the second pointing forward to machine art, the first surrounded by admirers, the second quite ignored by the crowd.

The trial devastated Ruskin. Even though the jury awarded Whistler only contemptuous damages of a farthing, there were still the lawyers to pay. Legal fees also left Whistler impoverished, but he emerged with his pluck intact and he gave us a hilarious account of the trial in *The Gentle Art of Making Enemies.* Whistler also took from the trial his trademark of a butterfly atop a farthing. But the case had deeper implications, since it dealt a psychological blow to Ruskin's theory of art and promoted that of Whistler.

In *The Stones of Venice* Ruskin had proclaimed the superiority of Gothic art, the art of free people, to the Neo-classical. The Gothic was rude, uneven, changeful, and this permitted the craftsman-artist to experiment and improvise. Neo-classical art expressed itself in straight lines and settled proportions, and in aiming for inhuman perfection dispensed with the creative artisan. It was machine art. Ruskin's theory assigned a positive role for the critic, as one who upheld the ideals of liberty and human art that he saw as increasingly threatened by a coarse Victorian machine age. By contrast, Whistler's high aestheticism dispensed with the critic: only the artist could comment on art, which indeed was what the lawsuit was about. Ruskin's target was poorly chosen, for the butterfly could paint as well as sting. Yet the denial of artistic responsibility, so plausible when asserted by a Whistler, sustains machine art when asserted by the Finleys; and if the artist truly is above criticism, the layman is not permitted to distinguish between the artist and the charlatan.

Machine Cities

Something similar has happened in architecture and urban planning. When I was a boy and saw pictures of different cities I could tell at a glance which country they were from. Today one cannot. Every city looks like K Street in Washington, with one box-like building after the other, each one the same, like the product of some dreary Victorian factory. The only difference is the modern sculpture dumped in front of the better buildings—Tom Wolfe's "turd in the Plaza."

In 1981, Wolfe's *From Bauhaus to Our House* described how the machine buildings of Bauhaus architects, designed in the 1920s by mitteleuropean Marxists for worker housing, became the official architecture of Western capitalism when bankers, lawyers, and accountants decided to become cutting edge. They bought into a theory that glorified technology, engineering, and machines. Le Corbusier even called his houses "machines for living," with the accent on the first word and not the last. There was little concern for comfort and eye-catching beauty, and none for the client's wishes. (Remember Ayn Rand's Howard Roark, who blew up the building he designed because the client had the temerity to want *balconies!*) What mattered was not people but fidelity to a theory. People could always be reshaped according to the theorist's Procrustian schemes. Le Corbusier, for example, was a Fourierist, who believed that families should be broken up and society reassembled into phalanxes of several hundred people each. Hence the large buildings, the small apartments, and the oversize common areas to foster communard solidarity.

If one is looking for an architectural butt, it would be hard to do better than Le Corbusier ("Otto Silenus" in Evelyn Waugh's *Decline and Fall*). "The problem of architecture as I see it," proclaimed Professor Silenus,

> is the problem of all art—the elimination of the human element from the consideration of form. The only perfect building must be the factory, because that is built to house machines, not men.

Le Corbusier's "Radiant City" was skyscraper after skyscraper—one for the city hall (and all its urban planners), another for the office workers, and others for universities and museums. Everyone would live in high-rise apartments, separated by vast empty spaces to keep population densities down. "I suppose there ought to be a staircase," said Professor Silenus gloomily:

> Why can't the creatures stay in one place? Up and down, in and out, round and round! Why can't they sit still and work? Do dynamos require staircases?

There is a short line from Professor Silenus to Albert Speer's plans for Germania, the new capital for the Thousand Year Reich. During his final weeks in the bunker, Hitler pored over Speer's plans, daydreaming about his legacy—the three-mile-long concourse, flanked by an Arch of Triumph at one end, and at the other by the People's Hall, a vast dome into which three St. Paul's cathedrals would fit, National Socialism writ in stone and concrete. Speer was imprisoned after the war, but Le Corbusier was luckier. Before the war, during the Soviet mass starvations and show trials, he had eagerly designed his Palace of Soviets for Stalin. Then he flirted with Fascist politics, and in 1941 courted Marshal Pétain in a vain quest to build his megalomaniacal cities for Vichy. However, he was a survivor, and after the war he emerged with his reputation unscathed.

Even Mies van der Rohe, the Bauhaus head, successfully shook off his past in 1945. When Hitler assumed power, some of the Bauhaus leftists had protested. But not van der Rohe. In 1934, when Hindenburg died and Hitler assumed his powers as head of state and commander of the armed forces, van der Rohe was one of the artists who signed a public declaration that read in part:

> We believe in this Führer, who has fulfilled our fervent wish for unity;
> We trust his work, which asks sacrifice beyond all carping sophistry;
> . . . we thus belong to the Führer's followers. The Führer has called upon us to stand by him in trust and faith. None of us will be missing when an affirmation of trust is needed.[2]

After all, the Nazi Party was the biggest client in Germany, and by no means hostile to machine architecture. What it disliked was bolshevism and the original Bauhaus communists. When it came to design, however, there was not a great deal of difference between Soviet and Nazi buildings: both favored an unadorned architecture of monumental size and straight lines that communicated that the state and its architects were everything and the individual nothing. Nor is this surprising. While Nazi ideology was antimodern, it was also antihuman and therefore modernist.

If anything, Nazi architecture had a more modern feel than Soviet architecture, though the visitor to the Paris Exhibition of 1937 would have been hard-pressed to tell the German and Soviet Pavilions apart, as they gloomily faced each other across the Palais Chaillot. From the outside, only the swastika and hammer-and-sickle told the tourist which brand of inhumanity the building represented.[3] Years afterward, when his past was safely forgotten, and when he became the official architect of modernism, did van der Rohe ever yearn for Nazi authoritarianism? In his Seagram office tower in New York, van der Rohe had insisted that the blinds could only be fully open, shut, or precisely half-closed; but the stubborn tenants insisted on marring the building's symmetry. Say what you will about the Nazis, *they* could have ensured compliance!

Le Corbusier's vision of machine cities made American city planners drool. But how to build them? The problem, as always, was that private developers lacked the planner's vision, and it therefore became necessary to enlist the aid of enlightened technocratic politicians: people like Chicago's Mayor Daley, who were only too happy to find construction work for their political allies in the building trades.

The cities had two other inestimable advantages over private developers. Cities had access to Other People's Money—the taxpayers; better still, they did not have to get anyone's consent before they tore down an old building and filled up a new one with tenants. They could expropriate land through the power of eminent domain and populate their new buildings with welfare recipients who had no say in the matter. And they could do all this with the blessing of the most respected urbanists, like Lewis Mumford. "Pleasant open spaces and parks and playgrounds were not an upper-class luxury, but could be incorporated without extra cost in the most modest housing scheme, simply by saving on needless utilities and streets," said Mumford. "Here was a way to make the stony urban desert bloom."[4]

What happened next we all know. The planners took neighborhoods that worked, called them slums, and had them torn down to build projects that quickly became violent and drug-infested hellholes. The "pleasant open spaces" between the buildings became a no-man's land. For older residents, afraid to leave their apartments, the Radiant Cities were prisons and sometimes tombs.[5] And when the city at length tried to evict the pushers and addicts, it ran into ACLU lawyers pleading machine law. Eventually, some of the worst projects, like St. Louis's Pruitt-Igoe, were dynamited. It wasn't that they were structurally unsound; it was rather that, so far as a building might have moral qualities, they were evil.

Jane Jacobs was one of the first to recognize that modern urban planning was antihuman. Her best-known book, *The Death and Life of Great American Cities,* is a modern classic and an indispensable commentary on the folly of top-down central planning. Written in 1961, when the experts were still pushing for "urban renewal," Jacobs was a nonexpert who recognized that true renewal was more likely to come from older buildings and that planners who sought to destroy old neighborhoods in servile obedience to inhuman machine theories had become ridiculous.

Jacobs saw all this at first hand, in a city she loved, New York. From her home in Greenwich Village she wandered throughout the city and did what the planner seldom does: she observed people. Like Yeats's *Seven Sages,* she hated the expert's Whiggery: she "walked the roads, mimicking what she heard, and understood that wisdom comes of beggary." She brought along with her only a notepad (for she was a reporter) and a sense of humor. She described how the city planners sought to revitalize Morningside Heights, a slum dangerously close to establishment sanctuaries such as Columbia University, Juilliard, and the Union Theological Seminary. And so the planners went to work. They wiped out the most run-down part of the area and built in its stead a middle-income cooperative project complete with shopping center, and a public housing project, all interspersed with air, light, sunshine and landscaping. This was hailed as a great demonstration in city saving.

After that Morningside Heights went downhill even faster.[6]

Early on in her book she described a foray into Boston's North End, an Italian area that today is one of the city's most charming neighborhoods. Back then it was poorer, of course, but still the "general street atmosphere of buoyancy, friendliness and good health" so impressed Jacobs that she stepped into a local bar and called a Boston planner she knew to ask him about it. "What in the world are you doing in the North End," he asked. "That's a slum!" "It doesn't seem like a slum to me," she answered. Smiling inwardly, the expert explained to Jacobs just why it was a slum. "It has two hundred and seventy-five dwelling units to the net acre!" Because of the population density it had to be a slum. Poring further in his books, the expert was surprised to discover that the North End had among the lowest delinquency, disease, and infant mortality rates in the city. "Well, they must be strong people. Of course it's a terrible slum."[7]

Like a good expert, Jacobs's friend never let real life get in the way of machine theories. And so, reported Jacobs, the North End became a recurring assignment for the budding planners at MIT and Harvard, who pursued "the paper exercise of converting it into super-blocks and park promenades, wiping away its nonconforming uses, transforming it into an ideal of order and gentility so simple it could be engraved on the head of a pin."[8] All Whiggery. "But what is Whiggery?" asked Yeats. "A levelling, rancorous, rational sort of mind / That never looked out of the eye of a saint / Or out of a drunkard's eye."

Jacobs recognized that planners were animated by what Friedrich Hayek called a fatal conceit. Cities need chaos, not planning, and so far as they are human must grow like Topsy. Order will emerge; not the artificial and deadly order of the planners, but the spontaneous order of real people coordinating their activities around each other. For example, Jacobs reported on how working neighborhoods were naturally self-policed by ordinary people who observed what passed before them on the street, when they were safe enough to attract pedestrians. No planner could ever hope to match the information produced by such microinstitutions of civic order. Nor could the planner's naked public square attract the number of people needed to ensure safety, as compared to a street in which property owners have a stake in its safety. What cities need are free markets, not top-down planning, for the choices that emerge in a market setting are human choices made by real people. Private developers could never build Germania or Pruitt-Igoe; only planners could.

Jacobs also recognized that we need cities to civilize us. Early planners such as Ebenezer Howard, with their suburban "Garden Cities," simply disliked large cities and sought to persuade people to move from them. Later, Hitler had similar, if more ruthless, plans for postwar Germany, as did that other notable urban planner, Pol Pot. What all such planners miss is that cities satisfy a human desire for solidarity, that we are naturally attracted to them and quit them only when they are utter failures. We need others to flourish. We are not born virtuous and then corrupted by civilization, as Rousseau thought. It is just the opposite, as Diderot, Freud, and Burke recognized. Solitude and self-indulgence corrupt; what saves us is the civilization and laughter of cities.

In sum, the hard version of the Normative thesis, in which laughter always signals a superior life, is clearly wrong. Nevertheless, a soft version of the thesis, which asserts that laughter provides valuable information about how to live, is highly persuasive. The soft version does not attribute inerrancy to laughter. In truth there are no infallible guides, or if they exist seldom speak *ex cathedra*. I cannot say that laughter never did betray the heart that loved her, as Wordsworth said of nature. Nothing on earth does that, and particularly not nature. Our laughter sometimes misleads? So does speech, but we would not give that up either. Speech and laughter are valuable gifts, which we could not abandon without cost.

PART THREE

The Experience of Laughter

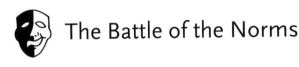 The Battle of the Norms

Let not us that are squires of the night's body be called
thieves of the day's beauty: let us be Diana's foresters,
gentlemen of the shade, minions of the moon; and let
men say, we be men of good government, being governed
as the sea is, by our noble and chaste mistress of the
moon, under whose countenance we steal.

1 Henry IV

We have sought to defend the normative thesis by showing how laughter signals a defective life plan or risible scholarship
(chaps. 6–10). Through the sting of laughter, we are recalled from
comic vice to the path of moderation and comic virtue. But if laughter is
such an effective sanction, why do comic vices persist? Where is the failure in comic norms?

Laughter can be modeled as a three-party game in which the parties
bargain for inclusion in a two-party coalition (wit and listener) that
excludes the third (the butt). No one party can dictate what is risible.
Instead, the selection of butts is a matter of negotiation between wit and
listener. The wit proposes a butt for laughter, and this offer may be
accepted by the listener through a return of laughter or rejected
through silence. In such a laughter exchange, individuals may be seen to
trade off butts through implicit agreements about who is risible. These
bargains determine what counts as a comic vice, since jokes must have a
content to amuse.

Laughter bargains lack an equilibrium solution when they are nothing more than status contests: the butt is degraded, and the wit and listener move up a notch (chap. 4). While each party has an incentive to
join the winning coalition, every coalition is unstable since the butt can
always offer an equal status gain to the listener by cracking his own joke

at the first joke-teller. Laughter then would signal an empty superiority, and the incentive to produce laughter would disappear. But if laughter does signal useful information about comic vices, as Bergson thought, the game will have a solution, in the sense that it will produce a single winning coalition and a single butt. The natural butt will never be able to deflect the laughter away from himself, and the process of coalition formation will promote value-maximizing (or efficient) comic norms.

Absent barriers to bargaining, the Coase theorem posits that all opportunities for gain will be exploited through private contracting.[1] Since failing to do so would be like leaving money on the table, the parties will take up all bargain opportunities. And since we can imagine a social contract in which social norms are adopted, we might extend Ronald Coase's insight about efficient bargaining to norm formation. In that case, all efficient norms would be created where the costs of norm formation are trivial. All our laughter would be benign, as the Normative thesis asserts, and we would laugh just as much as was necessary in order to police comic vices in an efficient manner.

The puzzle is then to explain why comic vices persist. Why do butts remain? And why do we still laugh? There would be no need for laughter signals if everyone knew just how to live. Yet satirists such as Menander never lack for targets, as Ben Jonson noted. "Whilst slaves be false, fathers hard, or bawds be whorish, / Whilst harlots flatter, shall Menander flourish." Moreover, comic norms might conflict when different groups trade off gibes. None of this could happen if laughter proclaimed a one, true, universal, and optimal set of comic norms.

The puzzle is answered when one recognizes that the Coase theorem does not predict that all bargain opportunities will be exploited. Instead, barriers to contracting will result in profit opportunities being left on the table. Similarly, our extension of the Coase theorem to norm creation does not predict that all efficient norms will be created, and directs our attention to the barriers to efficient norm formation.

Judgment Errors

Because laughter is immediate and unreflective, comic norms cannot exploit bargain gains as easily as private contracting might. In many cases, our laughter simply lacks the intelligence to pierce through a paradox and understand deeper meanings. Consider Stanley Kubrick's *Dr. Strangelove,* one of the most hilarious movies of the cold war, which it satirized. Jack D. Ripper, a mad U.S. general, obsessed with vital bodily fluids and fluoridation, exceeds his authority and launches a first-strike nuclear attack on the Soviet Union. Upon hearing this, the U.S. president summons the Soviet ambassador, who tells him devastating news: if the USSR is hit by nuclear weapons, this will trigger a "Doomsday Device" that will destroy all life on Earth. This possibility is discounted by the president's adviser, Dr. Strangelove, who notes that "such a device would not be a practical deterrent for reasons which at this moment must be all too obvious." That is, a Doomsday Device would only deter a nuclear attack if the enemy knows about it; yet the Soviets never announced it. But, alas, the story is true: the device had been built; Soviet Premier Kissoff had kept it a secret so that he could announce it with a splash at the next Party Congress.

What *Strangelove* mocked was a game of death that energized its players ("Mein Fuhrer, I can walk!") and an arms strategy that asserted the rationality of creating a bomb that could wipe out the world.

> PRESIDENT MERKIN MUFFLEY: But this is absolute madness, Ambassador! Why should you *build* such a thing?
>
> AMBASSADOR DE SADESKY: There were those of us who fought against it, but in the end we could not keep up with the expense involved in [listed with increasing disgust] the arms race, the space race, and the peace race. At the same time our people grumbled for more nylons and washing machines. Our doomsday scheme cost us just a small fraction of what we had been spending on defense in a single year.

Mistakes were made. General Ripper should never have been allowed to declare an emergency and launch a nuclear attack. But as General Buck Turgidson put it, "I don't think it's quite fair to condemn the whole program because of a single slip-up."

What Stanley Kubrick's movie satirized was Herman Kahn's doctrine of mutually assured destruction (MAD), under which the threat of destruction would deter both the United States and the Soviet Union from launching a nuclear attack. The Doomsday Device was simply a logical extension of MAD deterrence policies. And this was indeed a highly rational strategy, once nuclear weapons had been invented. A world in which only one power has nuclear weapons, or in which both powers have enough to inflict substantial but limited damage, is inherently unstable. However, a world in which both parties can entirely destroy each other and no party enjoys a first-strike advantage is highly stable in theory and practice. MAD strategies made a wonderful target for satire, as did the arms race during the cold war. However, Herman Kahn's prediction of a stable bipolar world proved accurate up to the fall of the Berlin Wall, which the arms race hastened. Happily, Pentagon strategists ignored the laughter of *Dr. Strangelove*.

The success of Kubrick's movie suggests a way in which the promptings of laughter might mislead. Laughter might seize on a paradox and have just enough sense to see the incongruity but not enough to fathom the deeper meaning. The wit in *Strangelove* was the paradoxical combination of the ideas of love and death, of defense and destruction. Without more reflection, the inner logic that made MAD strategies sensible would not be understood and a superficial wit would reject them.

Locke explained how simple-minded wit might be deficient in judgment in his *Essay Concerning Human Understanding*. The reason, he said, was that the two faculties are very different. Wit is a synthetic art, the ability to put together ideas "with quickness and variety, wherein can be found any resemblance or congruity, thereby to make up pleasant pictures and agreeable visions in the fancy." Judgment is the analytical ability to take apart ideas "wherein can be found the least difference, thereby to avoid being misled by similitude, and by affinity to take one thing for another."[2] Intelligence unties a knot; wit leaves the knot just as it is, but identifies a similar knot, in a different place, made of different materials. This is not to say that wit work is trivial, for the very existence of a knot might lie hidden till wit identifies it, and even then we may lack the desire to untie it until wit tells us how ridiculous it looks.

Large Numbers

Parties might be unable to exploit bargain opportunities through private contracting when there are simply too many people to be bound. In that case, the transaction cost of securing the consent of all parties might exceed the contractual gain, and the bargain will remain unexploited. Similarly, efficient comic norms might not arise because of the difficulties of coalition formation in large groups. With a group of three parties we would expect efficient laughter norms to dominate, but in large-number groups a stable set of inefficient norms might take hold and persist. For example, Edward Banfield described a society so riddled with envy—a precapitalist Italian town he called "Montegrano"—that any form of economic progress was unthinkable. The Montegranese thought that every politician was on the take, that every priest was corrupt, that every employer cheated his employees. Only the most basic forms of economic cooperation were possible.

> All those who stand outside the small circle of the family are at least potential competitors and therefore also potential enemies. Toward those who are not family the reasonable attitude is suspicion. The parent knows that other families will envy and fear the success of his family and that they are likely to do it injury. He must therefore fear them and be ready to do them injury in order that they may have less power to injure him and his.[3]

Banfield labeled this "amoral familism." It is a highly inefficient ethic, but once it takes root it is very difficult to break away from it. In the same way, a set of perverse comic norms might take hold and persist in a community. For example, think of the jokes directed from within an ethnic community at its members who rise above it in some way—the "Mick on the make" or the "inauthentic" African-American.

Perverse Norms and Factual Errors

To account for false beliefs, Sir Thomas Browne assembled a list of vulgar and common errors in his *Pseudodoxia*. Inefficient comic norms might also result from perverse norms or factual errors. The impulse to laugh, being human, might arise from unpleasant human sentiments like the envy in Banfield's Montegrano. The envious will not bargain with strangers, but might laugh at them. Some forms of racial prejudice might also rest on a foundation of envy, and the ethnic jokes told about such groups might celebrate a cult of nonachievement. Moreover, ethnic jokes might pander to other primitive instincts, such as the desire to scapegoat.

In addition, laughter might err through a want of factual information. It might settle issues by reference to simple signals, such as physical appearance and pedigree, without adequately examining the facts. "Remember Alger Hiss?" asked Mordecai Richler in *Joshua Then and Now.* "What a proper gent! Right schools. Right ideas. How dare that sewer rat [Whittaker Chambers] call him a lying Communist bastard! But the sewer rat was telling the truth and the gentleman was lying through his f——ing teeth."

The most famous example of misguided laughter in philosophy is the ridicule that greets the philosopher in Plato's Allegory of the Cave.[4] The world is like a cave, said Plato, in which we sit chained together facing a wall. Behind us, hidden from view, a fire glows, which casts up shadows on the wall in front of us. Chained as we are, all we see are the shadows and take them as constituting the real world. One day someone unlocks the secret of the cave and explains that what we thought was reality was simply shadows. Would we thank him for correcting our error? No, said Plato. Instead, we would ridicule him. Plato told the story because he thought his Theory of Forms gave us a deeper understanding of reality. There are few Platonists today, but we need not buy into Platonic Forms to recognize that laughter at times is premised on a factual error.

Uncertainty

Finally, differences in laughter norms might reflect differences in individual talents and skills or uncertainties about comic norms. Where physical grace is granted to some and withheld from others, we would not expect a uniform norm of comic virtue. The more clumsy will mock the excessive grace of the more agile, who in turn will ridicule the less agile. And what is true of grace is true as well of the other charismatic norms, where there are marked differences in aesthetic taste and intelligence. There is no one good life that is the same for all of us. In addition, the differences in laughter norms might reflect genuine uncertainty about what constitutes a good life. We would readily agree that learning, grace, fortitude, integrity, and all the other comic virtues are admirable; but how many of us would be so rash as to suppose that they can identify just where the mean lies and where the extremes of comic vice begin?

When laughter is contested, rival coalitions seek to define the golden mean by laughing at each other. Both sides proclaim, "We are sensible, they are risible." Because laughter norms are contestable, partisans on either side of the mean might stake out extreme positions to shift it in their direction. Today the grunge-lover sports drooping, baggy shorts and a baseball cap tilted backward to signal his ridicule for all aesthetic standards. In the 1830s, the partisans at the other extreme—the dandies—dug in their heels. *Le dandysme* was a French movement, for while English dandyism was mostly about neckcloths, French *dandysme* was a political movement that sought to unite artists and intellectuals against democracy, utilitarian ethics, and a rising business class.[5]

We may thus distinguish two kinds of laughter, across the Battle of the Norms. In the *Poetics*, Aristotle had said that all art is founded on "imitation" (*mimēsis*), and Northrop Frye employed the term to distinguish between the forms of tragedy: "high mimetic" when it portrays a super-hero and "low mimetic" when it depicts a more ordinary person. Frye saw satire on a lower plane than either, since it mocks an inferior person. But satire also has its high and low forms. High mimetic laughter mocks those who display an excess of a comic virtue, while low mimetic laughter ridicules those at the other extreme.[6]

High mimetic laughter is the carnival laughter we saw in chapter 5. It is heard in the vulgar laughter that mocks its betters and the self-satisfied mirth of Nietzsche's Last Man, and may therefore be repellent. At best, thought Freud, such laughter is a mixed blessing, for it might subvert valuable cultural norms. It does not ban but channels hostility, and permits us to evade irksome checks on our bile. Through obscene jokes and nasty gibes we surmount moral barriers and open up otherwise inaccessible sources of pleasure. "What is fine about [laughter] is the triumph of narcissism, the ego's victorious assertion of its own invulnerability.[7]

To the travails of the world, such laughter is a *je m'en fiche;* to stern moral codes, it is a thumbing of the nose; and to a restraining superego, it is the ego's cry of triumph. And even if it leaves a bitter aftertaste, high mimetic laughter might still teach us useful lessons. For example, it might be directed at the hypocrisy of morally pretentious faux-dévots. The hypocrite is a false superior, whose duplicity mocks the virtues to which he pretends. If he is risible, it is because we still regard these as virtues. We laugh at the hypocritical Jim Bakker, but not at Ste. Thérèse de Lisieux. In this way, we pay tribute to the moral code the Little Flower followed and that Bakker flouted.

One of the most amusing satires of hypocrisy is Lytton Strachey's *Eminent Victorians,* which did as much as any book to dissolve pious Victorian seriousness. Strachey's Cardinal Manning assumes a mantle of virtue while scheming for priestly power; Florence Nightingale bullies weak-willed men while affecting a pose of helplessness; Gladstone refuses to rescue General Gordon from Khartoum out of petty jealousy and not high policy. But for those whose lives he saw as circumscribed by repressive social norms—Cardinal Newman, Arthur Clough, Gordon—Strachey's satire was genial and good-natured. His real complaint was that a misplaced and excessive moral code rewarded the hypocrite and punished the truly devout and moral.

High mimetic laughter might also mock the false ideals of the morally or culturally pretentious, the *précieuses ridicules,* the aesthetes of Gilbert and Sullivan's *Patience,* the tiresome pedants, the hairshirt-wearers and the opera-lovers of the world. Such people are not hypocrites, for they are true to their ideals. But these are false ideals, that demand too much of one. What is honor, asked Falstaff?

> Who hath it? He that died o' Wednesday. Doth he feel it? no. Doth he hear it? no. 'Tis insensible, then? Yea, to the dead. But will it not live with the living? no. . . . Therefore I'll none of it. (*1 Henry IV* V.i)

High mimetic comedy may also deflate an over-the-top seriousness or passion. The balcony scene in *Romeo and Juliet* fairly cries out for the parody it received in Beaumont's *Knight of the Burning Pestle.* "Good night, twenty good nights, and twenty more, / And twenty more good nights— that makes threescore!"

There is nevertheless a tension in such laughter, since the choice between the pleasure-seeking and morally demanding life is often a near-run thing. Whose life is superior: Prince Hal in the tavern or Henry V in the field? It depends, we want to say. On what? On our mood of the moment, since both lives fascinate. Will we be libertines or penitents distinguished by the austerities of our devotions? We are reluctant to choose, and perch, with Hal and Julien Sorel and with all adolescents, between divergent and incommensurable life plans, unable to choose. We play at adulthood, along with Falstaff, without abandoning youthful pleasures. We visualize the grim moral life of adulthood, without seriously believing that its fetters will one day descend upon us.

> FALSTAFF. No, my good lord; banish Peto, banish Bardolph, banish Poins; but for sweet Jack Falstaff, kind Jack Falstaff, true Jack Falstaff, valiant Jack Falstaff, and therefore more valiant being, as he is, old Jack Falstaff, banish him not thy Harry's company: banish not

him thy Harry's company: banish plump Jack, and banish all the world. (*1 Henry IV* II.iv)

The tension underlies both parts of *Henry IV,* and becomes almost unbearable as we swing with Hal between the pull of inconsistent and equally attractive lives.

> PRINCE. Before God, I am exceedingly weary.
> POINS. Is't come to that? I had thought weariness durst not have attached one of so high blood.
> PRINCE. Faith, it does me; though it discolours the complexion of my greatness to acknowledge it. Doth it show vilely in me to desire small beer?
> POINS. Why, a prince should not be so loosely studied as to remember so weak a composition.
> PRINCE. Belike then my appetite was not princely got; for by my troth, I do now remember the poor creature, small beer. But, indeed, these humble considerations make me out of love with my greatness. What a disgrace is it to me to remember thy name! Or to know thy face tomorrow! (*2 Henry IV* II.ii)

The tension heightens both the pathos and the comedy, until the noble life at last claims Hal and betrays Falstaff. At his coronation, Henry V banishes Falstaff and laughter. "I know thee not, old man: fall to thy prayers, / How ill white hairs become a fool and wit!" (*Henry V* V.v).

High mimetic laughter therefore assumes a pose of superiority. We may share in the laughter if we agree with its criticism of false or excessive standards. But if we do not, we cannot laugh. We do not laugh along with bounders like Poins, nor do we laugh at television sitcoms that disgust us. Others might find such programs amusing, but only if they do not share our contempt.

Yet our laughter is often a little uncertain. A skilled jester might draw us into either high and low mimetic laughter. We can enjoy not only Falstaff's high mimetic but also the disdainful low mimetic of an Alexander Pope. Perhaps this reflects inconsistencies in our comic norms, for our laughter sometimes seems to place a stamp of approval upon inconsistent life plans. A more charitable explanation is that, through our openness to divergent kinds of laughter, we reject mechanistic rules of life and keep ourselves open to the endless possibilities of joy that life offers us.

12   Resistance to Laughter

> Christ is crucified and dost thou laugh?
>
> St. John Chrysothom, Homily XVII

We must all develop a degree of resistance to laughter. Comic norms are always contested, as we saw in the last chapter, and this means that one is always a butt for someone, somewhere. Wherever the golden mean of comic virtue might lie, some will think one excessively virtuous and others insufficiently so. We cannot hope to avoid all laughter and must therefore learn to tolerate some forms of it.

Who can shut himself off from laughter? It breaks through, even if we close our ears to it. We cannot will ourselves to be immune to its sting, however much we try. We can bear pain courageously and pressure gracefully, but we can never be indifferent to laughter. Nor can we will ourselves to be ignorant, and as laughter communicates information we can never decide not to hear it. "All men naturally desire to know," was how Aristotle began his *Metaphysics,* and this is particularly true of the information conveyed by laughter. Suppose that a friend tells you that everyone is laughing at you and asks "Would you like to know why?" Who would say no? No one could ever wish to be ignorant of his comic vices.

Nevertheless, some of us have a stronger resistance to laughter than others. The determined butt seems ridiculous to most people, but still persists in his comic vices. To do so, he must deaden his sensitivity to laughter. For the machine theorist, laughter is always the enemy. He senses, whenever he hears it, that his ideals are under attack, and he is right. Any willingness to join in the laughter, any smile, signals the machine lawyer's weakness and the machine politician's want of ideological fervor. Such people show no greater interest in laughter than Rousseau had in comedy.

In what follows I identify five ways in which the butt might resist the message of laughter. The butt must be ignorant of his comic vice, and *vanity* can almost make his ignorance invincible. Second, *acedia* or depression might lead the butt to despair of correcting his comic vices. Third, *cynicism* about social norms may lead one to disregard laughter's message. Fourth, the butt might have traded laughter away for power in a *Faustian Bargain*. Laughter tends to subvert power, and the powerful will frown when they hear it. Lastly, comic norms might seem trumped by a superior set of *moral or religious norms*.

Vanity

C. S. Lewis wrote that courage is not simply a moral virtue but the form of every virtue at the testing point.[1] Without courage, we lack the inner resources necessary for all the other virtues. Similarly, vanity is not so much a comic vice as its very form. Vanity hides his error from the butt and stops up his ears against laughter. Comic defects proceed from ignorance, and nothing promotes the ignorance of comic vice so much as vanity.

The butt must always be self-deluding. He is the hypocrite who thinks himself politic, the prig who thinks himself virtuous, and the miser who thinks himself frugal. We are all a little self-delusional and apt to think too highly of ourselves. We see ourselves as the hero of our own private movie, without recognizing that, as seen by others, it is a comedy. We might have sufficient self-awareness to recognize that we depart from the mean, but cannot see this as a vice. It is thus a simple matter to discover a person's most besetting vice: we have only to ask him what his most sterling virtue might be. The misanthrope will tell you of his integrity, the moral reprobate will boast of his liberal views, and the coward will preen over his prudence.

Our antipathy to evil is so strong that we rarely if ever recognize our own vices. We ache with envy and call it fairness; we burn with resentment and call it justice. Unlike those around us, we adhere to the highest code of ethics, one that holds up our hidden virtues for all to see, and that lets us feast in our hatred for others. We prize forgiveness, not for our own sins (since we are blameless), but always for sins that others have committed against us, which in our dreams we pardon out of the greatness of our souls.

We are all self-deluding, but the vain man is a special case. Ordinary self-delusion might be cured by ridicule, but the vain man resists our laughter. He cannot hear it and remains supremely pleased with himself. And the more he is vain, the more he is risible, for the more he will thrust himself where he has no right to be. He is the self-righteous sinner who thinks his good works have bought him a place in Heaven, and the self-important academic who thinks that thoughts become important when it is he who thinks them. In literature, he is M. Jourdain in Molière's *Bourgeois gentilhomme.*

M. Jourdain is a favorite butt of social comedies in less democratic times, the self-made merchant who seeks to buy his way into the upper classes. A society that welcomes its new men is always wealthier than one that freezes them out, and this kind of laughter might be costly. But where the parvenu's only claim to our attention is his money, our laughter defends aesthetic, moral, and comic norms that cannot be purchased. And that is why we laugh at M. Jourdain, who is delighted to hear the improbable news that his father was a gentleman.

> MONSIEUR JOURDAIN. What! . . . I simply can't understand. . . . There are some numskulls who want to tell me he was a merchant.
> COVEILLE. Him, a Merchant! That's utterly false, he never was. All he did, since he was so very obliging, and since he knew garments so well, he went about picking them from here and there, he brought them home, and he gave them to his friends . . . for money.*

Molière's satire mocks M. Jourdain's quick-and-dirty efforts to acquire the grace and education of a gentleman, with dancing lessons, fencing lessons, and a course in philosophy. After discarding logic and ethics as too difficult, M. Jourdain settles on a more congenial philosophical subject: pronunciation.

> PHILOSOPHY MASTER. Now for R one puts the tip of the tongue to the top of the plate, so that being shaken forcefully by the escaping air, it yields and then returns, making a kind of trembling: R, Ra.

Monsieur Jourdain. Comment dites-vous? . . . Je ne sais donc comment le monde est fait . . . Il y a des sottes gens qui me veulent dire qu'il a été marchand. *Coveille.* Lui marchand! C'est pur médisance, il ne l'a jamais été. Tout ce qu'il faisait, c'est qu'il était fort obligeant, fort officieux; et comme il connaissait fort bien en étoffes, il allait choisir de tous les côtés, les faisait apporter chez lui, et en donnait à ses amis pour de l'argent.

M. JOURDAIN. R, R, Ra, R, R, R, R, R, Ra. It's true! Ah, what a splendid teacher you are! And how I've wasted my time! R, R, R, Ra.*

If we laugh less today, vanity might have something to do with it. The self-esteem movement, which promotes vanity, cannot have helped. The movement began with a California task force on a hitherto neglected social problem. Incredibly, the study concluded that Americans had too *little,* not too much, self-esteem. But, said the authors, we asked people and they told us they sometimes felt down on themselves—as though occasional self-doubt was not a badge of health, and flaming self-certainty not a sign of madness. Nevertheless, the movement took hold, its goal "a High Self-Esteem existence . . . in the crusade to rid present-day society of its cruelest and most devastating social invader . . . low self-image."[2] The problem was global, and its consequences more profound than anyone had imagined. Following India's nuclear tests, President Clinton suggested that India (which he called "a perfectly wonderful country") might have been motivated by a lack of self-esteem.[3] But after a while doubts about the self-esteem movement set in, particularly when a sober review of the evidence failed to find a positive correlation between low self-esteem and teenage pregnancy, child abuse, and most cases of alcohol and drug abuse.[4] If anything, the correlation works the other way. American children consistently rank ahead of children from other first world countries on measures of self-esteem, and behind them in educational categories.[5] Within the United States, those who do poorest in math have the most inflated impression of their math ability. And the teenage hoodlum is more likely to be a raving egomaniac than a shrinking violet. Rather than nurturing that tender shoot, the adolescent ego, a teacher might at times more profitably prune it back through ridicule.

But let's talk about me. The newest trend in legal scholarship is autobiography, where legal rules are evaluated through the magnifying glass of "my personal experience" (161 Lexis cites).[6] All very well to say a rule is efficient and benign and just. What I want to know is: Does it accord

---

*Maître de philosophie. Et l'R, en portant le bout de la langue jusqu'au haut du palais, de sorte qu'étant frôlée par l'air qui sort avec force, elle lui cède, et revint toujours au même endroit, faisant une manière de tremblement. R, Ra. *M. Jourdain.* R, R, Ra, R, R, R, R, R, Ra. C'est vrai! Ah, l'habile homme que vous êtes! Et que j'ai perdu de temps! R, R, R, Ra.

with "my philosophy" (111 cites) or "my principles" (70 cites)? Perhaps I might refer you to "my scholarship" (96 cites) or "my previous article" (58 cites), where you might observe "my difference" (68 cites)? I should like to tell you of "my sympathies" (65 cites) and "my taste" (88 cites). Or would you rather hear of "my sexuality" (17 cites) or "my lover" (17 cites)? All in all, I think I may fairly say that I did it "my way" (564 cites).

If the lawyer's vanity leads him to take himself too seriously, part of the blame must be lain at the feet of Legal Realism, an academic movement that sought to explain legal rules through insights derived from other disciplines, such as sociology, psychology, and economics. The Legal Realist denied what an earlier academic movement called Formalism had asserted: that law was an independent science which could be understood on its own terms, without the need for interdisciplinary perspectives.

The Formalist shut himself up in his law library, surrounded by his law reports. For any legal problem, he thought, the answer might be found within the law alone. By contrast, the Realist was contemptuous of the Formalist's otherworldliness and his devotion to his profession, and sought to clear away the antique rules and legal fictions that the Formalist favored.

Realism had little use for ceremony; Formalism cherished it, and was therefore on better terms with laughter. Laughter flourishes best in an artificial environment, where things are not what they seem and the players wear masks. For this reason, laughter has always been welcome at court. "A magnificent and polite court, and by consequence a monarchy à la Louis XV, strongly promotes laughter," said Stendhal. "Such a court is an immense and unlimited source of a kind of laughter—satirical laughter."* For where would we most expect to find laughter? In a faculty committee? Or in a French court of Meredith's "hypocrites, posturers, extravagants, pedants, rose-pink ladies and mad grammarians, sonnetteering marquises, highflying mistresses, plain-minded maids, interthreading as in a loom, noisy as at a fair"?[7] So too, the English barrister with his wig and gown learns the law's potential for laughter. In the midst of his work he has entered a world of play, and thereafter can more easily move from the serious to the comic.

---

*"Une cour magnifique et polie, et par conséquent un gouvernement monarchique, à la Louis XV, est fort utile au rire. Une telle cour est une source immense, inépuisable, d'une espèce de rire, le *rire satirique.*" Stendhal, *Molière, Shakespeare, La comédie et le rire* (Liechtenstein: Kraus Reprint, 1968), 297–98.

The Realists were far too self-important for laughter. For the Formalists, who worried less about the social and economic consequences of their rules, the stakes were lower all around. A mistaken doctrine was an error, an embarrassment, possibly, but not an occasion for profound alarm. Not surprisingly, formal legal systems like those of England are better noted for their humorists. The English reader may smile at the gentle mockery of an A. P. Herbert or a Henry Cecil. By contrast, the American reader is Concerned and Appalled with Mary McGrory, or Shocked and Offended with Bill O'Reilly. The English Formalist is forgiving of human lapses and foibles; the American Realist asks, with Chrysothom, "Christ is crucified and dost thou laugh?" But in forswearing laughter, did we end up with better law? Was the exchange of Formalism and humor for Realism and serious policy analysis really benign? Modern American law is replete with absurd rules that could never have stood the test of ridicule, but which Realists welcomed—the enormous awards for spilt coffee and the damages for bruised feelings. Seventy years of Realism have left us with a humorless profession and what often seems an inferior law.

Acedia

Acedia is the spiritual sloth that shuts its eyes to joy, and is the mirror image of vanity. The vain man is too proud and the acedic man too depressed to notice his comic vices. By obsessing over themselves, both miss laughter's corrective message.

Acedia is the child of despair, as vanity is of presumption, and in Catholic dogma these are the two unforgivable sins because both prevent one from seeking God's assistance in the work of salvation. The presumptuous do not call on God because they do not believe they need Him; the despairing do not call on God because they do not think He can help them. By refusing grace, the acedic sin against the Holy Spirit, and for this they will not be forgiven. "Whoever says a word against the Son of Man will be forgiven but whoever speaks against the Holy Spirit will not be forgiven, either in this age or in the age to come" (Matt. 12:31). It is not that the Holy Spirit is deserving of more respect than the other members of the Trinity. Instead, as St. Thomas Aquinas noted, it is a question of a sin that is unforgivable by its very nature, since it excludes the elements through which the forgiveness of sin takes place.[8]

169

Aristotle called the acedic small-souled, in contrast to his great-souled man. If the vain man thinks too highly of himself, the small-souled man is unduly humble. Though worthy of good things, he robs himself of what he deserves. His humility is not a vice, but he still seems to have something bad about him since he thinks himself unworthy of good things (*Nicomachean Ethics* 1125a20). Because the small-souled man attempts little, his humility is a greater failing than vanity. The vain man tries to perform honorable deeds and, not knowing his limits, fails. He might look foolish, but at least he has made the effort. The small-souled man stands back from noble actions and undertakings, and Aristotle thought his failing was worse and more common than vanity.

In late Roman times acedia was a tiredness of life (*taedium vitae*) that sapped one's energy, and in late medieval times it was identified with sloth. The acedic may indeed be listless, for they lack a motive for action. With Kierkegaard, they simply can't be bothered.[9] When nothing matters, only indolence is rational—so long as that does not look like a choice. Nevertheless, the emphasis on physical action is misleading, since the slug might be joyous and the acedic industrious. What matters is an openness to joy, not indolence. Acedia is an inability to experience joy, and this may be very different from sloth.[10] Instead, acedia more closely resembles ingratitude, for the acedic refuse the joy that comes from God, including His gift of laughter.

Like vanity, acedia is not so much a comic vice as a source of vices. In the Catholic tradition it is one of the seven "capital" sins, so called because they engender other sins. The same is true of the comic vice of acedia. Since the acedic man does not attend to laughter's message of correction, he will be an all-around butt. He is the graceless man who does not care how others see him and the ill-educated person who is indifferent to learning. He needs to pulls himself together, and must set aside his sadness and listen to laughter before he can do so.

We are said to live in a hedonistic age, but it does not seem a particularly joyful one. Few things are less joyous than the frantic search for joy, few things more depressing than the desperate attempt to persuade ourselves that we are having a good time. We reach for joy, and as quickly lose it. The promised land is in view—and the promised land disappears. "Men grow accustomed to joy," said Hölderlin in *Bread and Wine,* and never more so than today. The besetting sin of our age is not hedonism but indifference to joy, not narcissism but acedia.

The Cynic

There are degrees of cynicism. Most of us are cynical about some things but quite sentimental about others. Karl Marx was famously cynical about religion and liberal institutions but not about the bonds of communitarian solidarity, and he bemoaned the breakup of feudal hierarchies and communities with the passion of an Edmund Burke. "All that is holy is profaned," said the author of *The Communist Manifesto.* "All that is solid melts into air." It sounds like an Anglican hymn, and so it was treated in a long-ago movie called *Morgan.*

The cynicism I have in mind is more extreme, however. Like Bacon's Pilate, it rejects all commonly accepted beliefs about the world. "*What is truth?* said jesting Pilate, and would not stay for an answer."[11] An extreme cynicism may also affect a pose of indifference to social norms, including those enforced by laughter. In such cases, the cynic may resist laughter's message of correction.

The most famous cynic of antiquity, Diogenes, thought it natural to use any place for any purpose, as a dog might. With his knapsack, staff, and short cloak, he took to the road to preach his doctrine: Greek society was unnatural, and its most cherished beliefs were false and unprofitable. As heuristic devices, he employed laughter and shamelessness, forcing his audience to reconsider its ideals and taboos. One day he visited a man who had a fine mosaic on his floor. Whatever you do, don't spit on the floor, he was told. And so Diogenes spat on the owner's face. Not surprisingly, he scandalized his audience—even Plato described him as Socrates gone mad.[12] Ridiculing others, the cynic is risible himself, for he has abandoned the respect for common opinion that works as a check on a risible eccentricity.

Does the assertion of a more authentic morality immunize the cynic from laughter? One of the best-known modern cynics was Jean-Jacques Rousseau, who like Diogenes deprecated social customs and urged a return to nature, and who also adopted the cynic's barking tone after he became a public figure. But the cynic's mask was false, for no one was more exquisitely concerned about how others regarded him than Rousseau. He once was told that a king wished to see him the next day, with the prospect of a pension held out. Rousseau stayed away and the pension was lost.[13] The story recalls a famous anecdote about Diogenes: Alexander found him lying in the street and asked what he might do for him. Just get out of my light, was the answer. But Rousseau was no Diogenes. He had stayed up all night and was enervated by the possibility that he would be seen as foolish at court. The pose of cynicism is usually false and seldom shields us from laughter.

The Faustian Bargain

Pascal is said to have wanted a life that began in love and ended in power.[14] A curious choice, perhaps, but in one respect this seems right. We cannot seek love and power simultaneously, for love comes only to those who surrender power. We are put to an election, as Julien Sorel discovered in *The Red and the Black*.

We must also make a choice between power and joy, and this was the theme of Marlowe's *Doctor Faustus*. In his bargain with the devil, Faustus will gain every imaginable intellectual power but will lose his soul and the infinite joy of Heaven. So the Faustian Bargain sacrifices joy; and since laughter is naturally joyful, the power seeker must turn his back on it as well. Laughter is a distraction from the aching ambition and narrow calculation of advantage and remembered slights that fuel his drive for power. The power seeker is also hostile to the sense of equality implicit in the *lien de rire* between wit and listener. That is why few things are more depressing than the forced laughter at the employer's joke, unless it is the dreary jollity of his New Year's Eve party. But give us a chance to mock a bumbling superior and we have the exhilarating laughter of *Dilbert*.

There is a second reason why power tends to exclude laughter. Our sense of humor polices the meddlesome and inhuman rules of petty tyrants. And the more arbitrary and mechanical his rules, the more we ridicule them. A perfect tyrant like Stalin is the font of pure machine law. In this sense, laughter naturally nudges us toward liberty.

To test these ideas, let us examine one Faustian Bargain, where joy was exchanged for power and where laughter took revenge upon power. Laughter is little heard in the academy today, and the turn to power and to politics explains why this is so. The English scholar who has lost interest in literature and who cares only for politics has exchanged the joy of beauty for the power to chastise those who do not share his political views, and his Faustian Bargain merits our laughter.

In the backlash against political correctness, what annoyed was not the message so much as the manner in which it was conveyed, and the indecent delight taken in reducing opponents to submission. These are the forms of petit apartheid, in which a privileged group humiliates an underclass through symbolic gestures—separate washrooms or sensitivity training—designed to rub its nose in the dirt. The subordinate group must acquiesce in second-class status, and this is more deeply resented than the inequality of power itself. That is why we laugh so delightedly when the powerful overreach themselves and take a tumble. And this is what happened when academic deconstructionists launched a takeover bid against the hard sciences.

Deconstructionism argues that we understand the world only through our language, which in turn is shaped by ideological biases—economic, racial, and sexual. Since every form of knowledge (even science) employs language, all efforts to understand and describe the world necessarily enshrine power relations, like poisoned fruit from a poisoned tree. Deconstructionism had therefore no choice but to contest every rival body of knowledge. If the hard sciences could somehow hold out, this would mean that scientists had somehow overcome the problems of radical skepticism that the deconstructionist thought he had identified. And in that case his claim that language and power relations are prior to any understanding of the world would be suspect.

The deconstructionist improbably sought support from the movement toward complexity in science and mathematics. Sociologist Stanley Aronowitz, who cofounded a leading deconstructionist journal called *Social Text,* claims that "we are witnessing the slow, discontinuous breakup of the old world-view according to which physical science offers context-free knowledge of the external world."[15] But how is the move from Newtonian to quantum physics related to deconstruction? The idea, familiar from New Age accounts of pop science, is that Einstein's theory of relativity is somehow related to moral relativity; that Heisenberg's uncertainty principle evidences a loss of faith in normative order; and that chaos theory is a dagger pointed at the heart of hierarchical political structures.[16] The goofiness of these ideas is immediately apparent, as is their similarity to Nazi dismissals of Einstein's "degenerate Jewish" theory of relativity.

G. K. Chesterton thought that more people become mad through an excess than an insufficiency of reason, and that few things are more dangerous to the simple mind than the One Big Idea. Kept within bounds, the notion that language constrains our thoughts is eminently plausible. For example, Victor Klemperer's *Lingua Tertii Imperii* showed how lan-

guage could be employed to influence political opinion. Had deconstructionism merely asserted that language shapes our beliefs, it would
therefore have been unexceptional. What was excessive was the primacy
it gave to language and the suggestion that linguistic usage was uncon-
strained by the physical world.

In retrospect, the linguistic turn was an enormous strategic blunder,
since success within the academy came at the cost of political irrelevance
without. In what used to be called the real world, an older breed of liberals was dismayed by the academic deconstructionists' retreat from
practical problems. Within the academy, these concerns were shared by
New York University physicist Alan Sokal. Like others before him, Sokal
might simply have identified the scientific errors the deconstructionists
made. What he did, however, was far more effective. He submitted a parody of scientific deconstructionism to *Social Text* to see whether it would
be accepted. The journal had planned a special issue on the "Science
Wars," and the kind of article it sought may be seen from its mission
statement on its web site:

> *Social Text* . . . is produced by an editorial collective that today com-
> prises a group of scholars, critics, artists and writers in New York City.
> The editors are committed to preserving and renovating the broad left
> tradition of cultural and political commentary that has sustained
> North American intellectual life in this century. . . . The journal is well
> known for its contributions to debates about cultural affairs, and has
> provided a home, over the years, for some of the most crucial essays on
> a whole range of topics. In recent years, for example, we have pub-
> lished special issues or sections on ecology, the public sphere, popular
> culture, postcolonialism, radical democracy, queer politics, sex work,
> technoscience, and global restructuring.[17]

Sokal described the experiment in *Lingua Franca,* where he revealed
the hoax on the day *Social Text* published the article. "Would a leading
North American journal of cultural studies—whose editorial collective
includes such luminaries as Fredric Jameson and Andrew Ross—publish
an article liberally salted with nonsense if (a) it sounded good and (b) it
flattered the editors' ideological preconceptions? The answer, unfortu-
nately, is yes."

The paper, "Transgressing the Boundaries: Toward a Transformative
Hermeneutics of Quantum Gravity" is a hilarious send-up of deconstruc-

tionism, replete with every scientific howler he could throw in. Sokal began by accusing his fellow physicists of clinging to

> the dogma imposed by the long post-Enlightenment hegemony over the western intellectual outlook, which can be summarized briefly as follows: that there exists an external world, whose properties are independent of any individual human being . . . and that human beings can obtain reliable, albeit imperfect and tentative knowledge of these laws by hewing to the "objective" procedures and epistemological strictures prescribed by the (so-called) scientific method."[18]

Having begun with the deconstructionists' favorite buzz words, Sokal then proceeded to pander to them by citing their discovery of an "ideology of domination concealed behind the mask of 'objectivity,'" concluding (without anything like evidence) that "physical 'reality,' no less than social 'reality,' is at bottom a social and linguistic construct."

By the end Sokal had thrown caution to the wind. He compared the axiom of choice in set theory to the pro-choice abortion rights movement; he appended four footnotes after a single, lonely comma; and he described the geometric term π, which one learns is a constant in third grade, as a variable. He then did the same for Einstein's constant c (the speed of light), quoting Derrida:

> The Einsteinian constant is not a constant, is not a center. It is the very concept of variability—it is, finally, the concept of the game. In other words, it is not the concept of some*thing*—of a center starting from which an observer could master the field—but the very concept of the game.

The wonderful thing about the parody is that Sokal invented nothing; he simply reproduced what the deconstructionists had said about science, and had the wit to recognize that it was hilarious.

When the hoax was revealed, the editors sputtered with indignation and launched personal attacks on Sokal. Andrew Ross, the Marxist scholar who organized the special issue, complained of a "breach of professional ethics," as though deconstructionists do not base their professional careers on transgressing norms. Others complained that the parody was not a reasoned argument. But as Sokal showed, ridicule can dissolve nonsense that withstands serious debate.

The Puritan

The fifth way in which one might fail to laugh is through an excessive concern for moral or political duties. In the past, the Puritan subordinated aesthetics and the sweetness of life to religious duty. The modern Puritan devotes himself to political rather than religious duties, but has little more interest in aesthetics and laughter than his dour ancestor.

Matthew Arnold applied the label *Hebraism* to the excessive concern for moral and religious duties to the exclusion of Hellenism's beauty and culture. Arnold praised Hebraism's moral message, but sought a balance between moral principles and aesthetic impulses. The Renaissance Church was a splendid patron of the arts, but might possibly have stood a greater dose of Hebraism. For the pious low churchmen of Arnold's nineteenth century, however, the desire and pursuit of beauty was suppressed, both in the Anglican Church after the political defeat of the Oxford Movement, and most particularly among the Dissenters whose schools Arnold visited as a government inspector. Through their exclusive focus on correct beliefs and blameable actions, Arnold's compatriots had lost the ability to experience joy from the best that had been thought and said.

Hebraism takes moral development as our sole end, and not simply as a contribution to our good. Anticipating Bergson, Arnold described the result as "machinery." A "mechanical" rule, according to Arnold, is one that has lost sight of true ends and takes means to be ends. Arnold wittily described the result, in an account of a conversation with a Nonconformist manufacturer who had opened a chapel for Dissenters who did not want to attend an Anglican church. The result was that

> Church and Dissent were pretty equally divided, with sharp contests between them. I said that this seemed a pity. "A pity?" cried he! "not at all! Only think of all the zeal and activity which the collision calls forth!" "Ah, but, my dear friend," I answered, "only think of all the nonsense which you now hold quite firmly, which you would never have held if you had not been contradicting your adversary in it all these years."[19]

The Dissenter's mistake was to confuse means and ends. Whatever the final end of religious experience might be, it is something other than "zeal and activity."

Today the Dissenter's Hebraism is as strong as ever. The difference is that politics has taken the place of religion, even in the pulpit. Beauty and culture matter no more than in Arnold's day, and radio and television are filled with politics. Incredibly, political discussion is thought a public good, like the manufacturer's debate between Church and chapel, and deserving of subsidy through public radio.

The emphasis on the political to the exclusion of the aesthetic is particularly pronounced in the academy. One amusing example, from the voluminous literature on the subject, will suffice. In 1998 Arizona State University found an effective way to publicize its theater department: it fired a professor for staging plays by noted antifeminist William Shakespeare. The professor, Jared Sakren, a prize-winning director who had taught at Yale and Juilliard and tutored actresses Annette Bening, Kelly McGillis, and Frances McDormand, had run afoul of his feminist superiors. Though urged to teach from the "postmodern feminist canon," he had remained "firmly wedded to the idea of classical training," according to a negative performance review. For example, he had objected to how his department had butchered *Medea*. Its version had six Medeas, all protesting domestic violence, with no Jason and no mention that Medea had murdered her own children. What is worse, Sakren had promoted sexist and Eurocentric playwrights, such as Shakespeare, Ibsen, and Congreve, and had encouraged his students to read Aeschylus, Molière, and Chekhov. The last straw came when he refused to stage that feminist classic, *Betti the Yeti*, an environmentally sensitive epic about the taming of a reactionary logger by a superhuman snowwoman.[20]

Arnold observed that there is a great deal one cannot understand unless one understands that it is beautiful. He did not consider how laughter might help us "see things as they really are." That was left for Bergson, who told us that there is a great deal one cannot understand unless one understands that its denial is risible. Yet the modern Puritan is as suspicious of laughter as he is of beauty, since both distract us from the serious business of remedying injustice. We are given a finite number of minutes to live, and those not spent in the struggle to end sexism or racism are wasted. All the worse if we seek a secret refuge of pleasure in the nonpolitical.

13   The Sociability Thesis

> To breed an animal capable of promising—isn't
> that just the paradoxical task which nature has
> set herself with mankind, the peculiar problem
> of mankind?
>
> Nietzsche, *On the Genealogy of Morals*

In part II we examined the claim that laughter offers signaling gains through its message about a superior life. By laughing, the jester and listener communicate to the butt that his life plan is defective. This chapter examines a second benefit offered by laughter. By establishing a bond between jester and listener, laughter permits them to promote their trust in each other. With the trust comes a greater ability to exploit profitable opportunities for joint gain.

We begin by examining why trust is so important and how laughter has a unique ability to create trust.

Signaling Trustworthiness

The Need for Trust

Although Adam Smith is remembered as the first economist, several of his key insights were anticipated by David Hume. In particular, the discovery that specialization of trade promotes economic growth should be attributed to Hume, who noted that "different men are by nature fitted for different employments, and attain to greater perfection in any one, when they confine themselves to it alone."[1] By specializing, the baker can restrict his business to bread-making; he can buy his flour from merchants and need not grow and mill his own grain. But this assumes that he can trust the merchant to supply him with flour when he needs it. Without trust, the parties cannot rely on each other and are driven back to producing all their own goods and forgoing the gains from specialization.

Hume's account of the gains available through specialization explains why the institution of contract law is valuable. When a party who breaches his contractual obligations knows that he may be made to pay damages, his incentive to perform the obligation is strengthened, and the other party is better able to trust him. What happens where contracts are not feasible, however? The promisor might live in a place where the normal writs of the common law do not run—in Mississippi, possibly. Alternatively, the promise might be too vague to be easily enforced (or to trust to an American jury). Long-term contracts between business parties necessarily leave many details to be decided at a later time.

In such cases, the problem of trust cannot readily be solved by contract. Yet the need for trust remains. It is a crucial element in the social norms that Jon Elster calls the cement of society. Without trust our friendships would becomes affairs of momentary convenience, on which no plans, no projects for future cooperation, could be formed. We rely so often upon friends and associates that we often forget we are doing so. We scatter our promises about, without paying much attention to what we are doing. We make seemingly trivial promises, to meet for lunch or to return a call, on whose performance deep friendships depend. And we make unspoken promises that are the foundation of trust: I will take your side; I will not betray you.

Self-Binding Gains

Let us suppose that the parties wish to enter into a long-term relationship and cannot do so by contract. Without contractual fetters, how can a promisor signal his good faith to a promisee? Rousseau thought that we should be forced to be free, but our promisor seeks the freedom to be forced. He wishes to restrict his ability to breach in order to persuade the promisee to trust him. In this he is like Ulysses, who wished to hear the song the Sirens sing.[2] Since those who hear the music are led to the reefs and a watery grave, he lashed himself to the mast and stopped the ears of his crew with wax. As they rowed past, he heard the music but could not untie his cords to unstop the ears of his crew and direct them to the rocks. So they rowed safely on, without hearing either the Siren song or the commands of their enchanted captain.

Like Ulysses, the promisor seeks to restrict his future freedom of action in order to exploit a gain. And, like Ulysses, he might have to bind his hands through noncontractual means where a contract cannot be written. This might happen when the parties deal with each other on a repeat basis, and both parties know that a breach will destroy a valuable relationship. A pattern of reciprocal altruism may then emerge, through which parties in repeated transactions may confidently adopt cooperative strategies to extract bargaining gains.

Before such a pattern can begin, however, there is a prior stage during which we know little about the party with whom we are dealing. How can promise keeping be signaled at this stage? And how can the promisee detect cheaters before the first round of the game? What is needed is deception-detection equipment, where we test other people for signs of reliability.

How can one pick out a friend or partner in a sea of strangers? The answer is written on our faces, the most public part of our body, where our emotions register for all to see. Facial signals reveal our deepest feelings to others and permit them to make reliable inferences about our future behavior.

We may express our sentiments in other ways, of course, but what is special about facial expressions is that they are so easy to recognize and hard to mimic. We show our anxiety when lying, for example. When our sins are detected, our blushes and downcast eyes may convict us; when accused falsely, as Hero was in *Much Ado About Nothing*, our innocence shines through.

> I have mark'd
> A thousand blushing apparitions
> To start into her face, a thousand innocent shames
> In angel whiteness bear away those blushes,
> And in her eye there hath appear'd a fire
> To burn the errors that these princes hold
> Against her maiden truth.
> (IV.i.160–66)

Blushing is a useful commitment device. It increases the likelihood of detection and the costs of lying, and strengthens the incentive to tell the truth. Others will repose greater confidence in us, and this will permit us to extract increased gains from joint cooperation.

The demand for facial signals is particularly strong in low-trust societies where patterns of reciprocal altruism are relatively rare. Luigi

Barzini reported that Italians prefer direct negotiations for this reason. "They read in their opponent's eyes (or catch in his voice or choice of words) the signs of his stubborn decision or hidden timidity."[3] Even in America, face-to-face negotiations remain of crucial importance despite the rise of new techniques of communication.

Sudden genuine laughter is also written on our faces, by muscles over which we lack full self-control. The counterfeit laugh, produced for purely strategic purposes, is a pale imitation. Imagine being told an unfunny joke by a boorish superior, where it is politic to affect a laugh. One might bare one's teeth and emit the sound of laughter, but this can ordinarily be distinguished from companionable, uproarious laughter. The subordinate's pretended laugh might usefully communicate subservience to a domineering superior, but does not signal a shared mirth and friendship.

In 1862 the French anatomist Duchenne du Bologne took a series of photographs to illustrate the difference between true and false smiles.[4] In one picture the man was in his normal state; in the second he was naturally smiling; but in the third the smile was false. The lips curled up but the signs of hilarity were absent, suggesting a masked threat. When Darwin tested the photos on a small group of subjects, everyone could tell the genuine from the false smile.[5]

The difference between the two kinds of smiles is physiological. In the false smile, the corrugator muscle is more contracted, causing a frown. In the true smile, the eyelid muscles are more contracted, and the upper lip is drawn up more. The corners of the mouth are retracted and the cheeks are drawn upward. In older people wrinkles are formed under the eyes. The eyes are bright and sparkling, as they are when one is in love. And all of this happens in a flash, without conscious effort.

What is remarkable about all of this is how complicated a thing it is to smile. The facial movements are unconscious and costless when the smile is genuine, of course. But if the smile or laugh is insincere, there are simply too many muscles to move, and no one is fooled. On command, we might move one facial muscle, mechanically, as we might lift an arm; but we cannot will *all* of the right muscles to move in the required way. When the smile passes into a laugh, the facial movements intensify. We move fifteen facial muscles in a coordinated manner and alter our breathing patterns.[6] For virtually everyone, the false smile or laugh is simply too hard to counterfeit. We must imagine ourselves laughing to produce the false laugh. We must fool ourselves. And even when we try, false smiles and laughter are usually detected. We learn to see through the politician's bonhomie and the car salesman's coprophagous grin.

The physiological account of laughter helps to explain why laughter is a more reliable indicator of beliefs than emotionally neutral expressions of opinion. When political dissent is suppressed by criminal sanctions (as in the former Soviet Union), people will learn to camouflage their true opinions. However, it is a harder thing to suppress one's emotions, and joke telling against the regime became one of the most reliable expressions of public opinion before the fall of communism. One could fake political speech much more easily than laughter. The same is true of beliefs that are punished by social sanctions. Even in a democracy with robust free speech rights, such as the United States, we may be taught to falsify our true opinions. When this happens, there may be more truth in our laughter than in the most scientific opinion poll. False political beliefs might unwind very quickly in an informational cascade, when each person's beliefs are in part dependent on what others think, and the realization that everyone is wrong comes all at once to each of us. But the quickest informational cascade is provided by our laughter, when we recognize the ludicrous immediately and without deliberation.

Durable Preferences

For laughter to serve as a trust-building device, the laugh must not only reveal private sentiments but these must be durable. If they were wholly plastic, if an expression of feelings today gave no clue about tomorrow's feelings, then facial expressions would not signal anything about promise keeping. Today's great friend might readily betray one tomorrow, and we would place no more stock on their transitory attachments than Pope thought one should on women's fancies.

> Nothing so true as what you once let fall,
> 'Most Women have no Characters at all.'
> Matter too soft a lasting mark to bear,
> And best distinguish'd by black, brown, or fair.
> (Of the Characters of Women)

We are not made that way, however. We are capable of durable preferences that cannot be abandoned without emotional pain. Such preferences impose a cost, to the extent that they constrain future choices. They might make it painful to betray one's family, and those who have gone through a divorce might have wished that it were easier to do so ("so that the healing process can begin," as liberal clerics put it). But were it painless to leave one's wife, then divorce rates would be higher. Marriage rates would also be lower, since a man would find it harder to persuade a lady to trust his promises. Fewer people would marry, and fewer married couples would make the kinds of investments that are placed at risk through divorce—notably children.

Durable preferences are therefore a useful self-binding device, like the cords that bound Ulysses to the mast. Binding oneself through preferences that are difficult to change restricts future choices, but permits one to exploit bargain opportunities that would otherwise be lost through a want of trust.

How Laughter Signals Durable Preferences

Laughter is one of the many private ceremonies through which we demonstrate durable preferences of loyalty or disloyalty to others. We may betray our friends in obvious ways, as when we tell tales about them behind their back. But we may also betray them in smaller ways when we fail to take their part, or when we fail to show sympathy for their reversals. Alternatively, we signal loyalty when we demonstrate our happiness for a friend's good fortune, or when we take delight and share in his high-spirited laughter.

Revealing a confidence is a special way to signal loyalty, particularly when the secret concerns the teller. The secret gives the listener the power to betray him by revealing it, and his disclosure sends a strong signal that he trusts the listener. Where both parties trade secrets, they seal their friendship with mutual confidences. Thereafter, the cost of betrayal increases for both parties, with the result that its likelihood declines. The parties can invest more strongly in their relationship, and this feedback effect will further strengthen their bond.

Telling a joke also reveals a vulnerability to the listener, who might betray the wit in a variety of ways. The listener might repeat the joke to the butt or to third parties as an example of the wit's indiscretion or political incorrectness. Or the listener might simply fail to laugh, to signal the jester's want of wit. Suppose instead that the listener does laugh. Not feigned laughter either, but honest, heart-easing mirth. By doing so he signals that he accepts the special tie, the *lien de rire*, that the wit has proposed between them. The listener has agreed to take the wit's side against the butt.

Joke telling is a means of sniffing out friends. Sincere friends laugh together in a special way that false friends cannot duplicate. The laughter is open, unreserved, and joyful. When Carlyle said "the man who cannot laugh is only fit for treasons, stratagems and spoils," this was what he had in mind.[7] The weaker the tie, the more strained the laughter. Where the listener has recently betrayed the wit, the laughter often has a lupine quality: the cheeks are pulled back and the teeth are barred; the listener's gaze rests on the wit, and the general expression is ironic. The emotional cost of hiding the enmity is simply too great for most false listeners, and the appropriate inference will be made. If you cannot laugh with me, how can I trust you? You say you like me, and share my interests? Then come into my bar and laugh at my jokes. Only then will I trust you. And the more risqué the joke, the stronger the signal of friendship.

As a community-building device, laughter resembles gossip, which also features teller, listener, and butt. The teller reveals a secret about the butt to the listener, who can either show his appreciation or disapproval. Should the listener reciprocate with gossip of his own he will create a bond between the two. The butt might not appreciate the gossip, but from the perspective of the participants it is a communitarian experience.[8]

Radcliffe-Brown noted that joking relationships often exist among equals, where each person is expected to make fun of the other. Evelyn Waugh and Nancy Mitford, Hope and Crosby, the friends who kibbitz each other, the in-laws who joke at each other's expense, the colleagues who trade off playful jabs, all demonstrate a momentary superiority through their wit. But this is of secondary importance if a return joke is expected and even invited. The momentary joke is less important than the stable relationship that is maintained and strengthened.[9]

Because laughter assumes an agreement about core values, joke telling also signals common sympathies. The wit and listener share not only the joke but also a common way of looking at the world. People who regard radical feminists or political correctness as ridiculous are apt to share many other beliefs as well. They are less ready to quarrel and more likely to form bonds of attachment. By contrast, an inability to laugh together signals either a profound disagreement about basic values or a mutual antipathy.

A Communitarian Perspective

While laughter promotes trust between wit and listener, it does so by isolating the butt. In that sense, it might be thought to weaken the bonds of solidarity that connect us to other people and to our communities. We must therefore ask whether laughter's gains come at the cost of weakening communitarian sentiment. We begin by describing an ideal community.

The Loss of Community

When a child reaches the age of seven in Siena, he takes his First Communion and swears loyalty to his *contrada*. Time out of mind, the city has been divided into seventeen *contrade*—neighborhoods that serve as focal points for local loyalties. Formally, each *contrada* is charged with presenting an entry in the twice-yearly *Palio,* a horse race around the square in the center of the city. There are parades, with flag-twirlers for each *contrada,* immense feasts, and then the race itself—a dangerous affair, in which horse and rider are sometimes hurt. Most of the city attends, packed into the square. When the race is over, members of the winning *contrada* erupt in an explosion of joy. Its name is shouted throughout the city, and both rider and horse are embraced and led to a feast.

City life in Siena is a far cry from that of decaying American cities. It is now the fashion to decry middle-class flight from inner cities to remote suburbs, to which one commutes along overcrowded roads while listening to talk radio, arriving at last at the cul-de-sac one calls home, miles from any restaurant, shop, or sidewalk. It was not always thus. A few generations back, local neighborhoods flourished in every American city. While not Sienese *contrade,* these were communities with strong local institutions in which one knew one's neighbors. The loss of urban communities has meant a decline in the sense of attachment to and sympathy with others that is called solidarity and that is one of the most basic of human goods.

It is easy to sentimentalize the change and to misdiagnose its cause. Many suburban communities are perfectly pleasant, with thriving libraries, little theaters, and ethnic restaurants. As compared to the range of choices offered all but the richest Americans forty years ago, the average suburbanite has a wealth of cultural options. Nor are the reasons for the change mysterious. The rise of "diversity" has nothing to do with it, for America was more diverse a hundred years ago. Indeed, diversity promotes solidarity. It permits people to satisfy their desire for community by choosing to live among people who resemble them. Some people foolishly believe that diversity means that every street in every neighborhood in every city must have the same percentage of Hispanics and opera lovers. But that is uniformity, not diversity. When it comes to creating communities, diversity *between* neighborhoods is far more valuable than diversity *within* them.

With diversity comes rivalry between groups, and rivalry might seem antisocial. However, rivalry and solidarity go hand in hand. I choose one religion in preference to another. I leave one Internet discussion group to join another. I root for the local high school and against the other team. It is a mistake to think that, in assessing solidarity, only the most encompassing communities count, and that laughter is necessarily suspect because it treats the butt as an outsider. What this forgets, in a world of natural rivalries, is that we cannot take the side of one community without taking sides against another. In the *Palio,* we cheer our *contrada;* we hope its rivals lose. We laugh with friends in our *contrada* at butts from other *contrade,* and the between-*contrade* communitarian loss is dwarfed by the within-*contrada* communitarian gain.

Communities of Laughter

The communitarian objection to laughter is therefore unpersuasive. The concern for the butt's isolation ignores the fact that every community excludes nonmembers. If no one is to be excluded, then all communities must be disbanded. And the same is true of laughter. If there are to be no butts, there will also be no laughter, and we will have sacrificed the communities of wit and listener that laughter creates.

Consider the joke told to a friend. The listener's failure to laugh, when common ties of affection were presumed, will be felt a betrayal. "You take the butt's side against me!" This feeling is particularly strong when the joke was told to establish a tie between wit and listener, and the unhearing butt is not closely implicated or deserving of sympathy. What would we think of a friend who objects to our Newfie jokes? His expression of distaste did not establish a bond between himself and Newfoundlanders: There were none in the room, and neither of us know any or harbor any particular feelings about them (droll though they might be).

Instead, he has frayed the relationship of solidarity he once had with me. This is not an act easily defended on communitarian grounds by anyone with normal human sympathies.

The only communities that count are those formed by ordinary, sensible people, with real passions and preferences, who naturally find the same kind of people amusing. We laugh at the butt, it is true, but we laugh at him together. Our mutual laughter seals a pact by which we participate in a community with similar tastes and aspirations. And with similar butts. I cannot imagine a community worthy of the name that does not share its butts in common.

Laughter is a supreme communitarian device because of the natural instinct to share it. Without an audience, comedy is incomplete. We may fully enjoy a piece of music without wanting to share it; but we no sooner hear a joke than we imagine telling it to a friend. With an audience, W. C. Fields's aversion for children is hilarious. (Do you believe in clubs for young people, Fields was asked. "Only when kindness fails," he answered.) Without an audience, a distaste for children is merely unpleasant.

As a social institution, comedy resembles religion. If religious impulses were entirely satisfied through private worship, there would be no need for church or synagogue. Indeed, if all that were required was a personal connection between the individual and God ("I and Thou"), the existence of public institutions of worship might seem puzzling. We could as easily pray at home, alone in a room. As places of public worship do exist, however, we must assume that religious experiences are more intense when they are shared with others. The impulse to solidarity is stronger still in laughter, which begs to be shared. The most profound religious experience—Pascal's night of fire, for example—is often passed in private. But this is never true of laughter. Even the most amusing play is funnier when seen in a theater than when read at home.

One of the most sparkling of communities was that found in Urbino, at the court of Guido of Montefeltro, which Yeats called a "mirror-school of courtesies / Where wit and beauty learned their trade."[10] Years later one of its members, Baldassare Castiglione, wrote an account of the court that became the best description of what it means to be a gentleman. In *The Book of the Courtier*, Castiglione recounted a dialogue among a group of brilliant wits and nobles about the special qualities sought in a *cortegiano* at the most polished court of the Italian High Renaissance. The courtier should be well-dressed but not ostentatious, amorous but not gross. He should be conscious of his honor and intrepid in defense of his lord. More than anything Castiglione emphasized the courtier's good humor, his jests and "merrie pranks."

> There was then to bee heard pleasant communications and merie conceits, and in everie man's countenance a man might perceive painted a loving jocundnesse. So that this house truely might wel be called the very Mansion place of mirth and joy.[11]

The greatest part of the book is devoted to amiable laughter. Wit was offered up like a gift between people who, out of "loving jocundnesse," sought each other's happiness through shared laughter. Those who wish to build a community could do worse than to study *The Courtier*.

What Is a Community?

Laughter's ability to cement a community is easily appreciated in a crowd, during a feast or carnival, when we are jostled about by our neighbors and share their hilarity. But where is the community when we read a satiric novel or poem? We do not know the author; he might be long dead; we no longer read novels aloud to each other. Something seems amiss. It is not that our notion of laughter is too broad, however; instead, our idea of community is too narrow. Physical presence is neither sufficient nor necessary to constitute a community. When we travel, we are still joined to our towns and families; on weekdays, we are still members of our churches; after graduation, we remain loyal sons of our colleges; on vacation, we are still members of our profession; off-line, we are still subscribers to our listservs. The bonds are invisible, yet they still hold us; the dialogue is imaginary, yet it is still real.

Through an imagined community,[12] we may remain in communion with parents and spouses long after their deaths, and these ties may be stronger than any we have with the living.[13] In Pascal Quignard's *Tous les matins du monde*, the austere Sieur de Sainte Colombe's inner dialogue with his dead wife is more intense than the worldly Martin Marais's merely physical liaison with Sainte Colombe's daughter. The Jansenist is more passionate than the courtier.

In the same way, laughter may be shared among members of an invisible, ideal community. Think again of the pleasure one takes, on hearing a joke, at the thought of retelling it to someone else. One takes just the same pleasure from writing or reading a polished satire. All that is needed is the expectation of a sympathetic audience when the pleasure is shared on a retelling.

We are apt to regard solidarity as a solemn rite of communitarian virtue, in which we formally express our ties to other people, like an oath of fealty to a *contrada*. But solidarity is not a joyless expression of civic virtue; instead it is the honest pleasure taken from the company of others, and shows itself most strongly in the laughter of close friends at a jest.

Few experiences are as sociable as laughter. The joy of listening to a Bach fugue is complete, alone in a church. When others arrive, we do not enjoy the music more fully. We might even enjoy it less, when they distract us. This was the truth that Glenn Gould expressed when he announced the death of the audience; henceforth music would be heard at home and in private, and not in the concert hall. Similarly, we do not appreciate a painting more when seen in a gallery than on our living room wall. And if we go to a gallery, do we not linger longer in front of the painting that the crowd has passed over?

Reading was at one time a communitarian activity. The Romans read aloud, often to an audience. Since they were reading a highly inflected word order, without breaks between the words, *praelectio* or spoken recitation greatly aided comprehension. Those who could read silently, like St. Ambrose, were prodigies of learning, and all Milan came to witness this feat of erudition.[14] In time, the elegant oral performance was replaced by the private consumption of *lectio in silentio*. Literature itself changed, with clarity preferred to sonority.

Today, only great poetry shares with satire the need for retelling. The poem asks to be memorized so that it can be recited before others. And when this happens, when we listen and allow the poem to take hold of us, we enter into a world as different from ordinary life as the play world of laughter. This is the world of solemnity, formality, and grandiloquence, the world of Racine's tragic drama, which offers "an image of what life might be like if it were lived at all times on a plane of high decorum and if it were at all instants fully responsive to the obligations of nobility."[15] When all life is ordinary life, *la vie et rien d'autre,* when life's poetry and drama are forgotten, then a community of high culture has disappeared. Bach may be appreciated alone in a room, but poetry needs company, and is thus the more fragile. The same is true of high satire, which requires a community of educated readers. The boundaries of the class might stretch across borders and generations. Yet were they wholly imaginary, were we never to meet anyone for years on end who shared our delight in refined satire, then our membership in the ideal community would lapse as well. That is why the attack on the canon of Western culture, ostensibly democratic in purpose, is so deeply anticommunitarian.

Communities of high culture were stronger in the past, and are stronger today in other countries. I once walked down Pigalle, past the strip clubs with their revealing posters, and past the barkers who try to nudge passersby inside. One barker was particularly insistent, and I looked away as I passed him. And after I did so I looked up at the posters. Evidently I reminded the barker of a famous hypocrite. "*Ah, regarde,*" he called after me. "He ignores me but he looks at the poster. *Le Tartuffe!*" There is something to be said for the way in which a French classical education builds a community.

14 Conclusion

Quia ignoro, adoro.
Nicholas of Cusa, *De deo abscondito*

My project has been a very conservative one. Modern scholarship is subversive of meaning and value, but I have argued that laughter signals meaningful and valuable information. The Positive thesis holds that laughter reveals the laugher's sense of superiority to a butt who is thereby degraded, and the Normative thesis asserts that the message of superiority is more often than not correct. In general, we should attend to laughter's message of the good life.

I sought to defend the Positive thesis by arguing that, in every apparent counterexample, a signal of superiority may always be found. However innocent the laughter might seem, a mocking wit always lurks in the background, hugging his sides as he ridicules a butt. By itself, the sense of superiority cannot raise a laugh. But if superiority is not a sufficient condition for laughter, it is a necessary one.

Like Hobbes, one might accept the Positive and reject the Normative thesis. Those who laugh might think themselves superior and really be very inferior after all. But it would be difficult to argue that laughter signals valuable standards of conduct, as the Normative thesis asserts, and reject the Positive thesis. There would be no reason to believe that our laughter reveals a true superiority if a mere incongruity might provoke it. That is why, even though my primary interest was the Normative thesis, I began by defending the Positive thesis.

Whether they recognize it or not, those who laugh are moralists, for they uphold a set of comic norms. Our laughter identifies a set of comic vices, and the sting of laughter contains its own sanction for transgressors. When we turn the signal about to ask how we might immunize ourselves from laughter, we reveal a set of comic virtues. Laughter communicates a thick set of standards about self-fulfillment. These standards are very different from legal, religious, and moral norms, for laughter teaches us how to extract joy from life by holding the joyless up to ridicule. Legal and moral rules are concerned with duties to others, but the principal beneficiary of laughter is the butt himself.

Life Considered as a Fine Art

Laughter norms invite us to think of life as a fine art. The best of lives have a harmonious composition that naturally pleases, surprising us with sudden joy. The moralist and the lawyer cannot explain the pleasure we take from living well, any more than they can explain the appeal of a timeless work of art. But the artist might, for a life lived poorly is ugly. And so might the comic, since laughter is an invaluable method of teaching us how to live well.

Like comedy, aesthetics requires a sense of play. "Man is only serious with the agreeable, the good, the moral duty, and the perfect," said Schiller, "but with beauty he plays." Schiller did not mean to trivialize aesthetics, for he thought play indispensable to man. Reason cannot tell us how to fulfill our natures. Only play does so, by supporting "the whole fabric of aesthetic art, and the still more difficult art of living." Man is "only wholly Man when he is playing."[1] Through play we enter into a realm of freedom, where choices are unfettered and results are not predetermined.

Schiller thought that the modern preoccupation with political obligation to the exclusion of deeper sources of joy was profoundly dehumanizing, and saw in aesthetics a way to cure the wound of modernity. By developing our aesthetic sense we might recover a more integrated sense of human nature, where play, prayer, and art might flourish. The turn to aestheticism is largely forgotten today, but it resounded throughout the nineteenth century and strongly influenced Baudelaire, Ruskin, Arnold, and Wilde, all of whom shared a hatred for the ugliness of machine rules that lack an understanding of what it is to be human. In this respect, Bergson may be seen, at the very end of the century, as the last representative of aesthetic humanism.

The closeness of the analogy between art and laughter may be observed in Ruskin's defense of the Gothic. Ruskin thought that the

Gothic represented the purest form of artistic creativity, and defined it in terms that also describe laughter. Like the Gothic, laughter may seem *savage*, and if the word seems harsh Ruskin saw no reproach in it. Instead, the Gothic offered a savage delight and revealed "the strong spirit of men who may not . . . bask in dreamy benignity." The Gothic was also *changeful*, for "the accurate and methodical habits in daily life are seldom characteristic of those who either quickly perceive, or richly possess, the creative powers of art." Or of laughter, which is withheld from accountancy. Next, said Ruskin, the Gothic is *natural*, for like laughter it prefers truth to mere prettiness. When heard in a carnival, laughter also shares the Gothic's taste for the *grotesque*. Finally, laughter and art are both *redundant*, in the sense that they represent a superfluity over quotidian needs. Summing up, Ruskin regarded the Gothic as the epitome of the artistic impulse that seeks to transcend the mechanical and ordinary in life. In terms that also describe laughter, he praised the Gothic's nobility, in which is found

> a magnificent enthusiasm, which feels as if it never could do enough to reach the fulness of its ideal; an unselfishness of sacrifice, which would rather cast fruitless labour before the altar than stand idle in the market; and, finally, a profound sympathy with the fullness and wealth of the material universe.[2]

In Ruskin's later writings and in Arnold's *Culture and Anarchy* the aesthetic movement stood athwart a modern age of machine life and degraded culture. Both writers had lost their faith and thought that religion no longer commanded a sufficient appeal to hold modernism at bay. In that case, they said, let beauty serve in place of religion. The aesthetic project was a colossal failure, of course. The Pre-Raphaelite Brotherhood did not retard socialism or fascism by a day, and we no longer pay the idea that it might have done so the compliment of remembering it. This is hardly surprising, since aesthetic tastes are seldom as strong as religious impulses, and one would not expect art to succeed where religion failed. But what of laughter, which is both more deeply and widely experienced than aesthetic impulses? Nietzsche believed that laughter might express our superiority to a debased modernism, and Bergson thought that it held the secret of forgotten joys. Neither idea is as foolish as the high aestheticism of Ruskin and Arnold.

The Dream of a Unified Field

From Kierkegaard on, morality, art, and religion have been seen as distinct dimensions of life, with frontiers that separate each from the other.[3] Yet the differences trouble us, and we seek an overarching perspective that erases all borders. There is a natural desire for integrity and unity, in which the love of beauty does not betray religious sentiments, and in which both impulses are harmonized with ethical imperatives.

Not infrequently, two dimensions are conjoined. A. J. Balfour thought that morality was parasitic upon religion and that a decline in religious sentiments in the nineteenth century would result in a moral decline in the twentieth. Like Balfour, George Santayana was not a believer, but he nevertheless thought that the arts flourished under religion and went to church to enjoy the aesthetic pleasure of the Tridentine mass. Aesthetics might even be employed to win the apostate back to his religion, as Chateaubriand sought to do in his *Génie du Christianisme*. Finally, those who abandon religion might seek a unity of aesthetic and moral impulses, as Arnold and Nietzsche did in their very different ways.

A unity of all three dimensions is more elusive, however. The part of morality that is excluded from the morality of laughter is iconoclastic and insists upon the priority of its rules over a morally indifferent beauty and a God who tolerates the existence of evil. There is thus a natural tendency for the ethical to insist on paramountcy over the aesthetic and the religious, and in the last century the latter two dimensions were quite submerged by the former. And as individuals were exempt from personal blame, in an era of moral relativism, the only questions left were political.

The spirit of the age is journalistic, and journalism flattens life down to the merely political. Conservatives bemoan the retreat from high culture but misdiagnose the cause. It is not so much that the canon has been abandoned, but that we no longer share the sense of transcendence that inspired Donne and Crashaw, Tallis and Bach, Bellini and Carpaccio, or makes them comprehensible to us. The anguished passion that finds its resolution through a mystical unity, the communion with those who speak to some secret part of our heart, the reverence for things that are hidden, all these inform our high culture; but for those without a sense of sanctity they are like a foreign language for which we lack the code.

We live today in a world of immanence, of the here-and-now, whose most revered principles are "self-evident" and not revealed. Like the rowers of Thomas Eakins, everything is on the surface, man and scull, as accessible and efficient as a machine. The intuition that a transcendent reality underlies ordinary experience, which Christians express through the Mystery of the Incarnation and Romantics through their awe of nature, is lost when the spirit is no longer made flesh and the world is no longer sacred or magical. The world of wonders recedes, and Max Weber's world of disenchantment (*Entzauberung*) takes its place. Wordsworth saw the problem coming, and blamed commerce–getting and spending. But balance sheets had very little to do with it, for a merchant like Joyce's Leopold Bloom might relive a Homeric epic in a walk through Dublin. The problem lies elsewhere. If we abandoned the desire and pursuit of the whole, the more plausible culprit is the modern tendency to reduce every question down to the banal level of politics.

No one satirized the modern obsession with politics more effectively than Théophile Gautier in the Preface to *Mademoiselle de Maupin*. Of what good is a novel, he asked? Its material use is to line the author's pockets with gold; and its spiritual use is that, when we read it, we cannot read useful and progressive newspapers. Indeed, Gautier thought his fellow subjects owed a great debt to Charles X, who had promoted civilization by suppressing newspapers. Before there were newspapers, a quatrain would occupy Paris for a week and a first performance for six months.

One hundred years from now, modernism's turn to politics might well seem as ridiculous as Arnold's low churchmen do today. Yet how are we to pursue a unified field in an age that denies the possibility of integration? The temptation is to retreat from the world to avoid the corrosion of a modernity that seems to deny the validity of at least one and sometimes all three dimensions. However, it is self-defeating to respond to the death of communities of high culture by withdrawing from all communities. We must make our way back slowly, seeking enchantment not outside but within the world, and I cannot think we will succeed if we do not remember the poor creature, laughter.

Our laughter affirms a morality of joy that aspires to the condition of aesthetics, and the canonization of laughter and laughter's joy also suggests a link to religious impulses. Laughter's goal is a wholeness that is unsatisfied if any source of joy is unexploited. At times laughter might perhaps be devilish, as Baudelaire recognized. Yet if laughter is engendered by the fall, it may also become the means of salvation.*

One of the special gifts of Heaven, said Dante, is holy laughter, which is death to ordinary mortals. In Canto xxi of the *Paradiso,* Beatrice explains why she does not laugh. If I did, she tells Dante, you would be reduced to ashes, as Semele was when she saw Zeus. To withstand such laughter, the poet must first experience Christ or Mary directly. Holy laughter is the laughter of the universe and a badge of the divine vision. Through its joy we approach the divine, even as Dante's earthly love for Beatrice was the forerunner of divine love. In laughter the word is made flesh and we share in the Mystery of the Incarnation.

Laughter might be likened to the Gift of the Holy Spirit (Acts 2:1–4), the special grace that provides an earthly substitute for the Gift of Eternal Life (Romans 6:23). The first great mystery of the Church, at its founding, was how it might continue after Christ's Death and Ascension. From where could it derive the strength to persevere, through all of the trials and persecutions it knew it must face? The answer, in the Mystery of the Pentecost, was the Gift of the Holy Spirit. The Holy Spirit is called the Paraclete or counselor, and His gifts are often represented as those of the missionary or lawyer: fortitude, confidence, and forensic skill. Yet this does not begin to capture the fulfillment and release of the human spirit that rejoices in the Holy Spirit.[4] What is missing is how James Joyce saw his epiphanies, or how Pier Paolo Pasolini portrayed the Pentecost in *The Gospel According to St. Matthew,* through laughter. And those who reject laughter risk committing the unforgivable sin against the Holy Spirit.

Comedy and tragedy both affirm joy, comedy through its presence and tragedy through its absence. There is no tragedy without a sense of joys withheld, no Fall without an Eden. A religion informed by a tragic sense of life, like Unamuno's Catholicism, must therefore be joyful and founded upon "the frenzied love of life, the love that would have life to be unending,"[5] a love that is tragically betrayed on earth and satisfied only through religion. Lovers of laughter who pursue joy down every dark and crooked alley, only to be broken in their quest, must like Wilde and Waugh come at last to the promise of everlasting joy, a joy we

---

*"Car les phénomènes engendrées par la chute deviendront les moyens du rachat." Charles Baudelaire, *De l'essence du rire,* 528.

glimpse through laughter; either that, or abandon the quest and settle on mere unbelief or the small-souled man's Laodician religion of journalism and petty political reform.

Waugh suggested that the great mystery is not whether God created the world, but why He did so. Why is there anything? To perform duties, perhaps? But what kind of duties? It cannot be to serve other people. Assume away the world and they would not exist either. To love and adore God, then? That is what my Baltimore Catechism said. But what need had God for adoration, when He was already complete? Only joy answers the fundamental question of existence, since it stills the question. An explosion of laughter, like the dance of the Hassidim, destroys philosophic doubts and gives us the confidence to know that we are worthy of life and do not wholly die.

Nevertheless, the dream of a unified field must, like every earthly wish, disappoint in the end. A morality of laughter might conjoin aesthetic and religious impulses, but cannot embrace all of our moral intuitions. A comic society that has lost its moral sense is as risible as an aesthetic society that has lost its conscience, like Thomas de Quincey's Society of Connoisseurs. De Quincey's 1827 essay "On Murder as One of the Fine Arts" wonderfully mocked an amoral aestheticism through ironic praise for the artistic murderer. When crime is viewed from a purely aesthetic perspective, it becomes clear that "all the Cains were men of genius" and that the canon of literature requires rethinking ("Milton was an amateur"). History also needs to be rewritten ("Greece, even in the age of Pericles, produced no murder, or at least none is recorded of the slightest merit"). De Quincey's aesthetes are delighted with their new discovery. But then a note of doubt sets in. Might a murder, however artistic, possibly be *wrong?* A novel thought, and the Society of Connoisseurs ponders whether an artistic murder might be condemned on moral grounds. Surprisingly, the answer is yes. "If once a man indulges himself in murder, very soon he comes to think little of robbing; and from robbing he comes next to drinking and sabbath-breaking, and from that to incivility and procrastination." This in a world where there is no morality and only aesthetics. So too, a world of laughter without morality is ludicrously incomplete—though not so ludicrous that the morality of laughter could substitute for the morality of reason.

Some defenders of laughter have sought to meet this objection by polishing it up. Yes, they say, vulgar comedy might be bawdy and celebrate low morals; but if the listener would only study more refined comedies he would find that they are more pleasing and their laughter more intense. He might turn to the polished French stage, where vice is held up for ridicule and butts are cardboard figures.

If only it were that simple. Comic and moral norms do not always overlap, and any attempt to assimilate the two must betray one or the other. Either morals are lowered by defining deviancy down, or laughter is lost by defining comedy up. This was the sin against laughter committed by George Meredith in his criticism of low comedy. Farce was simply a fumbling comic vulgarity, satire the work of a storage of bile,[6] and irony a complete immoralist. A grim philosophy, that trades off exuberant laughter for tepid smiles. Even with Molière, just how often does a moral lesson draw a laugh? Stendhal tested this at a performance of *Tartuffe*. The play was brilliantly acted, and there was frequent applause. But laughter? Twice only, and very lightly each time.[7]

Any attempt to assimilate comic to moral norms is bound to fail. If the gods do anything unseemly, said Euripedes, they are not gods at all. But the gods of laughter are not so nice: if *they* do nothing unseemly, they are not gods at all. Nevertheless, immoral laughter sometimes signals the true superiority of the Normative thesis. Such laughter reminds us that life is not to be judged from an ethical perspective alone and that a self-regarding morality of laughter might on occasion trump a wholly other-regarding morality of reason.

The great symbol of moral purity in Romantic literature is Bernardin de St. Pierre's Virginie. His *Paul et Virginie* describes the idyllic innocence of teenage castaways who grow to adulthood without losing their innocence. Baudelaire imagined how Virginie might fare were she to return to civilization. She leaves her island paradise and now must learn the ways of Paris, that great city. She wanders into the Palais Royal, the haunt of gamblers and prostitutes, and stops to look at a cartoon in a shop window. A Gillray, perhaps, full of vivid colors, violence, and G——d——mns. Virginie pauses before the cartoon, unable to understand it. The strange expressions—why would anyone draw another person that way? In time, said Baudelaire, she will lose her innocence, and then she will laugh, along with the rest of us.

Like Virginie, the truly innocent do not hear the world's laughter, and since they miss the signal of comic vice must be risible themselves. In *Paul et Virginie* itself, she dies—silly prude—because she refuses to disrobe in a shipwreck. We admire her purity, but there is still something repellent about an innocence born of ignorance and folly. Could we ever wish to be risible? We do not wish to be immoral, and we do not wish to be risible, and we really would not want to be put to an election between moral and comic vice.

Watteau portrayed the choice in his *Pierrot*. A player, dressed all in white, "pâle comme la lune, mystérieux comme le silence,"* stares blankly at us with sheep's eyes of deepest innocence and stupidity. Behind him a group of players tug at an ass, ridden by a man in black who smirks at the scene before him. There is no question with whom we more closely identify. Try as we might, we can never prefer virtuous imbecility to sophisticated wit. And that is how we must understand the painting. Watteau loved the *commedia dell'arte*, and no doubt laughed at Harlequin as much as the rest of us. What he chiefly loved, however, were the ancien régime's elegant fops and *jolies marquises*, and his *Pierrot* should be seen as a satire on the Rousseauian cult of simplicity. Our laughter at Virginie and Pierrot and at all unsophisticated innocence reminds us of the costs of trading off one set of virtues for another.

What is needed is balance. Laughter directs us to a middle way of comic virtue between extremes of comic vice. Similarly, we need to strike a balance between moral and comic virtues, between duties to others and the personal pursuit of happiness and joy. We have accorded too great a weight to abstract, ethical impulses and should attend more closely to the morality of laughter. To do so, we need only listen to laughter and seek to decode its message about how we should live.

Nevertheless, not everyone will heed the message of laughter, for how one feels about it must depend upon prior moral and political beliefs. Laughter has a tendency. It takes sides. It does not pick its butts haphazardly; and for his part the natural butt must fear and loathe laughter. Others might plead for broad toleration when it comes to ridicule, but he is not taken in.

We end, therefore, without false hopes that we have convinced the determined butt to abandon his comic vices. For the rest of us, however, especially those who shrink with horror before the dour, rationalist nightmares of machine law, machine art, and machine cities, we have an

---

*"Pale as the moon, mysterious as silence." Charles Baudelaire, "De l'essence du rire," in *Œuvres complètes* (Paris: Gallimard, 1976), 2:525, 538.

answer to *Lucky Jim*'s question: what can be done to slow the progress of the pathology I have described. Sound policy analysis and artistic criticism can identify the costs and ugliness of machine life, but cannot arrest the progress of the malady. Is there anything further that can be done? As it happens, there is.

We can laugh.

Notes

Preface

1. Roger Kimball, "'The Two Cultures' Today," in Roger Kimball, ed., *Against the Grain* (Chicago: Ivan R. Dee, 1995), 391, 392. For a balanced view of the dispute, see Lionel Trilling, "The Leavis-Snow Controversy," in *The Moral Obligation to Be Intelligent* (New York: Farrar, Straus, Giroux, 2000), 402.

2. Clifford Geertz, *Local Knowledge: Further Essays in Interpretive Anthropology* (New York: Basic Books, 1983), 160.

3. Roy Bhaskar, *Plato etc: The Problems of Philosophy and Their Resolution* (London: Verso, 1994).

Chapter 1. Laughter as Superiority

1. Sigmund Freud, "Wit and Its Relation to the Unconscious," in *The Basic Writings of Sigmund Freud* (New York: Modern Library, 1995), 599, 673, 620.

2. J. Y. T. Greig, *The Psychology of Laughter and Comedy* (New York: Cooper Square, 1923), 100–105.

3. Lawrence La Fave, Jay Haddad, and William A. Maesen, "Superiority, Enhanced Self-Esteem, and Perceived Incongruity Humor Theory," in Antony J. Chapman and Hugh C. Foot, eds., *Humor and Laughter: Theory, Research, and Applications* (New Brunswick, N.J.: Transaction, 1996), 63.

4. *Poetics* 5.1449a. There is a more extensive discussion of tragedy than comedy in the *Poetics*, which gave rise to the tradition of a lost second book on comedy—the subject of Umberto Eco's *The Name of the Rose*. A later fragment on comedy in the *Tractatus Coisilianus* appears to derive from Aristotle, though its author is unknown. See Lane Cooper, *An Aristotelian Theory of Comedy* (New York: Harcourt, Brace, 1922). For an attempt to flesh out an Aristotelian theory of comedy, see Richard Janko, *Aristotle on Comedy: Towards a Reconstruction of Poetics II* (Berkeley: University of California Press, 1984); Aristotle, *Poetics* (Richard Janko, ed.) (Indianapolis: Hackett, 1987).

5. Descartes's physical laughter is a joy mingled with hate in which we note some small fault in another. By contrast, his intellectual laughter—"modest raillery"—is a virtuous gaiety that usefully condemns vices by making them appear ridiculous. In both cases, laughter signals a butt's inferiority. See Susan James, *Passion and Action* (Oxford: Clarendon, 1998); Daniel C. Dennett, *Kinds of Minds: Toward an Understanding of Consciousness* (New York: Basic Books, 1996), 72–73.

6. Thomas Hobbes, *Leviathan* (London: Penguin, 1968 [1651]), 161.

7. Thomas Hobbes, "Human Nature," in *Human Nature and De Corpore Politico* (Oxford: Oxford University Press, 1994 [1640]), 48.

8. Hobbes, *Leviathan*, 125.

9. Tertullian, "Of Spectacles," in *I Translations of the Writings of the Fathers: The Writings of Tertullian* (Alexander Roberts and James Donaldson, eds.) (Edinburgh: Clark, 1869), 8–35. See also St. Thomas Aquinas, *Summa III* Supp. Q. 94, art. 1.

10. William Hazlitt, *Lectures on the English Comic Writers* (London: Oxford University Press, 1907 [1818]), 7.

11. Henri Bergson, *Le rire* (Paris: Presses Universitaires de France, 1940 [1900]).

12. Samuel Johnson, *The Critical Opinions of Samuel Johnson* (New York: Russell and Russell, 1953), 491.

13. Northrop Frye, *The Anatomy of Criticism: Four Essays* (Princeton: Princeton University Press, 1957), 223.

14. "Son crime est plutôt une punition des dieux qu'un movement de sa volonté." Racine, *Phèdre* (Paris: Livre de Poche, 1985), Préface, 13. On Jansenism's righteous sinner, see Leszek Kolakowski, *God Owes Us Nothing: A Brief Remark on Pascal's Religion and on the Spirit of Jansenism* (Chicago: University of Chicago Press, 1995), 9–14. "Jésus-Christ est venu . . . justifier les pécheures et laisser les justes dans leurs péchés." Blaise Pascal, *Pensées* 220, in *Œuvres complètes* (Paris: Pléiade, 2000), 2:623.

15. George Steiner, *The Death of Tragedy* (New Haven: Yale University Press, 1996 [1961]), 8.

16. *The Essays, Articles and Reviews of Evelyn Waugh* (Donat Gallagher, ed.) (London: Methuen, 1983), 304.

17. Elizabeth Longford, *Wellington: Pillar of State* (New York: Harper and Row, 1972), 77.

18. I take up the question again in chapter 9. For an overview of the debate, see John Searle, *The Rediscovery of the Mind* (Cambridge: MIT Press, 1992). For contrary views, see Daniel Dennett, *Consciousness Explained* (New York: Little, Brown, 1991), and (less provocatively) Owen Flanagan, *Consciousness Reconsidered* (Cambridge: MIT Press, 1992).

19. See John Searle, *The Mystery of Consciousness* (New York: New York Review, 1997), xiv.

Chapter 2. The Elements of Laughter

1. Animal laughter, said Beattie, "arises, not from any sentiment, or perception of ludicrous ideas, but from some bodily feeling, or sudden impulse, on what is called the animal spirits, proceeding, or seeming to proceed, from the operation of causes purely material." James Beattie, "On Laughter and Ludicrous Composition," in *Essays: On Poetry and Music* (Roger J. Robinson, ed.) (London: Routledge/Thoemmes, 1996 [1779]), 305.

2. See Arthur Koestler, *The Act of Creation* (London: Penguin, 1989 [1964]), 31.

3. Christine R. Harris, "The Mystery of Ticklish Laughter," *American Scientist* (July–August 1999), 344.

4. Francis Hutcheson, "Reflections upon Laughter," in John Moreall, ed., *The Philosophy of Laughter and Humor* (Albany: SUNY Press, 1987 [1750]), 26, 29.

5. Robert R. Provine, *Laughter: A Scientific Investigation* (New York: Viking, 2000), 75–80.

6. Henri Bergson, *Le rire*, 3. Addison's *Spectator* no. 203 made the same point.

7. On the infectiousness of laughter, see Robert R. Provine, "Contagious Laughter: Laughter Is a Sufficient Stimulus for Laughs and Smiles," *Bulletin of the Psychonomic Society* 1 (1992): 30; Antony J. Chapman, "Social Aspects of Humorous Laughter," in Chapman and Foot, *Humor and Laughter*, 155.

8. Jacob Burckhardt, *The Civilization of the Renaissance in Italy* (New York: Harper and Row, 1958 [1929]), 1:269–70.

9. W. B. Yeats, *Autobiography* (New York: Macmillan, 1965 [1916]), 234. See also Roger Shattuck, *The Banquet Years* (New York: Vintage, rev. ed., 1968), 205–9.

10. Robertson Davies, "Afterword," in Stephen Leacock, *Literary Lapses* (Toronto: McClelland and Stewart, 1957), 156.

11. Beattie began by noting that superiority was not a sufficient condition for laughter, and then announced his rival theory. "Laughter arises from the view of two or more inconsistent, unsuitable, or incongruous parts or circumstances, considered as united in one complex object or assemblage." Francis Hutcheson had earlier argued that laughter was caused by an "opposition of dignity and meanness," but this was too narrow, said Beattie. Instead, the opposition was between "relation and want of relation, united, or supposed to be united, in the same assemblage." James Beattie, "On Laughter and Ludicrous Composition," in *Essays: On Poetry and Music* (Roger J. Robinson, ed.) (London: Routledge/ Thoemmes, 1996 [1779]), 320, 321.

12. Immanuel Kant, *Critique of Judgment* (trans. J. C. Meredith) (Oxford: Oxford University Press, 1952), 199. See also M. Clark, "Humour and Incongruity," *Philosophy* 20 (1991): 45. Schopenhauer has also been identified as an incongruity theorist, though with less accuracy. Like Kant, Schopenhauer thought laughter arose from the apprehension of the incongruity between an intellectual concept and what we perceive. Arthur Schopenhauer, *The World as Will and Idea*, Book I sec. 13 (trans. R. B. Haldane and J. Kemp) (New York: Doubleday, 1961). Unlike Kant, however, Schopenhauer did not see the perception of incongruity as an intellectual affair. In the conflict between what is perceived and what is thought, what is perceived is always right. Laughter is an atavistic cry of triumph, and even an assertion of superiority, against one's reason. Schopenhauer's incongruity also signals a message about how life should be lived, as the superiority thesis maintains. Comedy affirms a "will to live" and looks forward to a future in which the vices we laugh at are corrected. As an explanation of laughter, this resembles Bergson's *Le rire* more closely than Kant's incongruity theory.

13. Sigmund Freud, "Wit and Its Relation to the Unconscious," in *The Basic Writings of Sigmund Freud* (New York: Modern Library, 1995), 703. Herbert Spencer offered a more general relief explanation of laughter. Nervous excitement seeks a release, he said, and laughter is one way in which surplus psychic

energy can be discharged. "Physiology of Laughter," *Macmillan's Magazine* 1 (1860): 395.

14. Lane Cooper inferred that Aristotle believed that, like tragedy, comedy purged the emotions through a catharsis. See *An Aristotelian Theory of Comedy* (New York: Harcourt, Brace, 1922), 131.

15. Max Eastman, *The Enjoyment of Laughter* (New York: Simon and Schuster, 1936), 3. See also Max Eastman, *The Sense of Humor* (New York: Scribner, 1921); James Sully, *An Essay on Laughter: Its Forms, Its Causes, Its Development, and Its Value* (London: Longmans Green, 1902), 145, 257, 411.

16. "Humor, in a good sense, means the talent for being able to put oneself at will into a certain frame of mind in which everything is estimated on lines that go quite off the beaten track." Immanuel Kant, *Critique of Judgment* I.1, 54 (trans. J. C. Meredith) (Oxford: Oxford University Press, 1952), 203. For an analysis of the need for an element of playfulness in joke settings, see W. F. Fry, *Sweet Madness: A Study of Humor* (Palo Alto, Calif.: Pacific Press, 1963).

17. Hugo Rahner, *Man at Play* (London: Burns and Oates, 1965), 66.

18. Charles Lamb, *The Essays of Elia and the Last Essays of Elia* (Garden City, N.Y.: Doubleday, n.d. [1823]), 209–10.

19. Lionel Trilling, *The Middle of the Journey* (New York: Scribner, 1947), 69–70.

Chapter 3. The One Necessary Thing

1. Beattie, 420. John Morreall adopts a similar tack in his description of incongruity as a kind of personal deficiency. Once again this comes down to a risible inferiority. John Morreall, *Taking Laughter Seriously* (Albany: SUNY Press, 1983), 64.

2. Richard Boston, *An Anatomy of Laughter* (London: Collins, 1974), 88.

3. Samuel Johnson, *Poetry and Prose* (Mona Wilson, ed.) (Cambridge: Harvard, 1957), 500.

4. John Aubrey, *Brief Lives* (Bury St. Edmunds: Boydell, 1982), 76.

5. Quoted in Barry Sanders, *Sudden Glory*, 48.

6. Mikhail Bakhtin, *Rabelais and His World* (trans. Hélène Iswolsky) (Bloomington: Indiana University Press, 1984), 12.

7. Friedrich Nietzsche, *The Genealogy of Morals* (trans. Walter Kaufmann) (New York: Vintage, 1967), Book 2, 6.

8. On the origins of Mennipean satire, see Michael Coffey, *Roman Satire* (Melksham, U.K.: Cromwell, 1976). Other prominent examples include Seneca's *Apocolocyntosis* and Petronius' *Satyricon*.

9. Mikhail Bakhtin, *The Dialogic Imagination: Four Essays* (trans. Caryl Emerson and Michael Holquist) (Austin: Texas University Press, 1981), 78–79. See also Mikhail Bakhtin, *Problems of Dostoevsky's Poetics* (trans. Caryl Emerson) (Minneapolis: University of Minnesota Press, 1984), 115; Bakhtin, *Rabelais*, 6.

10. Charles Darwin, *The Expression of the Emotions in Man and Animals* (New York: Oxford University Press, 1998 [1872]), 195. Up to about three years, children's laughter is thought to be simple, unreflective pleasure. Ernest Harms,

"The Development of Humor," *Journal of Abnormal and Social Psychology* 38 (1943): 351.

11. Darwin, *Expression of the Emotions*, 207.

12. Freud, "Wit and Its Relation to the Unconscious," 762.

13. Stephen Leacock, *Humor and Humanity: An Introduction to the Study of Humor* (London: Thornton, Butterworth, 1937), 26–27.

14. Max Eastman, *The Enjoyment of Laughter* (New York: Simon and Schuster, 1936), 331.

15. Frye, *The Anatomy of Criticism*, 164.

16. Perhaps the most amusing thing about The Absurd was the claims made about its staying power. "The Theater of the Absurd was . . . a response to the cultural and social changes of our epoch. That is why it could not and did not harden into just another rigid convention, why the driving force behind it continues to manifest itself in the manifold strivings of a Protean avant-garde." Martin Esslin, *The Theatre of the Absurd* (London: Penguin, 3d ed., 1980), 435. Nothing is so passé as the Protean avant-garde twenty years later.

17. Davis McElroy, *Existentialism and Modern Literature* (Westport, Conn.: Greenwood, 1964), 13.

18. There is an enormous literature on deconstruction. For a hostile but clear account of Derrida and his disciples, see John M. Ellis, *Against Deconstruction* (Princeton: Princeton University Press, 1989).

19. Georges Bataille, *Guilty* (trans. Bruce Boone) (Venice, Calif.: Lapis, 1988 [1961]), 203. "Laughing *in my own way*—and convulsed with laughter—I felt pain, a struggle to the death. It was dreadful and enticing. Which is *healthy*" (*Guilty*, 97). Michel Foucault's analysis of laughter in *Les mots et les choses* is similar.

20. Richard Rorty, *Contingency, Irony, and Solidarity* (Cambridge: Cambridge University Press, 1989), 88.

21. Hélène Cixous, "The Laugh of the Medusa," in *Literature in the Modern World: Critical Essays and Documents* (Dennis Walder, ed.) (Oxford: Oxford University Press, 1990), 316, 326.

22. Michael Ignatieff, *Isaiah Berlin: A Life* (New York: Metropolitan, 1998), 7.

23. Mark Twain, *Pudd'nhead Wilson* (New York: Grove, 1955), 68.

Chapter 4. Objections to the Normative Thesis

1. John Aubrey, *Brief Lives* (Bury St. Edmunds: Boydell, 1982), 307.

2. The term was invented by Robert Trivers to explain patterns of cooperation amongst animals. Robert Trivers, "The Evolution of Reciprocal Altruism," *Quarterly Review of Biology* 35 (1971): 46.

3. James Coleman, *Foundations of Social Theory* (Cambridge: Harvard University Press, 1990), 270–71. On free-rider problems, see Mancur Olson, *The Logic of Collective Action: Public Goods and the Theory of Groups* (Cambridge: Harvard University Press, 1965). Suppose that, in a society of 100 people, a valuable social norm offers a benefit of 1 to each person but costs 10 to produce for a net benefit of 90 to society. Will the norm be produced? The person who takes the

initiative to do so will expend 10 and get 1, for a net loss of 9. Those who hang back and free ride will gain 1 each. Each person has an incentive to wait for someone else to produce the norm. When everyone tries to free ride in this way, the norm will not be created.

4. Suppose that for wit and listener there is cost to joke-telling of 1 apiece but that the status gains are 2 apiece. Since the status gains sum to zero, the status loss for the butt is –4. Net of the costs of joke-telling, the payoffs for the parties will be 1 apiece for wit and listener and –4 for the butt. All parties will have an incentive to join in a winning coalition of wit and listener, and the free-rider problem will be eliminated.

5. Assume again that the status gains and losses of laughter sum to zero. But assume also that, in addition to the private status gains, there are social benefits associated with the enunciation of socially valuable comic norms: Each party derives a social gain is 2 when the natural butt is ridiculed and 0 otherwise. The status gains and losses cancel out, but not the social gains of laughter.

6. Thomas Hobbes, *Leviathan* (London, U.K.: Penguin, 1968), I.6, 125.

7. Thomas Hobbes, "Human Nature," in *Human Nature and De Corpore Politico* (Oxford: Oxford University Press, 1994 [1640]), 55.

8. Earl of Chesterfield, *Letters to His Son* (March 9, 1748) (Washington, D.C.: Walter Dunne, 1901). Similarly, Beattie warned that "a man of breeding will be careful not to laugh much longer, or much oftener than others." James Beattie, "An Essay on Laughter and Ludicrous Composition," in *Essays: On Poetry and Music* (London: Routledge, 1996 [1779]), 403.

9. Louis Maigron, *Fontenelle: L'Homme, L'Oeuvre, L'Influence* (Geneva: Slatkine, 1970 [1926]), 101.

10. "Quelle que soit la cause qui provoque [le rire], allez au fond, vous le trouvez constamment accompagné, qu'on se l'avoue ou non, d'une secrète satisfaction d'amour-propre, de je ne sais pas quel plaisir malin." Félicité de Lamennais, *Esquisse d'une philosophie* (Troyes: Cardon, 1840), III.9.II, 370.

11. John Dryden, "On Comedy, Farce, and Tragedy," in *Essays of John Dryden* (W. P. Ker, ed.) (New York: Russell and Russell, 1961 [1668]), 1:77.

12. John Dryden, *Essay of Dramatic Poesy*, in *Essays of John Dryden*, 1:21, 50. See also Pope's *Essay on Criticism*, 82–85.

13. Christopher Sykes, *Four Studies in Loyalty* (London: Collins, 1946), 27–28.

14. Samuel Johnson, *The Critical Opinions of Samuel Johnson* (New York: Russell and Russell, 1953).

15. W. Gunther Plaut, *The Torah: A Modern Commentary* (New York: Union of American Hebrew Congregations, 1981), 139; J. William Whedbee, *The Bible and the Comic Vision* (Cambridge: Cambridge University Press, 1998), 81.

16. "Qui pourrait se figurer le Christ riant?" Félicité de Lamennais, *Esquisse d'une philosophie* (Troyes: Cardon, 1840), III.9.II, 371.

17. G. K. Chesterton, *Orthodoxy* (Wheaton, Ill.: Harold Shaw, 1994 [1908]), 172.

18. Miguel de Unamuno, *The Tragic Sense of Life* (New York: Dover, 1954 [1921]), 111.

19. *Søren Kierkegaard's Journals and Papers* (Howard V. Hong and Edna H. Hong, eds.) (Bloomington: Indiana University Press, 1967), 2:274.

Chapter 5. Comic Virtues and Vices

1. "We are led to expect that an investigation of the specific type of mental activity involved in the creation of comic stimuli will lead us to the very core of the process of creative thought itself." Arthur Koestler, *Insight and Outlook* (New York: Macmillan, 1949), 15.

2. Hesketh Pearson, *The Smith of Smiths: Being the Life, Wit and Humour of Sydney Smith* (London: Folio 1977 [1934]), 209.

3. Lytton Strachey, *Eminent Victorians* (New York: Weidenfeld and Nicholson, 1988), 178.

4. R. H. Gronow, *The Reminiscences and Recollections of Captain Gronow* (New York: Viking, 1964), 260.

5. Friedrich Nietzsche, *Thus Spoke Zarathustra* (London: Penguin, 1961 [1885]), 68.

6. *Zarathustra*, 210.

7. *Zarathustra*, 140.

8. Nietzsche's positive moral theories are in disrepute for three reasons. First, the political ends to which the superman was put in Nazi Germany were so abhorrent that some would relegate the notion to "the pages of a philosophical bestiary." Alasdair MacIntyre, *After Virtue* (Notre Dame: Notre Dame University Press, 2d ed., 1984), 22. Second, Nietzsche's powerful critique of objective theories of ethics have led many conservatives to regard him as a founder of postmodern moral relativism. For more recent attempts to revive the older, heroic view of Nietzsche, see Peter Berkowitz, *Nietzsche: The Ethics of an Immoralist* (Cambridge: Harvard University Press, 1995); Leslie Paul Thiele, *Friedrich Nietzsche and the Politics of the Soul: A Study in Heroic Individualism* (Princeton: Princeton University Press, 1990); Richard Schacht, *Nietzsche* (London: Routledge, 1983), 344–51. For a contrary view, which emphasizes the indeterminacy of Nietzsche's ethics, see Alexander Nehemas, *Nietzsche: Life as Literature* (Cambridge: Harvard University Press, 1985), 200 ff. Third, Nietzsche's morality was anti-Christian, and *Zarathustra* is a parody of the Gospels.

9. *Zarathustra*, 306.

10. The revival of Hellenistic ethics and Natural Law theories marks a return to the traditional pursuits of philosophy. See Julia Annas, *The Morality of Happiness* (New York: Oxford University Press, 1993); Thomas Hurka, *Perfectionism* (Oxford: Oxford University Press, 1994); Martha C. Nussbaum, *The Therapy of Desire: Theory and Practice in Hellenistic Ethics* (Princeton: Princeton University Press, 1994); Ellen Paul, Fred D. Miller, and Jeffrey Paul, eds., *Human Flourishing* (Cambridge: Cambridge University Press, 1999). The most encompassing analysis of the philosophical return to man is Charles Taylor's *Sources of the Self* (Cambridge: Harvard University Press, 1989).

11. Friedrich Nietzsche, *The Gay Science*, 373.

12. *Nicomachean Ethics* 1176b28. Eudaimonia is sometimes defined as "that

which all men want." See J. L. Ackrill, "Aristotle on Eudaimonia," in Nancy Sherman, ed., *Aristotle's Ethics: Critical Essays* (Lanham, Md.: Rowman and Littlefield, 1999), 57, 61. If so, the question "Why do you seek *eudaimonia?*" would be meaningless.

13. C. S. Lewis, *Surprised by Joy* (San Diego: Harcourt, 1955), 18.

14. *The Life of Saint Teresa of Avila by Herself* (trans. J. M. Cohen) (London: Penguin, 1957), 201.

15. Charles Taylor, *Sources of the Self* (Cambridge: Harvard University Press, 1989), 418 ff.

16. James Joyce, *Stephen Hero* (New York: New Directions, 1959), 213. See Richard Ellman, *James Joyce* (Oxford: Oxford University Press, 1983), 83–85.

17. James Joyce, *Ulysses* (Harmondsworth: Penguin, 1971), 40.

18. For an admirable examination of the self-defeating pursuit of happiness, see Pascal Bruckner, *L'euphorie perpétuelle: Essai sur le devoir de bonheur* (Paris: Bernard Grasset, 2000). For a droll look at the self-help movement by a witty philosopher, see Mark Kingwell, *In Pursuit of Happiness: Better Living from Plato to Prozac* (New York: Crown, 1998).

19. "Intensely human, but always Queen, she upset, at her pleasure, the decisions of every court and the order of every authority, human or divine." Henry Adams, *Mont Saint Michel and Chartres* (Harmondsworth: Penguin, 1986 [1904]), 240.

20. Roger Crisp, "Modern Moral Philosophy and the Virtues," in Roger Crisp, ed., *How Should One Live: Essays on the Virtues* (Oxford: Oxford University Press, 1996), 1, 7.

21. Charles Taylor, "The Diversity of Goods," in *Philosophy and the Human Sciences: Philosophical Papers* (Cambridge: Cambridge University Press, 1985), 2:230.

22. According to George, "the most basic reasons for action are those reasons whose intelligibility does not depend on deeper and still more fundamental reasons. As basic reasons, they cannot be derived; for there is nothing more fundamental that could serve as a premise for a logical derivation. Therefore, they must be self-evident." Robert P. George, "Natural Law and Human Nature," in Robert P. George, ed., *Natural Law Theory: Contemporary Essays* (Oxford: Oxford University Press, 1992), 31, 34.

23. *The Rivals,* Preface.

24. "It would not be too much too much of an exaggeration to say that the whole of Bergson's philosophy is virtually contained in the few pages that Pascal dedicates to this fundamental distinction." William Barrett, *Irrational Man: A Study in Existential Philosophy* (New York: Anchor, 1958), 114.

25. The unitary view emerges most strongly in the *Nicomachean Ethics,* while the nonunitary view may be found in the *Eudemian Ethics.* Until recently, the *Nicomachean Ethics* was seen as the most complete statement of Aristotle's theory of ethics. Now, however, the *Eudemian Ethics* is increasingly seen as the later and more mature work. See generally Anthony Kenny, *Aristotle on the Perfect Life* (Oxford: Oxford University Press, 1992) and *The Aristotelian Ethics* (Oxford: Oxford University Press, 1978); Donald J. Monan, *Moral Knowledge and Its Methodology in Aristotle* (Oxford: Oxford University Press, 1968). But see Christo-

pher J. Rowe, *The Eudemian and Nicomachean Ethics: A Study in the Development of Aristotle's Thought* (Cambridge: Cambridge University Press, 1971).

26. Douglas J. Den Uyl, *The Virtue of Prudence* (New York: P. Lang, 1991); Martha C. Nussbaum, *The Fragility of Goodness: Luck and Ethics in Greek Tragedy and Philosophy* (Cambridge: Cambridge University Press, 1986), 297, and *Love's Knowledge: Essays on Philosophy and Literature* (Oxford: Oxford University Press, 1990).

27. See Thomas Nagel, *The View from Nowhere* (Oxford: Oxford University Press, 1986), 132–35.

28. *The Letters of John Keats: A Selection* (R. Gittings, ed.) (Oxford: Oxford University Press, 1970), 43.

29. For a neo-Aristotelian argument that Perfectionism might embrace agent-relative flourishing requirements, see Douglas B. Rasmussen, "Human Flourishing and the Appeal to Human Nature," in Paul, Miller, and Paul, *Human Flourishing*, 1.

30. George Orwell, *Collected Essays, Journalism, and Letters* (Harmondsworth: Penguin, 1970), 4:527.

31. "It is a mean between two vices, that which depends on excess and that which depends on defect; and again it is a mean because the vices respectively fall short of or exceed what is right in both passions and action, while virtue both finds and chooses what is intermediate." *Nicomachean Ethics* 1107a2. See also *Eudemian Ethics* 1220b21.

32. Nietzsche, *The Gay Science*, 283. On the difference between Nietzschean and Aristotelian ethics, see Solomon, *The Joy of Philosophy*, 33–35.

33. *Zarathustra*, 46–47.

34. Friedrich Nietzsche, "The Birth of Tragedy," in *Basic Writings of Nietzsche* (trans. Walter Kaufmann) (New York: Modern Library, 1992).

35. According to Nietzsche, both impulses were needed for the birth of tragedy: the audience was first swept up by a Dionysian excitement to identify with the chorus and actors, and thereafter was able to share in the tragedian's Apollonian vision. As an historical account of the development of Greek drama, this view was immediately rejected by scholars. In his later works, Nietzsche de-emphasized the Apollonian vision and championed a Dionysian ethos that affirmed life and strength and that rejected the "slave moralities" of Christian and utilitarian ethics.

36. Mikhail Bakhtin, *Problems of Dostoevsky's Poetics* (trans. Caryl Emerson) (Minneapolis: University of Minnesota Press, 1984 [1963]), 107.

Chapter 6. The Social Virtues

1. Charles Taylor, *The Ethics of Authenticity* (Cambridge: Harvard University Press, 1991) and "The Politics of Recognition," in *Philosophical Arguments* (Cambridge: Harvard University Press, 1995), 225. See also Ruth W. Grant, *Integrity and Hypocrisy: Machiavelli, Rousseau, and the Ethic of Politics* (Chicago: University of Chicago Press, 1997), 58–59.

2. Quoted in Heinrich Niehues-Pröbsting, "The Modern Reception of Cyn-

icism: Diogenes in the Enlightenment," in R. Bracht Branham and Marie-Odile Goulet-Cazé, *The Cynics: The Cynic Movement in Antiquity and Its Legacy* (Berkeley: University of California Press, 1996), 329, 350–53.

3. For the internal evidence that Diderot had Rousseau in mind as the nephew, see Donal O'Gorman, *Diderot the Satirist* (Toronto: University of Toronto, 1971), 136–84.

4. Albert Camus, Preface to *L'Étranger* (New York: Appleton-Century-Crofts, 1955). See Roger Shattuck's *Forbidden Knowledge: From Prometheus to Pornography* (San Diego: Harcourt Brace, 1996).

5. Sigmund Freud, *Civilization and Its Discontents* (trans. J. Strachey) (New York: Norton, 1961).

6. A man of integrity might also offend against the norm of truthfulness in other ways. The man who lies to his hostess about how he enjoyed his dinner, or the man who lies to save a friend, exhibits integrity but not truthfulness.

7. William Blake, *Poetry and Prose* (London: Nonesuch, 1967), 655.

8. Marc Escholier, *Port Royal: The Drama of the Jansenists* (New York: Hawthorn, 1968), 102.

9. Ian McEwan, *Amsterdam* (Toronto: Knopf, 1998), 67.

10. Jonathan Swift, *Gulliver's Travels* (London: Penguin, 1997 [1726]), II.vi.144.

11. In *Ordinary Vices* (Cambridge: Harvard University Press, 1984), 53, Judith Shklar expressed the hope that no one would marry "this archetype of the moral oppressor." However, few critics share her harsh judgment of Alceste, often because they identify Molière as the Misanthrope. Robert C. Elliott, *The Power of Satire: Magic, Ritual, Art* (Princeton: Princeton University Press, 1960), 168–69; René Jasinski, *Molière et Le misanthrope* (Paris: Colin, 1951). This misses the author's many suggestions that Alceste's views on virtue are excessive. Molière never dreamed of quitting the court for the "desert," whether in Port-Royal des Champs or elsewhere.

12. Ben Jonson, Song: "Though I am Young and Cannot Tell," from *The Sad Shepherd* I.v.

13. Louise Florence Petronille, Marquise d'Épinay, *Memoirs of Madame d'Épinay* (Leon Vallée, ed.) (Paris: Société des bibliophiles, 1903 [1818]), 3:62–63. On the break between the two, see O'Gorman, *Diderot the Satirist*, 167; Branham and Goulet-Cazé, *The Cynics*, 343.

14. William Roper, *The Life of Sir Thomas More, in Two Early Tudor Lives* (Richard S. Sylvester and David P. Harding, eds.) (New Haven: Yale University Press, 1962), 254.

15. Charles Péguy, *Notre jeunesse* (Paris: Gallimard, 1993 [1910]), 145.

16. Allan Young, *The Harmony of Illusions: Inventing Post-traumatic Stress Disorder* (Princeton: Princeton University Press, 1995).

Chapter 7. The Charismatic Virtues

1. Carlo Maria Franzero, *Beau Brummell: His Life and Times* (New York: John Day, 1958), 48; see also Venetia Murray, *An Elegant Madness: High Society in*

Regency England (New York: Viking, 1999); Henriette Levillain, *L'esprit dandy de Brummell à Baudelaire* (Paris: Corti, 1991).

2. R. H. Gronow, *The Reminiscences and Recollections of Captain Gronow* (New York: Viking, 1964), 202, 226.

3. Edith Sitwell, *The English Eccentrics* (Boston: Houghton Mifflin, 1933), 134–35.

4. Duncan Kennedy, "The Structure of Blackstone's Commentaries," *Buffalo Law Review* 28 (1979): 209.

5. Lionel Trilling, *The Middle of the Journey* (New York: Scribner, 1947), 246–47.

6. Sir Thomas Urquhart, *The Jewel* (Edinburgh: Scottish Academic, 1983 [1652]), 107–8.

7. Urquhart, *The Jewel,* 74.

8. Sir Thomas Browne, "Pseudodoxia," in *Selected Writings* (London: Faber, 1968), 149.

9. C. S. Lewis, *The Abolition of Man* (New York: Touchstone, 1975), 84.

10. Jeremy Bentham, "Auto-Icon; Or, Farther Uses of the Dead to the Living" (unpublished fragment [1832]). See David M. Levy, *The Economic Ideas of Ordinary People* (New York: Routledge, 1992), 164–65.

11. Schopenhauer, *The World as Will and Idea,* 76.

Chapter 8. Machine Law

1. U.S. v. Romani, 523 U.S. 517; 118 S. Ct. 1478, 1488; 140 L. Ed. 2d 710, 716 (1998). See also Blaine Const. Corp. v. Ins. Co. of North America, 171 F.3d 343 (6th Cir. 1999) (per Boggs J. dissenting).

2. A. P. Herbert, *Uncommon Law* (London: Methuen, 2d ed., 1936), 201–6.

3. U.S. v. Riverside Bayview Homes, Inc., 474 U.S. 121; 106 S. Ct. 455 (1985).

4. Rezza v. U.S., No. 87–6732, 12 May 1988 (E.D. Pa.), discussed in Charles J. Sykes, *A Nation of Victims: The Decay of the American Character* (New York: St. Martin's Press, 1992), 3.

5. Drew P. v. Clarke Cty. Sch. Dist., 676 F. Supp. 1559 (M.D. Ga. 1987), aff'd, 877 F.2d 927 (11th Cir. 1989), cert. denied, 494 U.S. 1046, 108 L. Ed. 2d 646, 110 S. Ct. 1510 (1990).

6. Linda Keene, "Beware, Retailers," *Seattle Times,* April 16, 1999, A1.

7. Wickard v. Filburn, 317 U.S. 111; 63 S. Ct. 82; 87 L. Ed. 122 (1942).

8. 765 F.Supp. 181, 183 (D. N.J.), rev'd, 958 F.2d 1242 (3d Cir. 1992).

9. Wesley R. Smith, "Don't Stand So Close to Me: Judges Are Giving Neighborhoods a Bum Rap," *Policy Review* 48 (fall 1994): 70.

10. Judge Sarokin's decision was overturned on appeal, but under threat of continued litigation the city of Morristown settled with Kreimer for $150,000, while the library settled with him for $80,000. The vagueness of the constitutional standard ensures that such issues will continue to be litigated.

11. 765 F.Supp. at 183.

12. The compelling evidence for the Gladstone-Grace theory is discussed in

Stephen Potter, *The Theory and Practice of Gamesmanship* (London: Moyer Bell, 1998 [1948]), 73–75.

13. 295 U.S. 495 (1935).

14. *Landmark Briefs and Arguments of the Supreme Court of the United States: Constitutional Law* (Philip B. Kurland and Gerhard Casper, eds.) (Arlington, Va.: University Publications, 1975), 28:735–36.

Chapter 9. Machine Scholarship

1. Tom Stoppard, *Jumpers* (London: Faber and Faber, 1972), 35.

2. Rudolf Carnap, "The Elimination of Metaphysics through Logical Analysis of Language," in A. J. Ayer, ed., *Logical Positivism* (New York: Free Press, 1959), 60, 69.

3. For a witty analysis of the problem, in an otherwise serious work, see "Nothing," in *Encyclopedia of Philosophy* (Paul Edwards, ed. in chief) (New York: Free Press, 1967), vol. 5.

4. Carnap, "The Elimination of Metaphysics," 80.

5. A. J. Ayer, *Language, Truth and Logic* (New York: Dover, 2d ed., 1952 [1936]), 44, 115, 120.

6. Ben Rogers, *A. J. Ayer: A Life* (London: Chatto, 1999).

7. J. L. Austin, "A Plea for Excuses," in *Philosophical Papers* (Oxford: Oxford University Press, 2d ed., 1970), 179.

8. Ved Mehta, *Fly and the Fly-bottle* (Boston: Little, Brown, 1962), 58–59. For other reminiscences of Austin's lecturing style, see the articles by Sir Isaiah Berlin, George Pitcher, and G. J. Warnock in Sir Isaiah Berlin et al., *Essays on J. L. Austin* (Oxford: Clarendon, 1973).

9. J. L. Austin, *Sense and Sensibilia* (reconstructed from the manuscript notes by G. J. Warnock) (Oxford: Oxford University Press, 1962), 6–7, quoting Ayer, 1–2.

10. Norman Malcolm, *Ludwig Wittgenstein: A Memoir* (London: Oxford University Press, 1958), 29. Wittgenstein appears to have been influenced by Lewis Carroll's nonsense stories, since the author of *Alice in Wonderland* was also fascinated by the ways in which simple linguistic errors might mislead. See George Pitcher, "Wittgenstein, Nonsense, and Lewis Carroll," *Massachusetts Review* (August 1966): 591, reprinted in K. T. Fann, ed., *Ludwig Wittgenstein: The Man and His Philosophy* (New York: Delta, 1967), 315.

11. Malcolm, *Ludwig Wittgenstein*, 31–32.

12. Bertrand Russell, "Ludwig Wittgenstein," *Mind* 60 (1951): 239, reprinted in Fann, *Ludwig Wittgenstein*, 30.

13. Bertrand Russell, "Philosophers and Idiots," *Listener*, Feb. 10, 1955, reprinted in Fann, *Ludwig Wittgenstein*, 31–32.

14. Ludwig Wittgenstein, *Philosophical Investigations* (trans. G. E. M. Anscombe) (Oxford: Blackwell, 1967), sec. 2.

15. Malcolm, *Ludwig Wittgenstein*, 69.

16. John R. Searle, *The Mystery of Consciousness* (New York: New York Review, 1997), 100.

17. Daniel C. Dennett, *Consciousness Explained* (Boston: Little, Brown, 1991), 73 (italics in original).

18. Searle, *The Mystery of Consciousness*, 107.

19. Edmund Burke, *Reflections on the Revolution in France* (Oxford: Oxford University Press, 1993), 87.

20. Burke, *Reflections*, 76.

21. Burke, *Reflections*, 81.

22. Burke's enemies, the Jacobins, agreed with him about the counterrevolutionary tendency of laughter and banned it during their parliamentary sessions. Laughter suggested an aristocratic disdain and chilled revolutionary fervor by revealing Jacobin nonsense. Georges Minois, *Histoire du rire et de la derision* (Paris: Fayard, 2000), 422–25.

23. Burke, *Reflections*, 37, 68.

24. Burke, *Reflections*, 62, 73, 77, 84.

25. Elisabeth M. Landes and Richard A. Posner, "The Economics of the Baby Shortage," *Journal of Legal Studies* 7 (1978): 323, 324. Judge Posner returned to the fray in "The Regulation of the Market in Adoptions," *Boston University Law Review* 59 (1987): 67. The issue was ventilated again in the Baby M litigation. See In re Baby M, 525 A.2d 1128 (N.J. Ch. Div. 1987); rev'd, 537 A.2d 1227 (1988) (holding that surrogate mothership contracts are illegal).

26. Landes and Posner, "The Economics of the Baby Shortage," 339 (italics in original).

27. Landes and Posner, "The Economics of the Baby Shortage," 339, 340, 341, 343.

28. Jonathan Swift, *A Modest Proposal and Other Stories* (Amherst: Prometheus, 1995 [1729]), 259, 263–64.

29. Or possibly Posner thought we were all hopeless sentimentalists and simply needed to be toughened up. In finding that a law banning partial-birth abortion was unconstitutional, Posner noted that the statute did "not outlaw a particularly cruel or painful or horrifying mode of abortion." Hope Clinic v. Ryan, 195 F.3d 857,879 (7th Cir. 1999). You think partial-birth abortion is revolting? So what's your point?

30. Michael Oakeshott, *Rationalism in Politics and Other Essays* (London: Methuen, 1962), 1, 3.

Chapter 10. Machine Art and Machine Cities

1. Under a 1990 amendment, the NEA was required to consider "general standards of decency and respect" in awarding grants, and since Finley had purposely set out to breach all such standards the agency concluded, with infinite regret, that she was a little too cutting-edge. The Finley case went to the courts, as all such controversies do, and the Supreme Court held that she had no right to the grant. N.E.A. v. Karen Finley, 524 U.S. 569; 118 S. Ct. 2168 (1998). Justice Scalia noted that "avant-garde artistes . . . remain entirely free to épater la bourgeoisie; they are merely deprived of the additional satisfaction of having the bourgeoisie taxed to pay for it."

2. Elaine S. Hochman, *Architects of Fortune: Mies van der Rohe and the Third Reich* (New York: Weidenfeld and Nicolson, 1989), 222–23. See also Stephanie Barron and Sabine Eckmann, *Exiles + Emigrés: The Flight of European Artists from Hitler* (New York: Abrams, 1997). See also Nicolai Ouroussoff, "Moral Dilemma of Architecture," *Los Angeles Times*, March 28, 1997, F1.

3. Robert R. Taylor, *The World in Stone: The Role of Architecture in National Socialist Ideology* (Berkeley: University of California Press, 1974), 150, and plates 29, 30.

4. Lewis Mumford, *The City in History: Its Origins, Its Transformations, and Its Prospects* (San Diego: Harcourt, Brace, 1961), 498.

5. The story is movingly told in Alan Ehrenhalt's *The Lost City: The Forgotten Virtues of Community in America* (New York: Basic Books, 1995). See also Fred Siegel, *The Future Once Happened Here: New York, D.C., L.A., and the Fate of America's Big Cities* (New York: Free Press, 1998).

6. Jane Jacobs, *The Death and Life of Great American Cities* (New York: Modern Library, 1993 [1961]), 9.

7. Jacobs, *The Death and Life of Great American Cities*, 13–14.

8. Jacobs, *The Death and Life of Great American Cities*, 12.

Chapter 11. The Battle of the Norms

1. Ronald H. Coase, "The Problem of Social Cost," *Journal of Law and Economics* 1 (1960): 3.

2. John Locke, *Essay Concerning Human Understanding* (London: Dent, 1965), 123, II.xi.2. Hobbes had proposed a similar distinction (*Leviathan*, 135), and Addison's *Spectator* no. 225 explicitly adopted the Lockean analysis of wit.

3. Edward C. Banfield, *The Moral Basis of a Backward Society* (Glencoe, Ill.: Free Press, 1958), 116.

4. *The Republic* VII, 514–18.

5. Charles Baudelaire, "Le dandy," in *Le peintre de la vie moderne, Œuvres complètes* 2:709 (Paris: Gallimard, 1976).

6. Frye's distinction between high and low mimetic comedy is different. Frye labeled the Old Comedy of Aristophanes as high mimetic, since there is something heroic about the protagonist's struggle against his society. By contrast, the New Comedy of Menander is rather more mundane, and Frye called it low mimetic. Northrop Frye, *The Anatomy of Criticism* (Princeton: Princeton University Press, 1957), 35–39.

7. Sigmund Freud, "Humor," in John Morreall, ed., *The Philosophy of Laughter and Humor* (Albany: SUNY Press, 1987 [1928]), 111.

Chapter 12. Resistance to Laughter

1. C. S. Lewis, *The Screwtape Letters* (New York: Simon and Schuster, 1996 [1961]), 104.

2. See the National Association of Self-Esteem web site at http://www.self-esteem-nase.org/cgi-bin/nase?links.hts (August 14, 2000).

3. James Bennet, "Clinton Calls Tests a 'Terrible Mistake' and Announces Sanctions against India," *New York Times*, May 14, 1998, A13.

4. Alfie Kohn, "The Truth about Self-Esteem," *Phi Delta Kappan* 76 (4) (1994): 272. See generally Charles J. Sykes, *Dumbing Down Our Kids: Why American Children Feel Good about Themselves But Can't Read, Write or Add* (New York: St. Martin's, 1995); David C. Berliner and Bruce J. Biddle, *The Manufactured Crisis: Myths, Fraud, and the Attack on America's Public Schools* (Reading, MA: Addison-Wesley, 1995).

5. Sykes, *Dumbing Down Our Kids*, 49.

6. All Lexis searches were conducted on May 24, 1999.

7. George Meredith, "An Essay on Comedy," in Wylie Sypher, ed., *Comedy* (New York: Anchor Books, 1956), 1, 12.

8. St. Thomas Aquinas, *Summa* IIa-IIae, Q. 14, art. 3.

9. "I can't be bothered to ride . . . ; I can't be bothered to walk . . . ; I can't be bothered to lie down, for either I'd have to stay lying down and that I can't be bothered with, or I'd have to get up again, and I can't be bothered with that either. In short: I just can't be bothered." Søren Kierkegaard, *Either/Or* (London: Penguin, 1992), 43.

10. "The opposite of *acedia* is not the industrious spirit of the daily effort to make a living, but rather the cheerful affirmation by man of his own existence, of the world as a whole, and of God—of Love, that is, from which arises that special freshness of action, which would never be confused by anyone with any experience with the narrow activity of the 'workaholic.'" Josef Pieper, *Leisure: The Basis of Culture* (South Bend: St. Augustine's Press, 1998 [1948]), 29.

11. Francis Bacon, *The Essays* (London: Penguin, 1985), 61.

12. *Lives of the Philosophers*, 6.43.

13. The story is told in Jean-Jacques Rousseau, *Les confessions* (Paris: Poche, 1995), 2:133–35.

14. "Qu'une vie est heureuse quand elle commence par l'amour et qu'elle finit par l'ambition! Si j'avais à en choisir une, je prendrais celle-là." *Discours sur les passions de l'amour* in *Œuvres complètes* (Paris: Pléiade, 2000), vol. 2, 200. Modern scholarship attributes the work to one of Pascal's followers.

15. Stanley Aronowitz, *Science as Power: Discourse and Ideology in Modern Society* (Minneapolis: University of Minnesota Press, 1988), 265.

16. See generally Paul R. Gross and Norman Levitt, *Higher Superstition: The Academic Left and Its Quarrels with Science* (Baltimore: Johns Hopkins University Press, 1998), chap. 3; Paul R. Gross, Norman Levitt, and Martin W. Lewis, eds., *The Flight from Science and Reason* (Baltimore: Johns Hopkins University Press, 1996).

17. http://www.nyu.edu/pubs/socialtext/ (July 7, 2002).

18. Alan D. Sokal and Jean Bricmont, *Fashionable Nonsense: Postmodern Intellectuals' Abuse of Science* (New York: Picador, 1998), 212; Alan D. Sokal, ed., *The Sokal Hoax: The Sham That Shook the Academy* (New York: Bison, 2000).

19. Matthew Arnold, *Culture and Anarchy* (Cambridge: Cambridge University Press, 1993 [1869]), 200.

20. See Suzanne Fields, "Theater of the Absurd on Campus," *Insight on the*

News, Dec. 7, 1998, 48; Michael Shelden, "Thought Police Ban the Bard," *Daily Telegraph,* Nov. 5, 1998, 24.

Chapter 13. The Sociability Thesis

1. David Hume, *Treatise of Human Nature* (Oxford: Oxford University Press, 1967 [1739]), III.2.iv, 514.

2. Jon Elster, *Ulysses and the Sirens: Studies in Rationality and Irrationality* (New York: Cambridge University Press, 1984); Oliver E. Williamson, "Credible Commitments: Using Hostages to Support Exchange," *American Economic Review* 73 (1983): 519.

3. Luigi Barzini, *The Italians* (New York: Touchstone, 1964), 188.

4. G. Duchenne, *The Mechanism of Human Facial Expression or an Electro-physiological Analysis of the Expression of the Emotions* (trans. A. Cuthbertson) (Cambridge: Cambridge University Press, 1990 [1862]).

5. Charles Darwin, *The Expression of the Emotions in Man and Animals* (New York: Oxford University Press, 1998 [1872]), 202. These findings have been replicated in recent tests. Paul Ekman, Wallace V. Friesen, and Maureen O'Sullivan, "Smiles when Lying," in Paul Ekman and Erika L. Rosenberg, *What the Face Reveals* (New York: Oxford University Press, 1997), 201; Paul Ekman, *Telling Lies: Clues to Deceit in the Marketplace, Politics, and Marriage* (New York: Norton, 1985). In addition to being hard to mimic, facial signals are easy to read. We appear to have a special skill in identifying facing expressions and recognizing faces. Victor S. Johnson, *Why We Feel: The Science of Human Emotions* (Cambridge: Perseus, 1999), 40.

6. Arthur Koestler, *The Act of Creation* (London: Penguin, 1989 [1964]), 29. EEG studies of brain activity also report that true and false smiles are wholly different mental events. Paul Ekman, R. J. Davidson, and W. V. Friesen, "The Duchenne Smile: Emotional Expression and Brain Psychology II," *Journal of Personality and Social Psychology* 58 (1990): 342–53.

7. Thomas Carlyle, *Sartor Resartus* (Oxford: Oxford University Press, 1987 [1833–34]), 26.

8. Patricia Meyer Spacks, *Gossip* (New York: Knopf, 1985), 29.

9. A. R. Radcliffe-Brown, *Structure and Function in Primitive Society* (New York: Free Press, 1965), 95. See Apte, *Humor and Laughter,* 50–66.

10. W. B. Yeats, "A wealthy man who promised a subscription to Dublin Municipal Gallery if it were proved that people wanted pictures."

11. Baldassare Castiglione, "The Book of the Courtier," in Burton A. Milligan, ed., *Three Renaissance Classics* (trans. Sir Thomas Hoby) (New York: Scribner's, 1953 [1528]), 241, 255.

12. The strongest "imagined community," in whose defense we might be prepared to sacrifice our lives, is the nation. Benedict Anderson, *Imagined Communities: Reflections on the Origin and Spread of Nationalism* (London: Verso, 1983).

13. In his *Dialogic Imagination,* Bakhtin saw inner dialogue not merely as the particular form of the novel but also as the way in which we live our lives. See James Wertsch, *Voices of the Mind* (Cambridge: Cambridge University Press,

1991); Charles Taylor, *Multiculturalism and "The Politics of Recognition"* (Princeton: Princeton University Press, 1992).

14. Paul Saenger, *Space between Words: The Origins of Silent Reading* (Stanford: Stanford University Press, 1997); Pascal Quignard, *Petits traités* (Paris: Folio, 1990), 2:54–55.

15. George Steiner, *The Death of Tragedy* (New Haven: Yale University Press, 1996 [1961]), 77.

Chapter 14. Conclusion

1. Friedrich Schiller, *On the Aesthetic Education of Man* (London: Routledge, 1954), 79–80 (15th letter). See Linda Dowling, *The Vulgarization of Art: The Victorians and Aesthetic Democracy* (Charlottesville: University of Virginia Press, 1996).

2. John Ruskin, *The Stones of Venice* (New York: Da Capo, 1960), 160–77. Ruskin's catalog of the Gothic's attributes also included rigidity, but by this he meant not a Bergsonian rigidity but rather the sense of inner tension that is absent in classical architecture.

3. Søren Kierkegaard, *Concluding Unscientific Postscript* (Princeton: Princeton University Press, 1992), 1:501 ff. See Anthony Rudd, *Kierkegaard and the Limits of the Ethical* (Oxford: Oxford University Press, 1993).

4. On the joyousness of the Gift of the Holy Spirit, see John Paul II's encyclical on the Holy Spirit, *Dominum et Vivificantem,* May 18, 1986.

5. Miguel de Unamuno, *The Tragic Sense of Life* (New York: Dover, 1954 [1921]), 44.

6. W. K. Wimsatt, *The Idea of Comedy: Essays in Prose and Verse* (Englewood Cliffs, N.J.: Prentice-Hall, 1969), 44.

7. Stendhal, *Racine et Shakespeare* (Utrecht: Bosch, 1965 [1823]), 56.

Bibliography

Many of the best recent books on laughter, such Barry Sanders, *Sudden Glory: Laughter as Subversive History* (Boston: Beacon, 1995), are by literary scholars. Useful studies of satire include Alvin Kernan's *The Cankered Muse: Satire of the English Renaissance* (New Haven: Yale University Press, 1959) and *The Plot of Satire* (New Haven: Yale University Press, 1965), as well as Dustin Griffin's *Satire: A Critical Reintroduction* (Lexington: University of Kentucky Press, 1994). Wayne C. Booth's *A Rhetoric of Irony* (Chicago: University of Chicago Press, 1974) and Morton Gurewitch's *The Ironic Temper and the Comic Imagination* (Detroit: Wayne State University Press, 1994) are the best studies of the dominant genre of our day. Other books that deserve mention are Harry Levin, *Playboys and Killjoys: An Essay on the Theory and Practice of Comedy* (New York: Oxford University Press, 1987) and Peter L. Berger, *Redeeming Laughter: The Comic Dimension of Human Experience* (New York: De Gruyter, 1997). Recent philosophical treatments of laughter include Ted Cohen's rambling and unfunny *Jokes: Philosophical Thoughts on Joking Matters* (Chicago: University of Chicago Press, 1999) and John Portmann's scholarly *When Bad Things Happen to Other People* (New York: Routledge, 2000) (an analysis of schadenfreude). While not a study of laughter, Judith Shklar's *Ordinary Vices* (Cambridge: Harvard University Press, 1984) are often comic vices too. See also John Morreall, *Taking Laughter Seriously* (Albany: SUNY Press, 1983).

While laughter has generally escaped their attention, philosophers, economists, and evolutionary theorists have written extensively on the emotions. Philosophic studies include Derek Parfit, *Reasons and Persons* (Oxford: Oxford University Press, 1986); Richard Wollheim, *On the Emotions* (New Haven: Yale University Press, 1999); Simon Blackburn, *Ruling Passions: A Theory of Practical Reasoning* (Oxford: Oxford University Press, 1998); and Ronald de Sousa, *The Rationality of Emotion* (Cambridge: MIT Press, 1997). For an analysis of emotions from an economic perspective, see Gary S. Becker, *Accounting for Tastes* (Cambridge: Harvard University Press, 1996); Robert Frank, *Passions Within Reason* (New York: Norton, 1988); and Thomas C. Schelling, *Choice and Consequence* (Cambridge: Harvard University Press, 1984). Psychologist Paul Ekman's studies of facial signaling buttress economic explanations of laughter as a signaling device. See Paul Ekman, ed., *Darwin and Facial Expression: A Century of Research in Review* (New York: Academic, 1973). One of the most influential students of the emotions is Jon Elster, whose work is strongly interdisciplinary. See *Ulysses Unbound* (Cambridge: Cambridge University Press, 2000); *Strong Feelings: Emotion, Addiction, and Human Behavior* (Cambridge: MIT Press, 1999); *Alchemies of the Mind: Rationality and the Emotions* (Cambridge: Cambridge University Press, 1999); *Sour Grapes* (Cambridge: Cambridge University Press, 1983).

Sociological and psychological examinations of laughter may be found in *Humor: International Journal of Humor Research*.

Adams, Henry. *Mont Saint Michel and Chartres*. Harmondsworth: Penguin, 1986.

Adorno, Theodor W. *The Jargon of Authenticity*. Kurt Tarnowski and Frederic Will, trans. Evanston: Northwestern University Press, 1973.

Anderson, Benedict. *Imagined Communities: Reflections on the Origin and Spread of Nationalism*. London: Verso, 1983.

Annas, Julia. *The Morality of Happiness*. New York: Oxford University Press, 1993.

Apte, Mahadev L. *Humor and Laughter: An Anthropological Approach*. Ithaca: Cornell University Press, 1985.

Aristotle. *Basic Works of Aristotle*. New York: Random House, 1966.

―――. *Nicomachean Ethics*. H. Rackham, trans. Cambridge: Harvard, 1982.

―――. *Poetics*. Richard Janko, trans. Indianapolis: Hackett, 1987.

―――. *Eudemian Ethics*. 2d ed. Oxford: Oxford University Press, 1992.

Arnold, Matthew. *Culture and Anarchy*. Cambridge: Cambridge University Press, 1993.

Aronowitz, Stanley. *Science as Power: Discourse and Ideology in Modern Society*. Minneapolis: University of Minnesota Press, 1988.

Aubrey, John. *Brief Lives*. Bury St. Edmunds: Boydell, 1982.

Austin, J. L. *Sense and Sensibilia*. Oxford: Oxford University Press, 1962.

―――. *Philosophical Papers*. 2d ed. Oxford: Oxford University Press, 1970.

Ayer, Alfred Jules. *Language, Truth and Logic*. 2d ed. New York: Dover, 1952.

―――, ed. *Logical Positivism*. New York: Free Press, 1959.

Bakhtin, Mikhail. *The Dialogic Imagination: Four Essays*. Caryl Emerson and Michael Holquist, trans. Austin: Texas University Press, 1981.

―――. *Problems of Dostoevsky's Poetics*. Caryl Emerson, trans. Minneapolis: University of Minnesota Press, 1984.

―――. *Rabelais and His World*. Hélène Iswolsky, trans. Bloomington: Indiana University Press, 1984.

Banfield, Edward C. *The Moral Basis of a Backward Society*. Glencoe, Ill.: Free Press, 1958.

Barrett, William. *Irrational Man: A Study in Existential Philosophy*. New York: Anchor, 1958.

Barron, Stephanie, and Sabine Eckmann. *Exiles + Emigrés: The Flight of European Artists from Hitler*. New York: Abrams, 1997.

Barzini, Luigi. *The Italians*. New York: Touchstone, 1964.

Bataille, Georges. *Guilty*. Bruce Boone, trans. Venice, Calif.: Lapis, 1988.

―――. *Inner Experience*. Leslie Anne Boldt, trans. Albany: SUNY Press, 1988.

Baudelaire, Charles. *Œuvres complètes*. Paris: Pléiade, 1975–76.

Beattie, James. *Essays: On Poetry and Music*. London: Routledge/Thoemmes, 1996.

Becker, Ernest. *The Denial of Death*. New York: Free Press, 1997.

Becker, Gary S. *Accounting for Tastes*. Cambridge: Harvard University Press, 1996.

Bennet, James. "Clinton Calls Tests a 'Terrible Mistake' and Announces Sanctions against India." *New York Times*, May 14, 1998.

Bentham, Jeremy. *Auto-Icon; Or, Farther Uses of the Dead to the Living*. Unpublished fragment, 1832.

Berger, Arthur A. *An Anatomy of Humor.* New Brunswick, N.J.: Transaction, 1993.
———. *Blind Men and Elephants: Perspectives on Humor.* New Brunswick, N.J. : Transaction, 1994.
Berger, Peter. L. *Redeeming Laughter: The Comic Dimension of Human Experience.* New York: De Gruyter, 1997.
Bergler, Edmund. *Laughter and the Sense of Humor.* New York: Intercontinental Medical Books, 1956.
Bergson, Henri. *Creative Evolution.* Arthur Mitchell, trans. New York: Henry Holt, 1911.
———. *Le rire.* Paris: Presses Universitaires de France, 1940.
———. *The Two Sources of Morality and Religion.* R. Ashley Audra and Cloudesley Brereton, trans. Notre Dame: Notre Dame University Press, 1979.
Berkowitz, Peter. *Nietzsche: The Ethics of an Immoralist.* Cambridge: Harvard University Press, 1995.
Berlin, Isaiah, et al. *Essays on J. L. Austin.* Oxford: Clarendon, 1973.
Bhaskar, Roy. *Plato etc: The Problems of Philosophy and Their Resolution.* London: Verso, 1994.
Blackburn, Simon. *Ruling Passions: A Theory of Practical Reasoning.* Oxford: Oxford University Press, 1998.
Bloom, Edward A., and Lillian D. Bloom. *Satire's Persuasive Voice.* Ithaca: Cornell University Press, 1979.
Boileau, Nicholas. *Satires, Épîtres, Art poétique.* Paris: Gallimard, 1967.
Booth, Wayne C. *A Rhetoric of Irony.* Chicago: University of Chicago Press, 1974.
Boskin, Joseph. *Rebellious Laughter.* Syracuse: Syracuse University Press, 1997.
Boston, Richard. *An Anatomy of Laughter.* London: Collins, 1974.
Branham, Bracht, and Marie-Odile Goulet-Cazé. *The Cynics: The Cynic Movement in Antiquity and Its Legacy.* Berkeley: University of California Press, 1996.
Brant, C. S. "On Joking Relationships." *American Anthropologist* 50 (1948): 160–62.
Broadie, Sarah. *Ethics with Aristotle.* Oxford: Oxford University Press, 1991.
Browne, Thomas. *Selected Writings.* London: Faber, 1968.
Bruckner, Pascal. *L'euphorie perpétuelle: Essai sur le devoir de bonheur.* Paris: Bernard Grasset, 2000.
Burckhardt, Jacob. *The Civilization of the Renaissance in Italy.* New York: Harper and Row, 1958.
Burke, Edmund. *Reflections on the Revolution in France.* Oxford: Oxford University Press, 1993.
Caillois, Roger. *Man and the Sacred.* Meyer Barash, trans. New York: Free Press, 1959.
———. *Les jeux et les hommes.* Paris: Gallimard, 1991.
Calasso, Roberto. *The Marriage of Cadmus and Harmony.* Tim Parks, trans. New York: Vintage, 1994.
———. *Literature and the Gods.* Tim Parks, trans. New York: Knopf, 2001.
Camus, Albert. *L'Étranger.* New York: Appleton-Century-Crofts, 1955.
Carlyle, Thomas. *Sartor Resartus.* Oxford: Oxford University Press, 1987.
Cavaliero, Glen. *The Alchemy of Laughter.* London: Macmillan, 2000.

Chapman, Anthony J. "Humorous Laughter in Children." *Journal of Personality and Social Psychology* 31 (1975): 42–49.

Chapman, Antony J., and Hugh C. Foot, eds. *Humor and Laughter: Theory, Research, and Applications.* New Brunswick, N.J.: Transaction, 1996.

Charney, Maurice. *Comedy High and Low: An Introduction to the Experience of Comedy.* New York: Oxford University Press, 1978.

Chesterfield, Earl of. *Letters to His Son.* Washington, D.C.: Walter Dunne, 1901.

Chesterton, G. K. *Orthodoxy.* Wheaton, Ill.: Harold Shaw, 1994.

Chiaro, Delia. *The Language of Jokes: Analysing Verbal Play.* London: Routledge, 1992.

Clark, M. "Humour and Incongruity." *Philosophy* 45 (1991): 20.

Coase, Ronald H. "The Problem of Social Cost." *Journal of Law and Economics* 3 (1960): 1.

Coffey, Michael. *Roman Satire.* Melksham, U.K.: Cromwell, 1976.

Cohen, Ted. *Jokes: Philosophical Thoughts on Joking Matters.* Chicago: University of Chicago Press, 1999.

Coleman, James. *Foundations of Social Theory.* Cambridge: Harvard University Press, 1990.

Comte-Sponville, André. *Petit traité des grandes vertus.* Paris: Presses Universitaires de France, 1996.

Connery, Brian A., and Kirk Combe. *Theorizing Satire: Essays in Literary Criticism.* New York: St. Martin's, 1995.

Conrad, Peter. *Modern Times, Modern Places.* New York: Knopf, 1999.

Cook, Albert. *The Dark Voyage and the Golden Mean: A Philosophy of Comedy.* Cambridge: Harvard University Press, 1949.

Cooper, John M. *Reason and Emotion.* Princeton: Princeton University Press, 1999.

Cooper, Lane. *An Aristotelian Theory of Comedy.* New York: Harcourt, Brace, 1922.

Cornford, F. M. *The Origins of Attic Comedy.* Garden City, N.J.: Anchor, 1961.

Crisp, Roger, ed. *How Should One Live? Essays on the Virtues.* Oxford: Oxford University Press, 1996.

Culler, Jonatha, ed. *On Puns: The Foundation of Letters.* Oxford: Basil Blackwell, 1988.

D'Alton, John Francis. *Horace and His Age.* New York: Russell and Russell, 1962.

Darwin, Charles. *The Expression of the Emotions in Man and Animals.* Oxford: Oxford University Press, 1998.

Davies, Christie. *Jokes Are about People.* Bloomington: Indiana University Press, 1988.

———. *Ethnic Humor around the World: A Comparative Analysis.* Bloomington: Indiana University Press, 1992.

Davis, D. Diane. *Breaking up [at] Totality.* Carbondale: Southern Illinois University Press, 2000.

Davis, Murray S. *What's So Funny? The Comic Conception of Culture and Society.* Chicago: University of Chicago Press, 1993.

Davis, Nathalie Zemon. *Society and Culture in Early Modern France.* Palo Alto: Stanford University Press, 1975.

Dennett, Daniel. *Consciousness Explained.* New York: Little, Brown, 1991.

———. *Kinds of Minds: Toward an Understanding of Consciousness.* New York: Basic Books, 1996.

Den Uyl, Douglas J. *The Virtue of Prudence.* New York: P. Lang, 1991.

Dodds, E. R. *The Greeks and the Irrational.* Berkeley: University of California Press, 1968.

Dowling, Linda. *The Vulgarization of Art: The Victorians and Aesthetic Democracy.* Charlottesville: University of Virginia Press, 1996.

Dryden, John. *Essays of John Dryden.* W. P. Ker, ed. New York: Russell and Russell, 1961.

Duchenne, G. *The Mechanism of Human Facial Expression or an Electro-physiological Analysis of the Expression of the Emotions.* A. Cuthbertson, trans. Cambridge: Cambridge University Press, 1990.

Duckworth, George E. *The Nature of Roman Comedy: A Study in Popular Entertainment.* Princeton: Princeton University Press, 1952.

Duncan, Hugh D. *Language and Literature in Society.* Chicago: University of Chicago Press, 1953.

———. *Communication and Social Order.* New York: Bedminster, 1962.

Eastman, Max. *The Sense of Humor.* New York: Scribner, 1921.

———. *The Enjoyment of Laughter.* New York: Simon and Schuster, 1936.

Ehrenhalt, Alan. *The Lost City: The Forgotten Virtues of Community in America.* New York: Basic Books, 1995.

Ekman, Paul. *Telling Lies: Clues to Deceit in the Marketplace, Politics, and Marriage.* New York: Norton, 1985.

———, ed. *Darwin and Facial Expression: A Century of Research in Review.* New York: Academic, 1973.

Ekman, Paul, R. J. Davidson, and W. V. Friesen. "The Duchenne Smile: Emotional Expression and Brain Psychology II." *Journal of Personality and Social Psychology* 58 (1990): 342–53.

———. "Facial Expression of Emotion." *American Psychologist* 48 (1993): 384–92.

Ekman, Paul, and Erika Rosenberg, eds. *What the Face Reveals: Basic and Applied Studies of Spontaneous Expression Using the Facial Action Coding System.* New York: Oxford University Press, 1997.

Elkin, P. K. *The Augustan Defence of Satire.* Oxford: Clarendon, 1973.

Elliott, Robert C. *The Power of Satire: Magic, Ritual, Art.* Princeton: Princeton University Press, 1960.

Ellis, John M. *Against Deconstruction.* Princeton: Princeton University Press, 1989.

———. *Literature Lost.* New Haven: Yale University Press, 1997.

Ellman, Richard. *James Joyce.* Oxford: Oxford University Press, 1983.

Elster, Jon. *Ulysses and the Sirens: Studies in Rationality and Irrationality.* New York: Cambridge University Press, 1984.

———. *The Cement of Society.* Cambridge: Cambridge University Press, 1989.

———. *Alchemies of the Mind: Rationality and the Emotions.* Cambridge: Cambridge University Press, 1999.

———. *Ulysses Unbound.* Cambridge: Cambridge University Press, 2000.

Encyclopedia of Philosophy. New York: Free Press, 1967.

Épinay, Marquise d' (Louise Florence Petronille). *Memoirs of Madame d'Épinay.* Paris: Société des bibliophiles, 1903.

Escholier, Marc. *Port Royal: The Drama of the Jansenists.* New York: Hawthorn, 1968.

Esslin, Martin. *The Theatre of the Absurd.* 3d ed. London: Penguin, 1980.

Fann, K. T., ed. *Ludwig Wittgenstein: The Man and His Philosophy.* New York: Delta, 1967.

Feibleman, James K. *In Praise of Comedy: A Study of Its Theory and Practice.* New York: Horizon, 1970.

Feinberg, Leonard. *The Satirist: His Temperament, Motivation, and Influence.* Ames: Iowa State Press, 1963.

Fields, Suzanne. "Theater of the Absurd on Campus." *Insight on the News,* Dec. 7, 1998.

Flanagan, Owen. *Consciousness Reconsidered.* Cambridge: MIT Press, 1992.

Frank, Robert H. *Passions Within Reason.* New York: Norton, 1988.

———. "If Homo Economicus Could Choose His Own Utility Function, Would He Want One with a Conscience?" *American Economic Review* 77 (1987): 593.

Franzero, Carlo Maria. *Beau Brummell: His Life and Times.* New York: John Day, 1958.

Freud, Sigmund. *Civilization and Its Discontents.* J. Strachey, trans. New York: Norton, 1961.

———. *The Basic Writings of Sigmund Freud.* New York: Modern Library, 1995.

Frye, Northrop. "The Nature of Satire." *University of Toronto Quarterly* 14 (1944): 75–89.

———. *The Anatomy of Criticism.* Princeton: Princeton University Press, 1957.

Geertz, Clifford. *Local Knowledge: Further Essays in Interpretive Anthropology.* New York: Basic Books, 1983.

Gelernter, David. *1939: The Lost World of the Fair.* New York: Avon, 1995.

George, Robert P. *Natural Law Theory.* Oxford: Oxford University Press, 1992.

———. *In Defense of Natural Law.* Oxford: Clarendon, 1999.

Goldmann, Lucien. *The Hidden God: A Study of Tragic Vision in the Pensées of Pascal and the Tragedies of Racine.* London: Routledge, 1964.

Goldstein, Jeffrey H., and Paul E. McGhee, eds. *The Psychology of Humor: Theoretical Perspectives and Empirical Issues.* New York: Academic, 1972.

Grant, Ruth W. *Integrity and Hypocrisy: Machiavelli, Rousseau, and the Ethic of Politics.* Chicago: University of Chicago Press, 1997.

Greig, J. Y. T. *The Psychology of Laughter and Comedy.* New York: Cooper Square, 1923.

Griffin, Dustin. *Satire: A Critical Reintroduction.* Lexington: University of Kentucky Press, 1994.

Gronow, R. H. *The Reminiscences and Recollections of Captain Gronow.* New York: Viking, 1964.

Gross, Paul R., and Norman Levitt. *Higher Superstition: The Academic Left and Its Quarrels with Science.* Baltimore: Johns Hopkins University Press, 1998.

Gross, Paul R., and Martin W. Lewis, eds. *The Flight from Science and Reason.* Baltimore: Johns Hopkins University Press, 1996.

Guiraud, Pierre. *Les jeux des mots.* Paris: Presses Universitaires de France, 1976.

Gurewitch, Morton. *The Ironic Temper and the Comic Imagination.* Detroit: Wayne State University Press, 1994.

————. *Comedy: The Irrational Vision.* Ithaca: Cornell University Press, 1975.

Hall, Peter. *Cities of Tomorrow.* Oxford: Blackwell, 1996.

Harris, Christine R. "The Mystery of Ticklish Laughter." *American Scientist* (July–August 1999): 344.

Hazlitt, William. *Lectures on the English Comic Writers.* London: Oxford University Press, 1907.

Herbert, A. P. *Uncommon Law.* 2d ed. London: Methuen, 1936.

Highet, Gilbert. *The Anatomy of Satire.* Princeton: Princeton University Press, 1962.

Hobbes, Thomas. *Leviathan.* London: Penguin, 1968.

————. *Human Nature and De Corpore Politico.* Oxford: Oxford University Press, 1994.

Hochman, Elaine S. *Architects of Fortune: Mies van der Rohe and the Third Reich.* New York: Weidenfeld and Nicolson, 1989.

Hodgart, Matthew. *Satire.* New York: McGraw-Hill, 1969.

Hölderlin, Friedrich. *Selected Poems and Fragments.* Michael Hamburger, trans. London: Penguin, 1998.

Horace. *Satires and Epistles.* Niall Rudd, trans. London: Penguin, 1979.

Howard, Philip. *The Death of Common Sense: How Law Is Suffocating America.* New York: Random House, 1994.

Hudson, Deal W. *Happiness and the Limits of Satisfaction.* London: Rowman and Littlefield, 1996.

Hughes, Robert. *The Shock of the New.* New York: Knopf, 1991.

Huizinga, Johan. *Homo Ludens.* Boston: Beacon, 1950.

Hume, David. *Treatise of Human Nature.* Oxford: Oxford University Press, 1967.

Hurka, Thomas. *Perfectionism.* Oxford: Oxford University Press, 1994.

Ignatieff, Michael. *Isaiah Berlin: A Life.* New York: Metropolitan, 1998.

Jacobs, Jane. *The Death and Life of Great American Cities.* New York: Modern Library, 1993.

Jaeger, Werner. *Paideia: The Ideals of Greek Culture.* 2d ed. New York: Oxford University Press, 1945.

James, Susan. *Passion and Action.* Oxford: Clarendon, 1998.

Janko, Richard. *Aristotle on Comedy: Towards a Reconstruction of Poetics.* Berkeley: University of California Press, 1984.

Jasinski, René. *Molière et Le misanthrope.* Paris: Colin, 1951.

John Paul II. *Dominum et Vivificantem.* May 18, 1986.

Johnson, Samuel. *The Critical Opinions of Samuel Johnson.* New York: Russell and Russell, 1953.

————. *Poetry and Prose.* Cambridge: Harvard University Press, 1957.

Johnson, Victor S. *Why We Feel: The Science of Human Emotions.* Cambridge: Perseus, 1999.

Joyce, James. *Stephen Hero.* New York: New Directions, 1959.

————. *Ulysses.* Harmondsworth: Penguin, 1971.

Juvenal. *The Satires.* Niall Rudd, trans. Oxford: Oxford University Press, 1992.

Kant, Immanuel. *The Critique of Judgment.* J. C. Meredith, trans. Oxford: Oxford University Press, 1952.

Kaufmann, Walter. *Nietzsche: Philosopher, Psychologist, Antichrist.* 4th ed. Princeton: Princeton University Press, 1974.

Keats, John. *The Letters of John Keats: A Selection.* Oxford: Oxford University Press, 1970.

Keene, Linda. "Beware, Retailers." *Seattle Times,* April 16, 1999.

Kempis, Thomas à. *The Imitation of Christ.* London: Collins, 1957.

Kennedy, Duncan. "The Structure of Blackstone's Commentaries." *Buffalo Law Review* 28 (1979): 209.

Kenner, Hugh. *Flaubert, Joyce and Beckett: The Stoic Comedians.* Boston: Beacon, 1962.

Kenny, Anthony. *The Aristotelian Ethics.* Oxford: Oxford University Press, 1978.

———. *Aristotle on the Perfect Life.* Oxford: Oxford University Press, 1992.

Kernan, Alvin. *The Cankered Muse: Satire of the English Renaissance.* New Haven: Yale University Press, 1959.

———. *The Plot of Satire.* New Haven: Yale University Press, 1965.

———. *The Death of Literature.* New Haven: Yale University Press, 1990.

Kierkegaard, Søren. *Journals and Papers.* Howard V. Hong and Edna H. Hong, trans. Bloomington: Indiana University Press, 1967.

———. *Fear and Trembling/Repetition.* Howard V. Hong and Edna H. Hong, trans. Princeton: Princeton University Press, 1983.

———. *The Concept of Irony.* Howard V. Hong and Edna H. Hong, trans. Princeton: Princeton University Press, 1989.

———. *Concluding Unscientific Postscript.* Howard V. Hong and Edna H. Hong, trans. Princeton: Princeton University Press, 1992.

———. *Either/Or.* Alastair Hannay, trans. London: Penguin, 1992.

Kimball, Roger. *Against the Grain.* Chicago: Ivan R. Dee, 1995.

———. *Experiments Against Reality.* Chicago. Ivan R. Dee, 2000.

Kingwell, Mark. *In Pursuit of Happiness: Better Living from Plato to Prozac.* New York: Crown, 1998.

Knox, Fr. Ronald A. *Essays in Satire.* New York: E. P. Dutton, 1930.

Koestler, Arthur. *Insight and Outlook.* New York: Macmillan, 1949.

———. *The Act of Creation.* London: Penguin, 1989.

Kolakowski, Leszek. *Bergson.* New York: Oxford University Press, 1985.

———. *Modernity on Endless Trial.* Chicago: University of Chicago Press, 1990.

———. *God Owes Us Nothing: A Brief Remark on Pascal's Religion and on the Spirit of Jansenism.* Chicago: University of Chicago Press, 1995.

Kramer, Hilton, and Roger Kimball, eds. *The Future of the European Past.* Chicago: Ivan R. Dee, 1997.

Kraut, Richard. *Aristotle on the Human Good.* Princeton: Princeton University Press, 1989.

Kurland, Philip B., and Gerhard Casper, eds. *Landmark Briefs and Arguments of the Supreme Court of the United States: Constitutional Law.* Arlington, Va.: University Publications, 1975.

Kuschel, Karl-Josef. *Laughter: A Theological Reflection.* New York: Continuum, 1994.

Lamb, Charles. *The Essays of Elia and the Last Essays of Elia.* Garden City, N.Y.: Doubleday, n.d.

Lamennais, Félicité de. *Esquisse d'une philosophie.* Troyes: Cardon, 1840.

Landes, Elisabeth M., and Richard A. Posner. "The Economics of the Baby Shortage." *Journal of Legal Studies* 7 (1978): 323.

Langer, Suzanne. *Feeling and Form: A Theory of Art.* New York: Scribner's, 1953.

Larmore, Charles. *The Morals of Modernity.* Cambridge: Cambridge University Press, 1996.

Lauter, Paul, ed. *Theories of Comedy.* Garden City, N.Y.: Anchor, 1964.

Leacock, Stephen. *Humour: Its Theory and Technique.* New York: Dodd, Mead, 1935.

———. *Humor and Humanity: An Introduction to the Study of Humor.* London: Thornton, Butterworth, 1937.

———. *Literary Lapses.* Toronto: McClelland and Stewart, 1957.

Lear, Jonathan. *Happiness, Death, and the Remainder of Life.* Cambridge: Harvard University Press, 2000.

Leuchtenburg, William E. *The Supreme Court Reborn: The Constitutional Revolution in the Age of Roosevelt.* New York: Oxford University Press, 1995.

Levillain, Henriette. *L'esprit dandy de Brummell à Baudelaire.* Paris: Corti, 1991.

Levin, Harry. *Playboys and Killjoys: An Essay on the Theory and Practice of Comedy.* New York: Oxford University Press, 1987.

———, ed. *Veins of Humor.* Cambridge: Harvard University Press, 1972.

Levy, David M. *The Economic Ideas of Ordinary People.* New York: Routledge, 1992.

Lewis, C. S. *Surprised by Joy.* San Diego: Harcourt, 1955.

———. *The Abolition of Man.* New York: Touchstone, 1975.

———. *The Screwtape Letters.* New York: Simon and Schuster, 1996.

Lewis, Paul. *Comic Effects: Interdisciplinary Approaches to Humor in Literature.* Albany: SUNY Press, 1989.

Lilla, Mark. *The Reckless Mind: Intellectuals in Politics.* New York: New York Review Books, 2001.

Locke, John. *Essay Concerning Human Understanding.* London: Dent, 1965.

Ludovici, Anthony. *The Secret of Laughter.* New York: Viking, 1933.

MacIntyre, Alasdair. *After Virtue.* 2d ed. Notre Dame: Notre Dame University Press, 1984.

Mack, Maynard. "The Muse of Satire." *Yale Review* 41 (1951): 80–92.

Maigron, Louis. *Fontenelle: L'Homme, L'Oeuvre, L'Influence.* Geneva: Slatkine, 1970.

Malcolm, Norman. *Ludwig Wittgenstein: A Memoir.* London: Oxford University Press, 1958.

———. *Dreaming.* London: Routledge, 1962.

Martin, Robert B. *The Triumph of Wit: A Study of Victorian Comic Vision.* Oxford: Oxford University Press, 1974.

McElroy, Davis. *Existentialism and Modern Literature.* Westport, Conn.: Greenwood, 1964.

McEwan, Ian. *Amsterdam*. Toronto: Knopf, 1998.

McFadden, George. *Discovering the Comic*. Princeton: Princeton University Press, 1982.

McGee, Paul E. "Development of the Humor Response: A Review of the Literature." *Psychological Bulletin* 76 (1971): 328–48.

———. *Humor: Its Origin and Development*. San Francisco: W. H. Freeman, 1979.

McGee, Paul E., and Jeffrey H. Goldstein, eds. *Handbook of Humor Research*. New York: Springer, 1983.

Mehta, Ved. *Fly and the Fly-bottle*. Boston: Little, Brown, 1962.

Michaut, Gustave. *Les luttes de Molière*. Geneva: Slatkine Reprints, 1968.

Miller, William Ian. *Humiliation*. Ithaca: Cornell University Press, 1993.

Milligan, Burton A., ed. *Three Renaissance Classics*. Thomas Hoby, trans. New York: Scribner's, 1953.

Minois, Georges. *Histoire du rire et de la dérision*. Paris: Fayard, 2000.

Molière. *The Misanthrope*. Richard Wilbur, trans. San Diego: Harcourt, Brace, 1965.

Monan, Donald J. *Moral Knowledge and Its Methodology in Aristotle*. Oxford: Oxford University Press, 1968.

Mongrédien, Georges. *La vie privée de Molière*. Paris: Hachette, 1950.

Montesquieu. *Persian Letters*. C. J. Betts, trans. London: Penguin, 1973.

Morreall, John. *Taking Laughter Seriously*. Albany: SUNY Press, 1983.

———. *Laughter and Humor*. Albany: SUNY Press, 1987.

———. *Comedy, Tragedy, and Religion*. Albany: SUNY Press, 1999.

———, ed. *The Philosophy of Laughter and Humor*. Albany: SUNY Press, 1987.

Mulkay, M. *On Humour*. Cambridge, U.K.: Polity, 1988.

Mumford, Lewis. *The City in History: Its Origins, Its Transformations, and Its Prospects*. San Diego: Harcourt, Brace, 1961.

Murray, Venetia. *An Elegant Madness: High Society in Regency England*. New York: Viking, 1999.

Nagel, Thomas. *The View from Nowhere*. Oxford: Oxford University Press, 1986.

Nash, W. *The Language of Humour*. London: Longman, 1985.

Nehemas, Alexander. *Nietzsche: Life as Literature*. Cambridge: Harvard University Press, 1985.

Nietzsche, Friedrich. *Thus Spoke Zarathustra*. R. J. Hollingdale, trans. London: Penguin, 1961.

———. *Beyond Good and Evil*. Walter Kaufmann, trans. New York: Vintage, 1966.

———. *The Genealogy of Morals*. Walter Kaufmann, trans. New York: Vintage, 1967.

———. *The Will to Power*. Walter Kaufmann and R. J. Hollingdale, trans. New York: Vintage, 1968.

———. *The Gay Science*. Walter Kaufmann, trans. New York: Vintage, 1974.

———. *Human, All Too Human*. R. J. Hollingdale, trans. Cambridge: Cambridge University Press, 1986.

———. *Basic Writings of Nietzsche*. New York: Modern Library, 1992.

———. *The Twilight of the Gods*. Duncan Large, trans. Oxford: Oxford University Press, 1998.

———. *The Birth of Tragedy*. Raymond Geuss and Ronald Speirs, trans. Cambridge: Cambridge University Press, 1999.

Nussbaum, Martha C. *The Fragility of Goodness: Luck and Ethics in Greek Tragedy and Philosophy*. Cambridge: Cambridge University Press, 1986.

———. *Love's Knowledge: Essays on Philosophy and Literature*. Oxford: Oxford University Press, 1990.

———. *The Therapy of Desire: Theory and Practice in Hellenistic Ethics*. Princeton: Princeton University Press, 1994.

Oakeshott, Michael. *Rationalism in Politics and Other Essays*. London: Methuen, 1962.

O'Gorman, Donal. *Diderot the Satirist*. Toronto: University of Toronto Press, 1971.

Olson, Mancur. *The Logic of Collective Action: Public Goods and the Theory of Groups*. Cambridge: Harvard University Press, 1965.

Orwell, George. *Collected Essays, Journalism, and Letters*. Harmondsworth: Penguin, 1970.

Parkin, John. *Humour Theorists of the Twentieth Century*. Lewiston: Edwin Mellen, 1997.

Pascal, Blaise. *Œuvres complètes*. Paris: Pléiade, 1998, 2000.

Paul, Ellen Frankel, Fred D. Miller, and Jeffrey Paul. *Virtue and Vice*. Cambridge: Cambridge University Press, 1998.

———. *Human Flourishing*. Cambridge: Cambridge University Press, 1999.

———. *Natural Law and Modern Moral Philosophy*. Cambridge: Cambridge University Press, 2001.

Paulos, John. *Mathematics and Humor*. Chicago: University of Chicago Press, 1980.

———. *I Think, Therefore I Laugh*. New York: Columbia University Press, 2000.

Pearson, Hesketh. *The Smith of Smiths: Being the Life, Wit and Humour of Sydney Smith*. London: Folio, 1977.

Péguy, Charles. *Œuvres*. 3 vols. Paris: Pléiade, 1987–92.

Pickard-Cambridge, A. W. *Dithyramb, Tragedy and Comedy*. Oxford: Clarendon, 1927.

Piddington, Ralph. *The Psychology of Laughter: A Study in Social Adaptation*. London: Figurehead, 1933.

Pieper, Josef. *Leisure: The Basis of Culture*. South Bend: St. Augustine's Press, 1998.

———. *In Tune with the Word: A Theory of Festivity*. South Bend: St. Augustine's Press, 1999.

Pitcher, George. "Wittgenstein, Nonsense, and Lewis Carroll." *Massachusetts Review* (August 1966): 591.

Placher, William C. *The Domestification of Transcendence*. Knoxville: Westminster John Knox, 1996.

Plato. *Collected Dialogues*. New York: Pantheon, 1963.

———. *Symposium*. Alexander Nehemas and Paul Woodruff, trans. Indianapolis: Hackett, 1989.

Plaut, W. Gunther. *The Torah: A Modern Commentary*. New York: Union of American Hebrew Congregations, 1981.

Polhemus, Robert M. *Comic Faith.* Chicago: University of Chicago Press, 1980.

Pollard, Arthur. *Satire.* London: Methuen, 1970.

Portmann, John. *When Bad Things Happen to Other People.* New York: Routledge, 2000.

Posner, Eric A. *Law and Social Norms.* Cambridge: Harvard University Press, 2000.

Posner, Richard A. "The Regulation of the Market in Adoptions." *Boston University Law Review* 67 (1987): 59.

Potter, Stephen. *One-upmanship: Being Some Account of the Activities and Teaching of the Lifemanship Correspondence College of One-upness and Gameslifemastery.* New York: Holt, 1952.

———. *The Sense of Humour.* London: Reinhardt, 1954.

———. *The Theory and Practice of Gamesmanship.* London: Moyer Bell, 1998.

Powell, Chris, and George E. Patton. *Humour in Society: Resistance and Control.* New York: St. Martin's, 1988.

Provine, Robert R. "Contagious Laughter: Laughter Is a Sufficient Stimulus for Laughs and Smiles." *Bulletin of the Psychonomic Society* 30 (1992): 1.

———. *Laughter: A Scientific Investigation.* New York: Viking, 2000.

Quignard, Pascal. *Petits traités.* Paris: Folio, 1990.

———. *Tous les matins du monde.* Paris: Gallimard, 1991.

———. *Rhétorique spéculative.* Paris: Folio, 1995.

Racine. *Œuvres complètes.* Paris: Pléiade, 1999.

Radcliffe-Brown, A. R. *Structure and Function in Primitive Society.* New York: Free Press, 1965.

Rahner, Hugo. *Man at Play.* London: Burns and Oates, 1965.

Rahner, Karl. *Foundations of the Christian Faith.* William V. Dych, trans. New York: Crossroad, 1978.

Rapp, Albert. *The Origins of Wit and Humor.* New York: E. P. Dutton, 1951.

Redfern, Walter. *Puns.* Oxford: Basil Blackwell, 1984.

Rogers, Ben. *A. J. Ayer: A Life.* London: Chatto, 1999.

Rorty, Richard. *Contingency, Irony, and Solidarity.* Cambridge: Cambridge University Press, 1989.

Rousseau, Jean-Jacques. *Les confessions.* Paris: Poche, 1995.

———. *Lettre à M. d'Alembert sur son article Genève.* Paris: Flammarion, 1967.

Rowe, Christopher J. *The Eudemian and Nicomachean Ethics: A Study in the Development of Aristotle's Thought.* Cambridge: Cambridge University Press, 1971.

Rudd, Anthony. *Kierkegaard and the Limits of the Ethical.* Oxford: Oxford University Press, 1993.

Ruskin, John. *The Stones of Venice.* New York: Da Capo, 1960.

Ryle, Gilbert. *The Concept of Mind.* London: Hutchinson's, 1949.

Saenger, Paul. *Space between Words: The Origins of Silent Reading.* Stanford: Stanford University Press, 1997.

Sanders, Barry. *Sudden Glory: Laughter as Subversive History.* Boston: Beacon, 1995.

Schacht, Richard. *Nietzsche.* London: Routledge, 1983.

Schaeffer, Neil. *The Art of Laughter.* New York: Columbia University Press, 1981.

Schelling, Thomas C. *Choice and Consequence.* Cambridge: Harvard University Press, 1984.

Schiller, Friedrich. *On the Aesthetic Education of Man.* London: Routledge, 1954.

Schopenhauer, Arthur. *The World as Will and Idea.* R. B. Haldane and J. Kemp, trans. New York: Doubleday, 1961.

Scruton, Roger. "Laughter." *Proceedings of the Aristotelian Society,* Supplement, 56 (1982): 197–212.

Searle, John R. *The Rediscovery of the Mind.* Cambridge: MIT Press, 1992.

———. *The Mystery of Consciousness.* New York: New York Review, 1997.

Segal, Erich. *Roman Laughter: The Comedy of Plautus.* New York: Oxford University Press, 1987.

———. *The Death of Comedy.* Cambridge: Harvard University Press, 2001.

Seidel, Michael. *Satiric Inheritance: Rabelais to Sterne.* Princeton: Princeton University Press, 1979.

Seligman, Adam B. *Modernity's Wager.* Princeton: Princeton University Press, 2000.

Seward, Samuel S. *The Paradox of the Ludicrous.* Stanford: Stanford University Press, 1930.

Sewell, Elizabeth. *The Field of Nonsense.* London: Chatto and Windus, 1952.

Shaftesbury, Earl of. *Characteristics of Men, Manners, Opinions, Times.* Indianapolis: Bobbs-Merrill, 1964.

Shattuck, Roger. *The Banquet Years.* Rev. ed. New York: Vintage, 1968.

———. *Forbidden Knowledge.* Harcourt, Brace: San Diego, 1996.

———. *Candor and Perversion.* New York: W. W. Norton, 1999.

Shelden, Michael. "Thought Police Ban the Bard." *Daily Telegraph,* Nov. 5, 1998.

Shklar, Judith. *Ordinary Vices.* Cambridge: Harvard University Press, 1984.

Siegel, Fred. *The Future Once Happened Here: New York, D.C., L.A., and the Fate of America's Big Cities.* New York: Free Press, 1998.

Sitwell, Edith. *The English Eccentrics.* Boston: Houghton Mifflin, 1933.

Sloterdijk, Peter. *Critique de la raison cynique.* Hans Hildenbrand, trans. Paris: Christian Bourgois, 1987.

Smith, Wesley R. "Don't Stand So Close to Me: Judges Are Giving Neighborhoods a Bum Rap." *Policy Review* 70 (fall 1994): 48.

Sokal, Alan D. "Transgressing the Boundaries: Toward a Transformative Hermeneutics of Quantum Gravity." *Social Text* 46/47 (1996): 217.

———, ed. *The Sokal Hoax: The Sham That Shook the Academy.* New York: Bison, 2000.

Sokal, Alan D., and Jean Bricmont. *Fashionable Nonsense: Postmodern Intellectuals' Abuse of Science.* New York: Picador, 1998.

Solomon, Robert C. *The Passions: Emotions and the Meaning of Life.* Indianapolis: Hackett, 1993.

———. *The Joy of Philosophy: Thinking Thin versus the Passionate Life.* New York: Oxford University Press, 1999.

Sontag, Susan. *Against Interpretation and Other Essays.* New York: Anchor, 1986.

Sousa, Ronald de. *The Rationality of Emotion.* Cambridge: MIT Press, 1990.

Spacks, Patricia Meyer. *Gossip.* New York: Knopf, 1985.

Spencer, Herbert. *Essays on Education, etc.* London: Dent, 1911.

Spender, Matthew. *Within Tuscany.* London: Penguin, 1993.

Steiner, George. *Real Presences*. Chicago: University of Chicago Press, 1989.

———. *The Death of Tragedy*. New Haven: Yale University Press, 1996.

———. *Grammars of Creation*. New Haven: Yale University Press, 2001.

Stendhal. *Racine et Shakespeare*. Utrecht: Bosch, 1965.

———. *Molière, Shakespeare, La comédie et le rire*. Liechtenstein: Kraus Reprint, 1968.

Stoppard, Tom. *Jumpers*. London: Faber and Faber, 1972.

Strachey, Lytton. *Eminent Victorians*. New York: Weidenfeld and Nicholson, 1988.

Sully, James. *An Essay on Laughter: Its Forms, Its Causes, Its Development, and Its Value*. London: Longmans Green, 1902.

Swabey, Marie. *Comic Laughter: A Philosophic Essay*. Hamden, Conn.: Archon, 1970.

Swift, Jonathan. *Prose Works*. Oxford: Blackwell, 1939–74.

———. *A Modest Proposal and Other Stories*. Amherst: Prometheus, 1995.

Sykes, Charles J. *A Nation of Victims: The Decay of the American Character*. New York: St. Martin's Press, 1992.

Sykes, Christopher. *Four Studies in Loyalty*. London: Collins, 1946.

Sylvester, Richard S., and David P. Harding, eds. *Two Early Tudor Lives*. New Haven: Yale University Press, 1962.

Sypher, Wylie, ed. *Comedy*. New York: Anchor Books, 1956.

Taylor, Charles. *Philosophy and the Human Sciences: Philosophical Papers*. Cambridge: Cambridge University Press, 1985.

———. *Sources of the Self*. Cambridge: Harvard University Press, 1989.

———. *Multiculturalism and "The Politics of Recognition."* Princeton: Princeton University Press, 1992.

———. *Philosophical Arguments*. Cambridge: Harvard University Press, 1995.

Taylor, Robert R. *The World in Stone: The Role of Architecture in National Socialist Ideology*. Berkeley: University of California Press, 1974.

Teresa, Saint. *The Life of Saint Teresa of Avila by Herself*. J. M. Cohen, trans. London: Penguin, 1957.

Tertullian. *Translations of the Writings of the Fathers: The Writings of Tertullian*. Edinburgh: Clark, 1869.

Thiele, Leslie Paul. *Friedrich Nietzsche and the Politics of the Soul: A Study in Heroic Individualism*. Princeton: Princeton University Press, 1990.

Thomas, Donald. *Charge! Hurrah! Hurrah!: A Life of Cardigan of Balaclava*. London: Routledge, 1974.

Timbs, John. *English Eccentrics*. Detroit: Singing Tree, 1969.

Trilling, Lionel. *The Middle of the Journey*. New York: Scribner's, 1947.

———. *Sincerity and Authenticity*. Harvard: Cambridge University Press, 1971.

———. *The Moral Obligation to Be Intelligent*. New York: Farrar, Straus, Giroux, 2000.

Truffaut, François. *Jules et Jim*. Paris: Seuil, 1971.

Twain, Mark. *Pudd'nhead Wilson*. New York: Grove, 1955.

Unamuno, Miguel de. *The Tragic Sense of Life*. New York: Dover, 1954.

Urmson, J. O. *Aristotle's Ethics*. Oxford: Blackwell, 1988.

Urquhart, Thomas. *The Jewel*. Edinburgh: Scottish Academic Press, 1983.

Verdon, Jean. *Rire au Moyen Age.* Paris: Perrin, 2001.

Vlastos, Gregory. *Socrates: Ironist and Moral Philosopher.* Ithaca: Cornell University Press, 1991.

Walder, Dennis, ed. *Literature in the Modern World: Critical Essays and Documents.* Oxford: Oxford University Press, 1990.

Waugh, Evelyn. *The Essays, Articles and Reviews of Evelyn Waugh.* London: Methuen, 1983.

Wertsch, James. *Voices of the Mind.* Cambridge: Cambridge University Press, 1991.

Whedbee, J. William. *The Bible and the Comic Vision.* Cambridge: Cambridge University Press, 1998.

Wickberg, Daniel. *The Senses of Humor: Self and Laughter in Modern America.* Ithaca: Cornell University Press, 1998.

Wieland, Christoph Martin. *History of the Abderites.* Max Dufner, trans. Bethlehem, Pa.: Lehigh, 1993.

Williams, Bernard. *Ethics and the Limits of Philosophy.* Cambridge: Harvard University Press, 1985.

Wilson, C. P. *Jokes: Form, Content, Use and Function.* London: Academic, 1979.

Wimsatt, W. K. *English Stage Comedy.* New York: Columbia University Press, 1955.

———. *The Idea of Comedy: Essays in Prose and Verse.* Englewood Cliffs, N.J.: Prentice-Hall, 1969.

Wittgenstein, Ludwig. *Philosophical Investigations.* G. E. M. Anscombe, trans. Oxford: Blackwell, 1967.

Wollheim, Richard. *On the Emotions.* New Haven: Yale University Press, 1999.

Worcester, David. *The Art of Satire.* New York: Russell and Russell, 1940.

Yeats, W. B. *Autobiography.* New York: Macmillan, 1965.

Young, Allan. *The Harmony of Illusions: Inventing Post-traumatic Stress Disorder.* Princeton: Princeton University Press, 1995.

Zillmann, Dolf, S. Rockwell, K. Schweitzer, and S. S. Sundar. "Does Humor Facilitate Coping with Physical Discomfort?" *Motivation and Emotion* 17 (1993): 1–21.

Zwart, Hub. *Ethical Consensus and the Truth of Laughter: The Structure of Moral Transformations.* Kampen, the Netherlands: Kok Pharos, 1996.

Index